ADVANCES IN ACCOUNTING EDUCATION

ADVANCES IN ACCOUNTING EDUCATION: TEACHING AND CURRICULUM INNOVATIONS

Series Editors: Thomas G. Calderon

Volume 1:	Edited by Bill N. Schwartz and David E. Stout
Volumes 2–7:	Edited by Bill N. Schwartz and J. Edward Ketz
Volumes 8–10:	Edited by Bill N. Schwartz and Anthony H. Catanach Jr.
Volumes 11 & 12:	Edited by Anthony H. Catanach Jr. and Dorothy Feldmann
Volume 13–15:	Edited by Dorothy Feldmann and Timothy J. Rupert
Volume 16:	Edited by Timothy J. Rupert
Volume 17–21:	Edited by Timothy J. Rupert and Beth Kern
Volume 22–27:	Edited by Thomas G. Calderon

STATEMENT OF PURPOSE

Advances in Accounting Education: Teaching and Curriculum Innovations is a refereed academic journal whose purpose is to help meet the needs of faculty members and administrators who are interested in ways to improve teaching, learning, and curriculum development in the accounting area at the college and university level. We publish thoughtful, well-developed articles that are readable, relevant, and reliable.

Articles may be either empirical or non-empirical and should emphasize innovative approaches that inform faculty and administrators as they seek to advance their classrooms, curricula, and programs. All articles should have well-articulated and strong theoretical foundations. Establishing a link to the non-accounting literature is desirable. Further, we expect all manuscripts to address implications for the scholarship of teaching and learning.

Normally, articles that emphasize pedagogy and classroom innovation (e.g., cases, exercises, specific approaches to teaching a topic, etc.) must demonstrate efficacy in a college setting. That is, the authors offer evidence to show that the innovation has been tried and it is effective.

Non-empirical manuscripts should be academically rigorous. They can be theoretical syntheses, conceptual models, position papers, discussions of methodology, comprehensive literature reviews grounded in theory, or historical discussions with implications for efforts to enhance teaching, learning, and curriculum development. Reasonable assumptions and logical development are essential.

Sound research design and execution are critical for empirical reports. Reviewers focus on the quality of method, data, results, and analysis as well as the implications for teaching, learning, and curriculum development.

Review Procedures

Advances in Accounting Education: Teaching and Curriculum Innovations provides authors with timely reviewer reports that clearly indicate the status of the manuscript. Each manuscript is reviewed by at least two reviewers. Authors receive initial reviews normally within eight to twelve weeks of manuscript submission.

EDITORIAL REVIEW BOARD

William Baker
Queens University of Charlotte, USA

Reza Barkhi
Virginia Tech, USA

Ryan Baxter
Boise State University, USA

Cathleen Burns
Creative Action Learning Solutions, USA

Cory Campbell
Indiana State University, USA

Anne Christensen
Montana State University, USA

Ann Davis
Tennessee Tech University, USA

Nina Dorata
St. John's University, USA

Cintia Easterwood
Virginia Tech, USA

Carol Fischer
St. Bonaventure University, USA

Michael Fischer
St. Bonaventure University, USA

Dan Fisher
Kansas State University, USA

Mary Anne Gaffney
Temple University, USA

Brian Patrick Green
University of Michigan-Dearborn, USA

Kelly Green
University of Louisiana – Lafayette, USA

Lei Gao
University of North Florida, USA

Brian Hogan
University of Pittsburgh, USA

Kerry Inger
Auburn University, USA

Joan Lee
Fairfield University, USA

Linda Lovata
Southern Illinois University Edwardsville, USA

Barry Marks
University of Houston – Clear Lake, USA

Shawn Mauldin
Mississippi State University, USA

Michele D. Meckfessel
University of Missouri St. Louis, USA

Jared Moore
Oregon State University, USA

Albert Nagy
John Carroll University, USA

Susanne O'Callaghan
Pace University, USA

Philip Olds
Virginia Commonwealth University, USA

Colin Onita
San Jose State University, USA

Arianna Pinello
Florida Gulf Coast University, USA

Sri Ramamoorti
University of Dayton, USA

Colin Reid
Washington and Lee University, USA

Timothy Rupert
Northeastern University, USA

Michael Schadewald
University of Florida, USA

William Stout
University of Louisville, USA

Michael Turner
The University of Queensland, Australia

Gerald (Jerry) Weinstein
John Carroll University, USA

Todd White
The University of North Carolina at Pembroke, USA

Matthew Wieland
Miami University, USA

Aaron Wilson
Ohio University, USA

Li Xu
Washington State University, USA

Yan Zhang
New Mexico State University, USA

ADVANCES IN ACCOUNTING EDUCATION: TEACHING
AND CURRICULUM INNOVATIONS   VOLUME 28

ADVANCES IN ACCOUNTING EDUCATION: TEACHING AND CURRICULUM INNOVATIONS

EDITED BY

THOMAS G. CALDERON
The University of Akron, USA

United Kingdom – North America – Japan
India – Malaysia – China

Emerald Publishing Limited
Emerald Publishing, Floor 5, Northspring, 21-23 Wellington Street, Leeds LS1 4DL.

First edition 2025

Editorial matter and selection © 2025 Thomas G. Calderon.
Individual chapters © 2025 The authors.
Published under exclusive licence by Emerald Publishing Limited.

Reprints and permissions service
Contact: www.copyright.com

No part of this book may be reproduced, stored in a retrieval system, transmitted in any form or by any means electronic, mechanical, photocopying, recording or otherwise without either the prior written permission of the publisher or a licence permitting restricted copying issued in the UK by The Copyright Licensing Agency and in the USA by The Copyright Clearance Center. Any opinions expressed in the chapters are those of the authors. Whilst Emerald makes every effort to ensure the quality and accuracy of its content, Emerald makes no representation implied or otherwise, as to the chapters' suitability and application and disclaims any warranties, express or implied, to their use.

British Library Cataloguing in Publication Data
A catalogue record for this book is available from the British Library

ISBN: 978-1-83797-187-9 (Print)
ISBN: 978-1-83797-186-2 (Online)
ISBN: 978-1-83797-188-6 (Epub)

ISSN: 1085-4622 (Series)

INVESTOR IN PEOPLE

CONTENTS

List of Contributors   *xi*

THEME 1
DATA SCIENCE AND ANALYTICS IN ACCOUNTING

Chapter 1   Data and Analytics in Introductory Managerial Accounting Courses
Yuxin Shan and Vernon J. Richardson   *3*

Chapter 2   A Framework for Integrating Python Programming into the Accounting Curricula
Kelly Green and Angel Littlejohn   *21*

Chapter 3   Data Science in Accounting: Budget Analytics Using Monte Carlo Simulation
Hemantha S. B. Herath and Tejaswini C. Herath   *55*

THEME 2
INNOVATIVE TEACHING CASES IN TAXATION

Chapter 4   Albert's Family Pet Store: A Case Exploring Guaranteed Payments, Book to Tax Differences, and Form 1065
Jodi Olson and Brian Huels   *77*

Chapter 5   Veterans Golf and Social Club: An Instructional Case for Not for Profits
Mitchell Franklin   *95*

THEME 3
PIPELINE ISSUES AND THE CPA EXAM

Chapter 6   Why Graduate Accounting Students Do Not Sit for the CPA Exam: Perceptions of the CPA Credential
Deirdre Collier, Hannah Rozen and Alexander J. Sannella   *115*

Chapter 7 CPA Exam Pass Rates and the Role of a CPA Review Course
Jiayin Li, Hussein Issa and Alexander J. Sannella   *131*

Chapter 8 Developing and Assessing Wellbeing in the Accounting Curriculum
Matt Bjornsen, Sarah Borchers and Steven Hall   *149*

THEME 4
PERSPECTIVES ON ACCOUNTING THEORY AND INTEGRATED THINKING AND LEARNING

Chapter 9 A Model to Develop Integrated Thinking Skills of Prospective Professional Accountants
Erica du Toit, Ben Marx and Rozanne Smith   *161*

Chapter 10 Theory and Its Absence in Accounting Education Research
Timothy J. Fogarty   *187*

Chapter 11 A Commentary on Teaching a Financial Accounting Theory Course
Jerry E. Trapnell and Michael T. Dugan   *199*

LIST OF CONTRIBUTORS

Matt Bjornsen	University of Nebraska at Kearney, USA
Sarah Borchers	University of Nebraska at Kearney, USA
Deirdre Collier	Fairleigh Dickinson University, USA
Erica du Toit	University of Johannesburg, South Africa
Michael T. Dugan	University of Alabama, USA
Timothy J. Fogarty	Case Western Reserve University, USA
Mitchell Franklin	Le Moyne College, USA
Kelly Green	University of Louisiana – Lafayette, USA
Steven Hall	University of Nebraska at Kearney, USA
Tejaswini C. Herath	Brock University, Canada
Hemantha S. B. Herath	Brock University, Canada
Brian Huels	University of Wisconsin – Whitewater, USA
Hussein Issa	Rutgers Business School, The State University of New Jersey, USA
Jiayin Li	University of International Business and Economics, China
Angel Littlejohn	University of Louisiana – Lafayette, USA
Ben Marx	University of Johannesburg, South Africa
Jodi Olson	Winona State University, USA
Vernon J. Richardson	University of Arkansas, USA
Hannah Rozen	Fairleigh Dickinson University, USA
Alexander J. Sannella	Rutgers Business School, The State University of New Jersey, USA
Yuxin Shan	University of Wisconsin – Eau Claire, USA
Rozanne Smith	University of Johannesburg, South Africa
Jerry E. Trapnell	Clemson University, USA

THEME 1
DATA SCIENCE AND ANALYTICS IN ACCOUNTING

CHAPTER 1

DATA AND ANALYTICS IN INTRODUCTORY MANAGERIAL ACCOUNTING COURSES

Yuxin Shan[a] and Vernon J. Richardson[b]

[a] University of Wisconsin – Eau Claire, USA
[b] University of Arkansas, USA

ABSTRACT

Managerial accounting has traditionally played an important role in analyzing data, estimating performance, and offering suggestions. Modern management accountants face evolving expectations, such as contributing strategically to long-term goals and communicating information using visualizations. We specifically focus on how managerial accounting courses and textbooks should integrate data analytics to better prepare accounting students for the current working requirements. This study presents survey findings encompassing perspectives from 23 accounting professors and 46 practitioners. The survey revealed a prevalent endorsement for data analytics integration, with 91% of practitioners and 78% of professors advocating for inclusion. Specifically, 64% of professors support substantial integration compared to 36% of practitioners. About 25% of both groups believe in discussing data analytics in every management accounting topic if not deeply integrated. This study significantly contributes to accounting education literature by combining insights from educators and practitioners regarding the inclusion of data analytics in management accounting. While professors offer guidance on essential materials and practices, practitioners enrich the discussion with practical, workplace-relevant techniques.

Keywords: Data analytics; integrating data analytics; accounting curriculum; managerial accounting; survey; accounting educators; accounting practitioners

Management accountants are facing the opportunities and challenges that come along with powerful information systems and advanced analytics tools. The escalation in business competition, parallel to advancements in technology, has led to an augmented scope within managerial accounting. This evolution extends beyond conventional historical value reporting, transitioning toward a focus on real-time reporting and predictive reporting (Cokins, 2013).

Contemporary management accountants are important in strategic cost management to attain long-term goals, implement operational checks to assess corporate performance, formulate internal cost activity strategies, and craft financial statements to support managerial decision-making processes. While they are taking heavier duties on data analytics, the managerial accounting course hasn't been changed much in support of their intended roles. To better prepare students, consideration should be given to adding data analytics techniques to management accounting courses to help students analyze and visualize historical data, make meaningful predictions under different scenarios, and explore hidden patterns behind the data using broader sources of internal and external data.

Embracing the changes brought by big data and data analytics, the 2018 Association to Advance Collegiate Schools of Business (AACSB, 2018) standards emphasize the critical role of data analytics with an expectation for accounting faculty to integrate these across undergraduate and master's programs. Specifically, it requires faculty and students to master contemporary and emerging technologies, such as statistical techniques, clustering, data management and analysis, predictive analytics, and visualization. Following that, the CPA exam underwent a significant change in 2022, effective in January 2024 (The American Institute of CPAs (AICPA), 2022b). In particular, technology-focused questions are incorporated throughout all sections of the updated CPA exam. Additionally, accounting educators and professionals have worked together diligently to blend accounting into established STEM (science, technology, engineering, and mathematics) programs through coordinated efforts (The American Institute of CPAs (AICPA), 2022a).

As for how data analytics should be integrated into the accounting curriculum, accounting educators hold different views about whether it should be infused into individual accounting courses or covered in standalone accounting data analytics courses (Richardson & Shan, 2019). Our study specifically focuses on accounting educators' and practitioners' views about whether and how data analytics should be included in introduction-level managerial accounting courses. We surveyed 23 managerial accounting professors and 46 management accounting practitioners to collect their opinions about the data, software, and specific techniques they expect students to learn in introductory managerial accounting courses.

This study contributes to the accounting education literature by presenting survey results on the perspectives of both accounting educators and practitioners regarding the inclusion of data analytics in the introductory managerial accounting course and the techniques to be integrated. Specifically, accounting professors offered valuable insights into the combination of required teaching materials and laboratory practices, while practitioners contributed significantly by sharing their experiences with the techniques crucial for students to master in a professional environment.

The remainder of this study provides background information on the accounting industry's changes in response to deeper integration with data analytics, a description of research questions and survey methodology, and a discussion of findings and conclusions.

BACKGROUND

Data Analytics Skills Requested by the Accounting Accreditation

In response to technological advancements, the 2018 AACSB standards underscored the significance of data analytics, particularly reflected in standard A5. This standard necessitates that faculty and students cultivate proficiency in contemporary technologies while remaining adaptable to emerging ones. These technologies encompass a spectrum including statistical techniques, clustering, data management, modeling, analysis, text analysis, predictive analytics, learning systems, and visualization (AACSB, 2018).

Data Analytics Skills Requested by the AICPA via the CPA Exam

In the transformative landscape of the CPA exam, 2022 witnessed significant adjustments in its testing contents. Traditionally, the CPA exam encompassed four integral sections: auditing and attestation (AUD), business environment and concepts (BEC), Financial Accounting and Reporting (FAR) and regulation (REG). Starting from January 1, 2024, candidates are required to take three mandatory examinations in AUD, FAR, and REG, along with one out of three specialized discipline exams: business analysis and reporting (BAR), information systems and controls (ISC), or tax compliance and planning (TCP). An important point to highlight is that while the BAR and ISC sections rigorously assess candidates on various aspects including data analytics, technical accounting, information systems, information security, and IT audit, the expanded CPA exam format also integrates technology-related questions across all its sections. This comprehensive approach to technological aspects signifies a significant shift in the examination structure, emphasizing the broader relevance of technology across the entire accounting landscape. This shift not only demands a broader skill set from candidates but also acknowledges the indispensable role of technology in shaping the future of accounting practice and expertise.

In the revised uniform CPA examination blueprint, managerial accounting and cost accounting are primarily tested in the BAR section, with a specific emphasis on variance analysis techniques. From a data analytics perspective, candidates are expected to showcase their ability to select the appropriate variance analysis method for evaluating key cost drivers within diverse business scenarios. Meanwhile, they are required to hone their skills in interpreting sales outcomes by conducting comprehensive analyses involving price, volume, and mix assessments. This comprehensive evaluation not only tests candidates' understanding of fundamental accounting principles but also underscores the critical role of analytics and cost assessment in contemporary business contexts.

Data Analytics Skills to Show Evidence of Technology in Accounting

In response to the growing combination of technology and accounting, concerted efforts have been undertaken by accounting educators and professionals to integrate accounting into established STEM programs. This strategic initiative seeks to ensure congruence between the knowledge and skill sets of accounting graduates and the evolving requisites of a fiercely competitive global market. An instance of this endeavor materialized through the introduction of the H.R. 3855 Accounting STEM Pursuit Act of 2021 before the United States House of Representatives Education and Labor Committee on June 11, 2021, during the 117th Congress. This legislative proposal aimed to amend the Student Support and Academic Enrichment Grant program, advocating for the inclusion of accounting within STEM education. The proposal intended to foster early career awareness in accounting within a comprehensive STEM educational framework, especially targeting elementary and secondary school students. This legislative proposal garnered substantial support from esteemed bodies such as AICPA, the Center for Audit Quality, the Diverse Organization of Firms, the National Association of Black Accountants Inc., and the American Accounting Association.

In tandem with this legislative endeavor, the AICPA made a compelling case on July 29, 2022. It proposed the inclusion of accounting and relevant Classification of Instructional Program codes within the Department of Homeland Security's STEM Designated Degree Program List, categorically under the "T" for technology. This proposed reclassification sought to better articulate the requisite skill sets and competencies expected of accounting professionals. Upon approval, this reclassification would offer foreign students enrolled in STEM-designated accounting programs an extended optional practical training period of up to 24 additional months in U.S. post-graduation programs, beyond the standard year. These programs underscore specialized areas encompassing data analytics, software development, cloud computing, and other burgeoning technological innovations.

Data Analytics Skills Increasingly Needed in Management Accounting

In recent years, the function of management accountants has undergone substantial evolution. Traditionally, management accountants typically rely on accumulated historical data to illustrate the financial situation of a company. However, as the current business environment increasingly demands more immediate and pertinent insights, financial statements often prove inadequate as a primary information source for managerial decision-making. In the contemporary landscape, management accountants play a pivotal role in aiding management by evaluating organizational performance through internal data analysis and offering decision-centric insights derived from both internal and external data sources. Their responsibilities encompass more than just generating descriptive reports to address past queries but include forecasting future scenarios (Nielsen, 2015). Specifically, modern management accountants now engage in various facets of business: contributing to strategic cost management for achieving long-term objectives, implementing operational controls to measure corporate performance, devising internal cost activity plans, and preparing financial statements to aid decision-making processes alongside management (Brands & Holtzblatt, 2015).

The Institute of Management Accounts (IMA) published its Management Accounting Competency Framework[1] (MACF) in 2019. It offers valuable insights and demonstrates the significance of management accounting as a bridge that enables students to integrate knowledge spanning both accounting and non-accounting domains. This integration aims to prepare them for careers in accounting and finance, ensuring their relevance in the digital age. The framework delineates six core domains of management accounting knowledge and skills, encompassing (1) Strategy, Planning, and Performance; (2) Reporting and Control; (3) Technology and Analytics; (4) Business Acumen and Operations; (5) Leadership; and (6) Professional Ethics and Values. Within these domains, there are 33 competencies identified. Furthermore, the MACF provides detailed guidance on the subject knowledge and techniques required to attain proficiency at five levels: limited, basic, applied, skilled, and expert.

Following the MACF, Venkatesh et al. (2023) recommended a three-course management accounting model which suggests a step-by-step advancement from limited to skilled proficiency levels that students ought to attain in each course within the six domains. The three courses are Course 1 – Principles of Management Accounting, Course 2 – Intermediate Management Accounting, and Course 3 – Advanced Management Accounting. They suggested that the first course (the focus of our study) should prioritize focusing on the overall strategy of a company. From the technology and analytics perspective, the first management accounting course should incorporate discussions about the important role of data analytics and visualization, such as the effects of Big Data, Machine Learning (ML), and Artificial intelligence (AI) on management accounting (Venkatesh et al., 2023). The study of Losi et al. (2022) provides survey results showing that asking the right questions (supported by 43.4% of participants), applying appropriate data analytic techniques (supported by 21.2% of participants), and effectively communicating (supported by 27.4% of participants) results, interpreting results (supported by 28.3% of participants) are the top four skills that should be included in the cost accounting course. Basis programming languages associated with ML and AI are suggested to be covered in accounting information systems (18.6%), data analytics courses taught by the accounting department (38.9%) or other departments (22.2%), or graduate level courses (22.3%) (Losi et al., 2022).

Responded to the rapidly increasing demand for incorporating data analytics into the accounting curriculum, many accounting scholars have provided teaching cases as supplementary teaching material to conventional textbooks. For example, Peters and Chiu (2022) designed 34 interactive Excel spreadsheets that cover 8 core calculative principles included in management accounting. Calderon et al. (2022) offer a framework to integrate "R" programming at multiple levels of complexity into the accounting curriculum.

Especially, visualizations have become commonplace in business applications (Dilla et al., 2010). Traditional accounting techniques have long relied on quantitative and statistical methodologies predominantly derived from structured data. Contemporary management accounting is facing rising demands for both explanatory visualizations and exploratory visualizations. Managers are seeking effective and interactive visualizations, such as dashboards, to deliver performance matrices as well as using clustering or other analytical visualizations to detect groups, trends, and common behaviors.

Moreover, the broader sphere of business management prefers analysis outcomes to be presented in easily comprehensible formats (Davenport, 2014; Kohavi et al., 2004). Consequently, reports often employ pie charts, heat maps, geographic maps, and similar graphical representations to facilitate swift comprehension (Davenport, 2014). Typically, management prefers streamlined and easily understandable analyses and reports. Although enterprise systems are designed to enable intricate predictions and optimizations, management accountants are expected to adeptly communicate these findings using clear and easily interpretable visualization tools (Appelbaum et al., 2017).

Additionally, contemporary accounting has expanded the realm by integrating methods rooted in ML, AI, deep learning, text mining, and data mining (Calderon & Cheh, 2001; Oracle, 2015; Schneider et al., 2015; Warren et al., 2015). A better understanding of ML and AL can help accounting professionals automate repetitive working processes, validate the effectiveness of AI tools, review source documents, analyze business transactions (Cho et al., 2020), improve accounting estimates (Ding et al., 2020) and recognize the cybersecurity risk that is associated with audit risks (Calderon & Gao, 2020). PWC firms in mainland China and Hong Kong reinvested AI-enabled productivity gains to elevate the quality, quantity, or efficiency of producing goods and services and generating expanded output from the same level of input (Likens & Wakefield, 2023). Consequently, their reinvestment achieves a 30% reduction in time for systems design, realizes a 50% increase in efficiency for code generation, and experiences an 80% decrease in time dedicated to internal translations (Likens & Wakefield, 2023).

RESEARCH QUESTIONS

To comprehend the necessity and methods to integrate data analytics into managerial accounting courses, we surveyed managerial accounting professors as well as accounting practitioners within the managerial accounting domain. This survey seeks to gather viewpoints from both academic and industry angles regarding the relevance and incorporation of data analytics in the managerial accounting field. Specifically, participants were asked to answer the following 10 questions included in the survey (the detailed survey is presented in the Appendix):

1. Do you think data analytics should be covered in the intro managerial accounting class/textbook?
2. To what extent should data and analytics be covered in the intro managerial textbook/course?
3. To what extent and where should labs teaching analytics techniques be included in the textbook materials? These labs take 15–20 minutes each to learn.
4. The extent and level of coverage of data and analytics in the intro managerial textbook would be one of the most important elements in choosing a text within the next three years.
5. There should be a discussion of internal and external data sources as part of the intro managerial accounting.
6. Which software tools should be included for intro managerial accounting (select all that apply)?
7. Would your students need a substantive Excel tutorial before completing Excel assignments in the intro to managerial accounting?
8. Students can either create visualizations, evaluate visualizations, or both in the intro managerial class. Which do you prefer (choose one)?
9. Which analytics techniques should be covered in the intro managerial class/text (choose all that apply).
10. Which visualization techniques should be covered in intro managerial class/text (choose all that apply).

METHOD

We disseminated a voluntary anonymous survey with the above questions to managerial accounting professors and managerial accounting practitioners in 2023 to learn their views about how data analytics should be incorporated in managerial accounting courses to better prepare students for the competitive working environment. We reached out to 82 managerial accounting professors (all-ranks) through emails and received 23 responses. Professors were asked to utilize the link provided in the email to complete the survey. Professors were selected based on their field of interest as described on universities' website. We also asked them to indicate whether they had experience in teaching managerial accounting. To increase the response rate of this unpaid survey from accounting practitioners, the hard copy of the survey was disseminated during the Accounting Career Fair and the Accounting Advisory Board meeting at a mid-west 4-year public university. Researchers first introduced the survey briefly to accounting practitioners. Accounting practitioners were asked if they were management accountants or familiar with the work content of management accountants. If they answered "yes" to this question and also indicated they would like to take the survey, then we asked them to complete the survey privately. Otherwise, we asked them to forward the survey to their management accountants with instructions to send the completed survey to the researchers via email. Out of approximately 100 practitioners, the researcher engaged with, a total of 46 responses were received. All participants retained the option to skip questions as they progressed through the survey. The entirety of this survey yielded a total of 69 responses.

RESULTS

Do You Think Data Analytics Should Be Covered in the Introductory Managerial Accounting Class/Textbook?

In some sense, managerial accounting and data analytics are the same. Management accountants can access and analyze accounting and other data to address management questions. Seeing this, in recent years introductory managerial accounting textbooks have started including data analytics. While some textbooks currently include one to two paragraphs in their 500-page textbooks, other texts have slightly longer discussions. Some assess students on analytics based on already created Tableau charts, while others offer other resources to create visualizations without integrating them into the chapter material. The first question of the survey aims to learn about participants' views on whether data analytics should be included in the introductory managerial accounting class or textbook. We observe differences between professors' and practitioners' responses. Among the professors who participated in this survey, about 61% of them strongly agree that data analytics should be integrated into the introductory managerial accounting class/textbook, and 17% of them agree data analytics should be integrated into the introductory managerial accounting class/textbook. Thirteen percent of them believe it's unnecessary to include data analytics, and 9% don't express a strong opinion on the matter. Among practitioners, 91% believe it's crucial to add data analytics to the introductory managerial accounting class/textbook (48% strongly agree, 43% agree), while 7% neither agree nor disagree, and 2% disagree. Notably, a higher proportion of practitioners endorse the inclusion of data analytics in the introductory managerial accounting class/textbook.

To What Extent Should Data and Analytics Be Covered in the Intro Managerial Textbook/Course?

In the second question, we want to go further and investigate how deeply data analytics should be embedded in the introductory managerial course/textbook. The survey results reveal a noticeable contrast between responses from professors and practitioners. Roughly 14% of professors feel that introducing data analytics in the initial chapter suffices. Another 23% of professors advocate for brief mentions of data analytics in every chapter, while a majority – 64% – support a substantial integration of data analytics with managerial accounting content. One professor opted not to respond to this question. While more practitioners lean toward integrating data analytics into the introduction of the managerial accounting course/textbook, only 37% of them support deep integration in each chapter alongside traditional managerial accounting topics. Approximately a quarter of practitioners endorse a brief discussion about data analytics in every chapter, and 35% believe data analytics should feature solely in the opening chapter. Consistent with the first question, 2% of practitioners don't view the inclusion of data analytics in the introductory managerial accounting class/textbook as necessary.

To What Extent and Where Should Labs Teaching Analytics Techniques Be Included in the Textbook Materials? These Labs Take 15–20 minutes Each to Learn

Hands-on labs serve as practical applications of analytics techniques, utilizing real company data or simulated data scenarios. They offer students step-by-step guidance and additional opportunities for practice. According to the survey results, over half of the professors advocate for integrating labs into textbook chapters, written by the authors, with up to four labs featured in each chapter. Around a third of professors support the inclusion of labs in the e-learning platform, outside the textbook, while 9% oppose incorporating labs in the textbook altogether. From the perspective of practitioners, about 24% prefer labs designed by the authors to be included in the textbook chapters, while 59% consider it essential to have labs within the e-learning platform. Additionally, 17% of practitioners believe labs shouldn't be included in the textbook.

The Extent and Level of Coverage of Data and Analytics in the Intro Managerial Textbook Would Be One of the Most Important Elements in Choosing a Text Within the Next 3 Years

This particular inquiry, given its direct correlation to textbook selection, has been exclusively included in the survey distributed solely to professors. It intends to gauge the significance professors place on integrating data analytics as essential components within their existing courses. The results indicate that approximately 52% of professors prioritize a comprehensive inclusion of data and analytics within their teaching materials for introductory managerial accounting courses. Additionally, about 26% of professors would take into account the level of coverage concerning data and analytics, while 9% express uncertainty about its importance. The remaining respondents express neither disagreement nor strong agreement on this matter.

There Should Be a Discussion of Internal and External Data Sources as Part of Intro Managerial Accounting

In the realm of managerial accounting, data serves as the foundation for informed decision-making, sourced from both internal and external avenues. Internally, organizations draw upon a rich repository of data generated within their operational sphere. Externally sourced data broadens this perspective, incorporating market dynamics, economic indicators, and regulatory landscapes. By leveraging internal and external data sources, managerial accountants are able to gain a comprehensive understanding of organizational performance, market positioning, and potential future trajectories, allowing for strategic initiatives and prudent resource management.

About 80% of professors (40% strongly agreeing and 44% agreeing) and accounting practitioners (26% strongly agreeing and 54% agreeing) concur that internal and external data sources should be discussed in the course of the introduction to managerial accounting. Thirteen percent of professors hold the view that this inclusion may not be deemed necessary within the confines of the managerial accounting course. The remainder of professors and practitioners do not lean toward either agreement or disagreement on this issue.

Which Software Tools Should Be Included for Intro Managerial Accounting?

Excel has been pervasively applied in the managerial accounting area. However, many students are familiar only with some basic functions. From our informal communications with employers, many of them consistently highlight concerns about students' proficiency in utilizing Excel to conduct analysis efficiently. Furthermore, there's widespread agreement on the necessity for students to acquaint themselves with data visualization tools such as Tableau and Power BI. In our survey, participants were presented with four options – Excel, Tableau, Power BI, and others – and were tasked with selecting the software they deemed essential for integration into the managerial accounting course or textbook.

Survey results unanimously highlight professors' consensus regarding the indispensability of Excel. Additionally, 52% of the professors endorse Tableau, while 30% advocate for the inclusion of Power BI. One professor expressed interest in alternative software options but didn't specify further details. The majority of accounting practitioners (96%) emphasize the significance of Excel in managerial accounting education, 20% of them recommend Tableau, and 39% support the inclusion of Power BI. Additionally, 3 practitioners suggest covering Alteryx in the managerial accounting courses, 1 practitioner suggests including Teammate and 1 practitioner suggests covering SAP.

Would Your Students Need a Substantive Excel Tutorial Before Completing Excel Assignments in Intro Managerial?

This question is included in the survey sent exclusively to professors. It is specifically designed to gather insights into professors' perspectives regarding students' familiarity with Excel, based on their previous experiences. Approximately 43% of professors believe that a comprehensive Excel tutorial would be beneficial, while 57% of respondents don't consider it necessary.

Students Can Either Create Visualizations, Evaluate Visualizations, or Both in the Intro Managerial Class. Which Do You Prefer?

Tableau and Power BI stand as popular, user-friendly data visualization tools. These platforms facilitate the easy creation of various visual graphs like bar charts, pie charts, line graphs, geographic maps, word clouds, heat maps, and box and whisker plots, among others. Additionally, students can utilize reference lines to make predictions or engage in exploratory analysis such as clustering. The tools also allow for the development of interactive dashboards that dynamically present crucial graphs and metrics. Furthermore, users can leverage the story function to craft a narrative around data, emphasizing key insights. While visualizations efficiently communicate information, they also hold the potential to distort or mislead audiences, often through inappropriate baselines, benchmarks, or scales. Thus, we sought insights from professors and practitioners regarding their expectations for student skills – whether focused on creating visualizations, evaluating them, or both.

The survey findings reveal that 4% of professors consider it sufficient for students to learn solely through visualization creation. In contrast, 31% advocate for proficiency in evaluating visualizations. The majority, constituting 65% of professors, emphasizes the importance for students to acquire expertise in both creating and evaluating visualizations. Practitioners hold differing views compared to professors. About 9% of practitioners emphasize the ability to learn to create visualizations, 13% of them believe that learning to evaluate visualizations is sufficient, while 78% think it is important to acquire both skill sets.

Which Analytics Techniques Should Be Covered in the Intro Managerial Class/Text?

Survey participants were asked to select all the techniques they believed should be covered, with the option to add additional techniques to the list. All professors answered this question, but three practitioners skipped this particular question. Similarly, among the responses we received, 83% of professors and 85% of practitioners concur that a comprehensive overview of Excel Formulas should be integrated into the managerial accounting course. Regarding formulas like mean, median, etc., utilized for calculating descriptive statistical information, 74% of professors advocate for their inclusion in the managerial accounting course, while less than half of practitioners (49%) perceive it as necessary. Excel's Data Analysis Toolpak, which can also be used to generate descriptive statistics, is suggested by about 65% of professors and 47% of practitioners for coverage in managerial accounting classes. Cost analysis holds significant importance in managerial accounting. While approximately 92% of professors recommend incorporating Job Costing Calculations into the course, only 47% of practitioners support this inclusion. In terms of Process Costing Calculations, 48% of professors and 37% of practitioners believe it should be included. Professors and practitioners hold similar views on the utilization of Slope() for Cost Behavior, with 35% of professors and 28% of practitioners advocating for its inclusion. Regression analysis for Cost Behavior is suggested by about 57% of professors and 28% of practitioners. Additionally, 65% of professors and 40% of practitioners suggest incorporating Goal-seek/Break-even Analysis. Similarly, around half of both professors and practitioners suggest including NPV(), IRR(), and PMT() for Cash Flow Analysis. About 30% of professors and 47% of practitioners propose including

Forecasting, while 57% of professors and 49% of practitioners suggest covering sensitivity analysis. Additionally, 4.35% of professors mentioned other techniques that should be included but did not specify which ones. One practitioner left a comment querying whether these topics are covered in other accounting classes.

Which Visualization Techniques Should Be Covered in Intro Managerial Class/Text?

Survey participants were prompted to select all the techniques they deemed necessary for inclusion, with the opportunity to supplement the list with additional techniques. All professors answered this question, but four practitioners skipped it. Among the responses received, 95% of professors (64% of practitioners) recommend including bar charts, 82% of professors (60% of practitioners) suggest incorporating line charts, and 86% of professors (48% of practitioners) advise the inclusion of pie charts. A higher proportion of practitioners (76%) advocate for incorporating pivot charts in the managerial accounting course compared to professors (55%). While most professors (73%) believe scatterplots and trend lines should be included, approximately half of practitioners (57%) share this perspective. Conditional formatting garnered support from around half of professors (55%) and practitioners (57%) for inclusion in the managerial course. A slightly larger percentage of professors (45%) favor including dashboards/slicers compared to practitioners (38%). Approximately one-fourth of professors (23%) and practitioners (26%) suggest the inclusion of sparklines.

CONCLUSION

Historically, management accounting encompassed diverse calculations and analyses aiding managerial decisions. However, contemporary management accountants confront a deluge of diverse data from disparate sources and formats. Combined with advanced analytical techniques, modern management accountants today are expected to contribute to strategic cost management for long-term goals, implement operational controls to gauge corporate performance, devise internal cost activity plans, and prepare financial statements to support decision-making within management. Despite this evolution in the profession, managerial accounting courses and textbooks have slightly adapted to this shifting managerial landscape. In light of this disparity, our paper presents survey findings reflecting the perspectives of accounting professors and practitioners regarding the integration of data analytics within managerial accounting coursework and textbooks.

The survey results highlight a strong consensus favoring the integration of data analytics, with 91% of practitioners and 78% of professors advocating for its inclusion. A higher percentage of professors (64%) support deep integration compared to practitioners (36%). About a quarter of both groups advocate for discussing data analytics across all management accounting topics. Approximately 80% of both professors and practitioners suggest discussing internal and external data sources. Additionally, both groups emphasize the importance of incorporating hands-on Excel practices and visualization tools (either Tableau or Power BI).

In terms of the survey responses, we propose that data analytics should be widely integrated into the introductory managerial accounting course. Managerial accounting textbooks should include hands-on lab practices to help students master data analysis and visualization techniques. The course should cover both internal and external data sources, utilizing Excel and at least one visualization tool such as Tableau or Power BI.

This study contributes to the accounting education literature by sharing survey findings from both accounting educators and practitioners on integrating data analytics into the introductory managerial accounting course and textbook. As accounting professors provide valuable insights into combining essential teaching materials and lab practices, practitioners can offer feedback based on their experiences with crucial techniques for students to master in a professional workplace. We note that our conclusions are subject to sample selection bias and response bias. The in-person survey was disseminated in the mid-west area of the United States, and the results may not be generalizable to other areas.

NOTE

https://www.imanet.org/insights-and-trends/the-future-of-management-accounting/ima-management-accounting-competency-framework?ssopc=1

REFERENCES

Association to Advance Collegiate Schools of Business (AACSB). (2018). *AACSB accounting accreditation standards*. https://www.aacsb.edu/educators/accreditation/accounting-accreditation/aacsb-accounting-accreditation-standards/

Appelbaum, D., Kogan, A., Vasarhelyi, M., & Yan, Z. (2017). Impact of business analytics and enterprise systems on managerial accounting. *International Journal of Accounting Information Systems*, 25, 29–44.

Brands, K., & Holtzblatt, M. (2015). Business analytics: Transforming the role of management accountants. *Management Accounting Quarterly*, 16(3), 1–12.

Calderon, T. G., & Cheh, J. J. (2001). A framework for incorporating data mining into an accounting curriculum. *Review of Business Information Systems*, 5(1), 45–58.

Calderon, T. G., & Gao, L. (2020). Cybersecurity risks disclosure and implied audit risks: Evidence from audit fees. *International Journal of Auditing*, 25(1), 24–39.

Calderon, T. G., Hesford, J. W., & Turner, M. J. (2022). A framework for integrating "R" programming into the accounting curriculum. *Advances in Accounting Education*, 26, 209–232.

Cho, S., Vasarhelyi, M. A., Sun, T., & Zhang, C. (2020). Learning from machine learning in accounting and assurance. *Journal of Emerging Technologies in Accounting*, 17(1), 1–10.

Cokins, G. (2013). Top 7 trends in management accounting. *Strategic Finance*, 95(6), 21–30.

Davenport, T. (2014). *Big data at work: Dispelling the myths, uncovering the opportunities*. Harvard Business Review Press.

Dilla, W., Janvrin, D. J., & Raschke, R. (2010). Interactive data visualization: New directions for accounting information systems research. *Journal of Information Systems*, 24(2), 1–37.

Ding, K., Lev, B., Peng, X., Sun, T., & Vasarhelyi, M. A. (2020). Machine learning improves accounting estimates: Evidence from insurance payments. *Review of Accounting Studies*, 25, 1098–1134.

Kohavi, R., Mason, L., Parekh, R., & Zheng, Z. (2004). Lessons and challenges from mining retail e-commerce data. *Machine Learning*, *57*, 83–113.

Likens, S., & Wakefield, N. (2023). *Do you have an "early days" generative AI strategy?* www.pwc.com/generative-ai-strategy

Losi, H., Isaacson, E., & Boyle D. (2022). Integrating data analytics in the accounting curriculum: Faculty perceptions and insights. *Issues in Accounting Education*, *37*(4), 1–23.

Nielsen, S. (2015). The impact of business analytics on management accounting. SSRN http://dx.doi.org/10.2139/ssrn.2616363

Oracle. (2015). Big data analytics with Oracle advanced analytics. www.oracle.com/docs/tech/database/oaa-12c-technical-briefv6.pdf

Peters, M., & Chiu, C. (2022). Interactive spreadsheeting: A learning strategy and exercises for calculative management accounting principles. *Issues in Accounting Education*, *37*(4), 47–60.

Richardson, V. J., & Shan, Y. (2019). Data analytics in the accounting curriculum. *Advances in Accounting Education: Teaching and Curriculum Innovations*, *23*, 67–79.

Schneider, G. P., Dai, J., Janvrin, D. J., Ajayi, K., & Raschke, R. L. (2015). Infer, predict, and assure: Accounting opportunities in data analytics. *Accounting Horizons*, *29*(3), 719–742.

The American Institute of CPAs (AIPCA). (2022a). Nomination of accounting and related CIP codes for inclusion in DHS STEM designated degree program list. https://nasba.org/wp-content/uploads/2022/08/2022-AICPA-Accounting-Profession-STEM-Nomination.pdf

The American Institute of CPAs (AIPCA). (2022b). *Uniform CPA examination Blueprints*. https://www.aicpa-cima.com/resources/article/learn-what-is-tested-on-the-cpa-exam

Venkatesh, R., Riley, J,. Eldridge, S., Lawson, R., & Church K. (2023). Management accounting – A rising star in the curriculum for a globally, integrated, technology–driven business age. *Issues in Accounting Education*, *38*(4), 109–129.

Warren, J. D., Moffitt, K. C., & Byrnes, P. (2015). How big data will change accounting? *Accounting Horizons*, *29*(2), 397–407.

APPENDIX: SURVEY OF DATA AND ANALYTICS IN THE INTRO MANAGERIAL ACCOUNTING COURSES

1. **Do you think data analytics should be covered in the intro managerial accounting class/textbook?**

    A. Strongly agree
    B. Agree
    C. Neither agree nor disagree
    D. Disagree
    E. Strongly disagree

2. **To what extent should data and analytics be covered in the intro managerial textbook/course?**

    A. No coverage of data analytics is needed in the intro managerial accounting course.
    B. An introduction to data analytics should be included in the opening chapter.
    C. Brief mention of data analytics should be in every chapter.
    D. Integrated coverage of data analytics should be in every chapter supporting traditional managerial accounting topics.

3. **To what extent and where should labs teaching analytics techniques be included in the textbook materials? These labs take 15–20 minutes each to learn.**

    A. No labs are needed in the intro textbook.
    B. Labs can be in the e-learning platform, outside of the textbook.
    C. Labs should be integrated into the textbook chapter and written by the authors.
    D. There would be up to four labs in each chapter.

4. **The extent and level of coverage of data and analytics in the intro managerial textbook would be one of the most important elements in choosing a text within the next three years.**

    A. Strongly agree
    B. Agree
    C. Neither agree nor disagree
    D. Disagree
    E. Strongly disagree

5. **There should be a discussion of internal and external data sources as part of intro managerial accounting.**
   A. Strongly agree
   B. Agree
   C. Neither agree nor disagree
   D. Disagree
   E. Strongly disagree

6. **Which software tools should be included for intro managerial accounting (select all that apply)?**
   A. Excel
   B. Tableau
   C. Power BI
   D. Other (please specify)_____

7. **Would your students need a substantive Excel tutorial before completing Excel assignments in intro managerial?**
   A. Yes
   B. No

8. **Students can either create visualizations, evaluate visualizations, or both in the intro managerial class. Which do you prefer (choose one)?**
   A. Create visualizations only
   B. Evaluate visualizations only
   C. Both create and evaluate visualizations

9. **Which analytics techniques should be covered in intro managerial class/text (choose all that apply)?**

General coverage of Excel formulas
Descriptive statistics (mean, median, etc.) using formulas
Descriptive statistics (mean, median, etc.) using Excel's Data Analysis Toolpak
Job costing calculations
Process costing calculations
Slope () for cost behavior
Regression analysis for cost behavior
Goal-seek/Breakeven analysis
NPV(), IRR(), PMT() for cash flow analysis
Forecast sheet
Sensitivity analysis
Other (please specify)

10. **Which visualization techniques should be covered in intro managerial class/text (choose all that apply)?**

Bar charts
Line charts
Pie charts
Pivot charts
Scatterplots and trend lines
Conditional formatting
Dashboards/Slicers
Sparklines
Other (please specify)

CHAPTER 2

A FRAMEWORK FOR INTEGRATING PYTHON PROGRAMMING INTO THE ACCOUNTING CURRICULA

Kelly Green and Angel Littlejohn

University of Louisiana – Lafayette, USA

ABSTRACT

In a ranking created by using data from multiple data sources, including CareerBuilder, GitHub, Google, Hacker News, the IEEE, Reddit, Stack Overflow, and Twitter, Python was shown to be the top programming language of 2023. Created in 1990, Python has seen a recent uptick in popularity driven primarily by its ability to sustain the use of artificial intelligence. Focus on data analytics proficiencies have gained significant traction especially now that the AICPA has incorporated data analytics as a key component in the CPA exam and the AACSB has made data analytics and other information technology skills a vital element of accounting accreditation. In response, accounting students and professors alike must respond to the growing need for data analytics skills. Currently, much of the data analytics course materials offered within textbooks include exercises working with Excel; however, this tool only scratches the surface of what is becoming expected of newly minted CPAs on the market. Therefore, we adapt a two-dimensional framework from contemporary accounting education literature for incorporating Python, a highly sought after programming language among employers, into the accounting curriculum.

Keywords: Data analytics; Python; programming; accounting curriculum; simple data sets; complex datasets; simple tasks; complex tasks; Calderon et al. framework

INTRODUCTION

This chapter provides professors with a framework for integrating the open-source program, Python, into the accounting curriculum. Python is a dynamic scripting language that allows for more simplicity and ease of use making it attractive for individuals wanting to perform data analysis. Because of Python's flexibility and simplicity, it is already a popular choice for teaching data analytics skills within Information Systems courses (Shein, 2015; Xu & Frydenberg, 2021). In 2018 Python was ranked the most popular coding language by IEEE (Cass, 2023), and in the same year named "Language of the Year" by the Application Development Trends Magazine (Ramel, 2019; Xu & Frydenberg, 2021). Python has consistently been the top ranked programming language on the TIOBE Index for several years.[1] Thus, it is easy to see why Python might be an excellent choice of programming language for newly minted accounting professionals just entering the job market.

As big data and data analytics continue to proliferate, accountants are increasingly expected to possess expert level skills in data analytics (Drew, 2018). This expectation is evident in ever increasing requirements from accrediting institutions (e.g., AACSB), professional bodies (e.g., AICPA), and employers. This has motivated an increased focus on data analytics within the classroom. As part of its CPA Evolution project, the AICPA created a new structure for the CPA exam that comprises of three mandatory core sections and three specialized electives, one of which is Business Analysis and Reporting which is expected to emphasize data analytics (NASBA, 2022).

Already, graduates are commonly running into issues arising from a lack of exposure to data analytics software during their undergraduate education. Andiola et al. (2020), surveyed higher education institutions across the US and found that while 92.8% of colleges surveyed had already incorporated lower-level data analytics learning tools such as electronic spreadsheets (primarily Microsoft Excel) into their curriculums, these same institutions were deficient in offering programming and query language skills such as Python. Further, we observe such trends communicated within whitepapers published by the Big 4 professional accounting firms. KPGM, for example, recently listed intelligent automation such as machine learning and data analytics as the numbers 1 and 2, respectively, on their "Top 10 in 2020: Considerations for impactful audit departments" (KPMG, 2019). The consensus among the Big 4 is that integrating technology into the internal audit process is of paramount importance for auditors as well (Green & Green, 2019). Therefore, accounting graduates entering the job market are currently in critical need of data analytics literacy.

Integrating data analytics into the curriculum is seen as the single biggest obstacle accounting instructors currently face (Dow et al., 2022). This is especially true for accounting programs with the onset of Standard A7 introduced by AACSB accreditation, which currently requires universities to bolster the technology skills of their graduates by integrating learning objectives associated with data analytics and information technology skills within the curriculum (Dzuranin et al., 2018). Additionally, accounting programs that are separately accredited

A Framework for Integrating Python Programming 23

from their respective business schools, are now required to create learning experiences to include "mastery of current technology" and to foster "agility in technology" (AACSB, 2018; Vien, 2018).

Emerging technologies such as ChatGPT further enhance the accessibility of Python for both students and instructors. ChatGPT's ability to generate Python code with the use of natural language queries now makes the programming language more readily accessible than nowadays without the assistance of generative artificial intelligence technologies. Additionally, ChatGPT is able to assist students and instructors instantaneously, allowing for students to adapt skills for real world applications beyond what is detailed in their coursework. For a very simple example, a student can compose and enter the query "create python code to find the sum of two groups" and the code in Fig. 2.1 will be generated in an instant. Here you can see that we are given step by step coding instructions on inputting the data of two potential groups, calculating the sum of each, finding the overall sum of the two groups, and finally printing those results. We are also provided helpful notes and information on how to customize these model groups to suit our needs.

 You
Create python code to find the sum of two groups

ChatGPT
Certainly! Here's a simple Python code snippet to find the sum of two groups:

```python
# Define two groups of numbers
group1 = [10, 20, 30, 40]
group2 = [5, 15, 25, 35]

# Calculate the sum of each group
sum_group1 = sum(group1)
sum_group2 = sum(group2)

#Find the overall sum of the two groups
Total_sum = sum_group1 + sum_group2

# Print the results
print("Sum of group1:", sum_group1)
print("Sum of group2:", sum_group2)
print("Total Sum of both groups;", total_sum)
```

This code defines two lists '**group1**' and '**group2**', and then calculates the sum of each group using the '**sum()**' function. The sums are stored in the variables '**sum_group1**' and '**sum_group2**', which are then printed to the console.

Fig. 2.1. ChatGPT Natural Language Python Code Generation.

In this chapter, we adapt an implementation method derived from Calderon et al. (2022). For this purpose, we distinguish two dimensions of data analytics (task and data complexity) to align material so that they may be integrated across a spectrum of post-secondary educational levels while providing guidance on appropriate comprehension expectations at sophomore through graduate levels. Applying Calderon et al.'s (2022) model, we utilize dataset complexity (simple and complex datasets) and analytics task difficulty (simple and complex tasks) to illustrate examples of tasks and datasets that are appropriate for both undergraduate and graduate level accounting courses. We also provide sample code and application instructions to empower students with the ability to apply data analytics skills to authentic real world analytic needs at varying levels of the accounting curricula.

In the remainder of this chapter, we first provide background to establish the need for students in higher education to learn data analytic skills, especially widely used and free data software such as Python. We also describe why Python is a preferred data analytics software based on ease of use and accessibility, making it ideal for a classroom setting for beginner to intermediate skill levels. Next, we develop and apply the framework adapted from Calderon et al. (2022) to provide guidance for implementing Python coding exercises within the classroom. Consistent with Calderon et al. (2022), we lay out a 2 × 2 platform with varying levels of difficulty by task complexity (simple vs complex) and data complexity (simple vs complex) along with applicable course levels for each combination of task/data complexity in the matrix. Like Calderon et al. (2022, p. 212), we define simple data sets as "highly structured data in a flat file" needing little transformation for analysis, and complex data sets as those that "require users to manipulate/transform the data and/or data structures in order to prepare for data analytics." We also provide both simple and complex tasks for students to execute, utilizing both simple and complex data sets. To aid instructors and students, we offer illustrations and sample codes to implement within the classroom. Finally, we provide conclusions and implications.

BACKGROUND

With big data becoming more pervasive and more utilized to create value in the business world, there is a strong need for individuals entering the workforce to attain higher levels of data analytics capabilities (Augustine et al., 2020). To achieve this, it is essential for post-secondary educational institutions to begin equipping students with programming acumen so that they can manage tasks beyond what had once been required of entry level accountants (Richins et al., 2017). Much of the routine tasks previously executed by entry level accounting professionals have become increasingly automated, allowing accountants and auditors to focus on more analytical tasks that require new skill sets such as coding. At the same time, accounting programs struggle to incorporate such advanced skills as coding into the curriculum. In a recent survey conducted by the Association of Chartered Certified Accountants drawing from 992 of its members, 57% of the respondents had no knowledge of coding even at a basic level (ACCA, 2021). Further, the importance of students' needs for such skills while entering the job market was very evident with 85% of respondents agreeing that coding is an "in-demand skillset and would improve their market value." Additionally, in a report from PwC. the first suggestion to get students ready for the modern accounting workforce is to include "basic programming skills using a contemporary coding language such as Python or Java" (PwC, 2015). Unfortunately, some professors do not believe that the type of analytical approach to thinking that is needed for effective coding is being incorporated into the accounting curriculum (AICPA, 2015).

Python offers multiple advantages for integration into the accounting curriculum. First, Python is a relatively easy-to-learn programming language due to its similarity to English and visual formatting, making it relatively straightforward to understand while skimming through code (Blackmon, 2021). In other words, Python is a beginner-friendly language that accounting students can readily learn. Python also has a large and active community of developers. This translates to a wealth of online tutorials, forums, and documentation, providing students with ample resources for learning and troubleshooting.

Additionally, Python has a well-established and continually growing set of open-source tools for data analytics. While Python is utilized in professional business settings, it is open source, which means students can download and utilize this powerful coding tool for free, making it available for classroom purposes without additional financial burden to the student and institution. Python excels at data visualization with specialized libraries such as Matplotlib and Seaborn, which support a variety of techniques for exploring and identifying patterns in large datasets. Accounting students can use these tools to create clear and compelling charts and graphs, effectively communicating financial information to stakeholders. Similarly, Python has capabilities of machine learning, which is stated to be one of the top business focuses for upcoming accounting professionals and the number one on KPMG's list of considerations for impactful internal audit departments (Arvind & Yaseen, 2022).

Python skills are currently in high demand in the job market (Blackmon, 2021; Cass, 2023; Daws, 2020; Goh et al., 2022; Robert Half, 2021). Equipping accounting students with Python proficiency strengthens their resumes and makes them more attractive to potential employers. A skillset like Python programming is portable to various projects, firms, and industries. It is a cornerstone in such fields as data science and machine learning, which are increasingly impacting accounting. Accordingly, learning Python equips students with skills relevant not just today, but also for the future of accounting and business. Consequently, it is easy then to see why Python is an excellent choice for accounting programs to adopt into their respective courses, particularly to satisfy information technology and data analytics requirements in the classroom (AACSB 2018, Standard A5).

FRAMEWORK

Table 2.1 presents the two-dimensional matrix framework adapted from Calderon et al. (2022). In the columns, we first distinguish between simple and complex

Table 2.1. A Framework for Integrating Python into the Accounting Curricula.

Task Complexity	Dataset complexity	
	Simple Dataset	Complex Dataset
Simple	The dataset consists of a single flat file (a two-dimensional table containing rows and columns, with each row representing a case and each column representing an attribute of that case). No other files are associated with the flat file and only limited data manipulation and transformations are needed for data analytics. The task is usually descriptive or diagnostic. Simple visualizations (e.g., scatter plots, histograms, bar charts, etc.) may also fall into this classification. Accounting and business students at the sophomore level should have no difficulty with the semantics and cognitive dimensions of such tasks.	The dataset consists of multiple flat files (a two-dimensional table containing rows and columns, with each row representing a case and each column representing an attribute of that case). The files must be merged by using a primary key in one table (main) and foreign keys in different tables. Each primary key uniquely defines a case in the main table, and each foreign key points to that case. Other file formats may exist but will significantly complicate the data preparation process. Files are often large and not easy to work with in such tools as Excel. The task is usually descriptive or diagnostic. Simple visualizations (e.g., scatter plots, histograms, bar charts, etc.) may also fall into this classification. Accounting and business students at the sophomore level should have no difficulty with the semantics and cognitive dimensions of such tasks. Depending on the learning group, instructors may modify the complexity of the dataset to make it more manageable and doable.
COMPLEX	Dataset same as above (simple dataset) but the task is complex. The task is usually predictive or involves complex pattern recognition, clustering, or advanced visualization. Accounting and business students at the senior and graduate level should have no difficulty with the semantics and cognitive dimensions of such tasks. Depending on the learning group, instructors may modify the complexity of the task to make it more manageable and doable.	The dataset is the same as above (complex dataset). The task is usually predictive or involves complex pattern recognition, clustering, or advanced visualization. Accounting and business students at the senior and graduate level should have no difficulty with the semantics and cognitive dimensions of such tasks.

Note: We use Python to illustrate and discuss each quadrant in this framework.

data sets. Simple data sets consist of single flat files that require little to no grooming or manipulation of the data prior to analysis. Conversely complex data sets, which can be expanded into the concept of Big Data, are comprised of multiple flat files which must be merged by utilizing primary keys and associated foreign keys to link appropriate data relationships. This grooming and manipulation of data is often the source of most data analytics work, many times taking up 80% of a specialist's working time (Press, 2016).

The second dimension within this framework categorizes task complexity. Davenport and Dyche (2013) define the most common categories of analytic tasks as descriptive, predictive, and prescriptive. Similarly, for the purpose of this chapter, we categorize tasks as either "simple" or "complex." Simple tasks are those that can be considered descriptive in nature, often utilizing data to create simple visualizations. For the purposes of our exercises, we utilize box plots and scatterplots, but other examples can include charts, infographics, and other similar graphics. Conversely, complex tasks are those that can be considered predictive or prescriptive in nature. While complex tasks can either utilize simple or complex data sets, the focus shifts from the question of "what is?" to "what could we expect?" Complex tasks are typically associated with multifaceted pattern recognition, clustering, or advanced visualization. In our model, we define differing task levels to coincide with the presumed skills of different students: sophomore level for simple tasks and senior or graduate level for complex tasks.

DATA SET COMPLEXITY

Simple Dataset

We adapt a single, proprietary data set utilized in Calderon et al. (2022) to illustrate our framework. The dataset covers information from a company operating a chain of 48 hotels within 4 Southwestern states. It consists of 45 variables, offering a range of both financial (e.g., revenue, profit, customer refunds, and similar operating information) and non-financial data (e.g., general manager tenure, training, supervisor name, year of last renovations, and other similar variables). Appendix 1 provides a complete list of variables included in the dataset. Because many of these variables span multiple years, we can measure changes in these variables over time. Because the data is comprised of only 48 rows, with each row corresponding to observations for a distinct hotel, the data set utilized requires little merging or any sort of significant transformations in order to uncover patters for further investigation. Due to the simplicity of the dataset, the instructor can readily focus students' attention on exploring relevant patterns and relationships within a relatively compact classroom session.

Understanding the intricacies of hotel profitability is crucial for strategic decision-making within the hospitality industry. To facilitate comprehensive analyses, we provide additional code in Appendix 2 for professors to generate a synthetic dataset that mirrors key characteristics of real-world hotel data. This process utilizes Python's pandas library and NumPy for numerical simulations.[2] This allows individuals to simulate a dataset resembling hotel-related financial information, including factors such as room occupancy, revenue, and costs.

Simple Task

Our first analysis is a simple task, which requires students to calculate firm profits by state. Students group the data by state and then calculate the sum for each group. The code required first to import the file and set the working directory appears below. It is important to note that lines beginning with '#' are lines of code for notation purposes only and are meant to guide the user on what the lines of code are executing, they will not execute any function having '#' preceding it.

```
import pandas as pd

# Set the working directory (optional in Python)
# Note: In Python, we typically don't need to set the
working directory # for file operations.
# You can specify the full path directly.
# Example:
# project_directory = "/Your/Project/Directory/Here"

# Read the Excel file
file_path = "Pueblo_Hospitality.xlsx"
pueblo = pd.read_excel(file_path)

# Group the data by State and calculate the sum of
Profit for each #group
result  =  pueblo.groupby("State")["Profit"].sum().
reset_index()
result.rename(columns={"Profit": "totalProfit"}, inplace
=True)

# Print the result (or save it to a file)
print(result)
```

The first line imports the Pandas library and assigns it the alias "pd."[3] Scientific notation is used to display large numbers, which is not appropriate for accounting functions. If a user wishes to suppress scientific notation in the pandas library temporarily and specify two decimal places as the default you may enter the following line of code after pandas has been imported:

```
'pd.set_option('display.float_format', lambda x: f'
{x:,.2f}')'
```

We then set the working directory (optional in Python), it is important to note that in Python, we typically do not need to set the working directory for file operations. You can specify the full path directly. For example,

```
project_directory = "/Your/Project/Directory/Here"
```

This comment section mentions setting the working directory, but in Python, it is not necessary to set the working directory explicitly for file operations. You can explicitly specify the full path to the file you want to read.

```
file_path = "Pueblo_Hospitality.xlsx"

pueblo = pd.read_excel(file_path)
```

Here, we use the `pd.read_excel` function from the Pandas library to read the Excel file named "Pueblo_Hospitality.xlsx" and store the data in a Pandas DataFrame called `pueblo`. This line reads the Excel data into a tabular format that can be easily manipulated. Next, we group the data by State and calculate the sum of Profit for each group using the fourth and fifth lines of code. These two functions accomplish the following:

- `pueblo.groupby("State")` groups the data in the DataFrame by the "State" column.
- `["Profit"].sum()` calculates the sum of the "Profit" column within each group.
- `reset_index()` resets the index of the resulting DataFrame.
- `result.rename(columns={"Profit": "totalProfit"}, inplace=True)` renames the "Profit" column to "totalProfit" for clarity.

Finally, we can print the result (or save it to a file) using the function found in the last line of code, giving us the following Table 2.2.

We are then able to print the result DataFrame to the screen. You can also choose to save this DataFrame to a file or perform further analysis on it depending on your needs.

Table 2.2. Simple Dataset, Simple Task: Total Profit by State.

State	totalProfit
CA	39,068,601.01
FL	34,592,383.99
NY	33,800,725.59
TX	40,771,771.58

Complex Task

Next, we look to deploy a more intricate data analysis task with the simple, single data set. To do so, we use the task of visualizations of the data for the purpose of finding the distribution of hotel profit per available room, by state. Visualization methods can be diverse and vary in their levels of complexity. Following Calderon et al. (2022), we choose to employ a simple box blot. A box plot, sometimes referred to as a box-and-whisker plot, is a graphical representation of the distribution and statistical summary of a data set. Specifically, it provides a visual way to understand a central tendency, spread, and presence of outliers in our datasets. This visualization method depicts first the box representing the interquartile range (IQR), spanning from the first quartile to the third. Whiskers (or adjacent lines) then extend form the edges of the box to indicate the range of the data. Finally, all outliers in our figure are indicated as dots beyond these whiskers. Outliers are typically considered extreme data points or anomalies well outside of the general population.

The code required for the aforementioned task appears below. Again, it is important to note lines beginning with # indicate that they are notes to allow the user to better follow the individual task each line is executing.

```
#import necessary libraries:
import seaborn as sns
import matplotlib.pyplot as plt

# Create a new variable "ProfitPAR" by dividing Profit by (Number of
# rooms * 365)
pueblo['ProfitPAR'] = pueblo['Profit']/(pueblo['Number of rooms'] * 365)

# Create a box plot
plt.figure(figsize=(10, 6))
sns.boxplot(x='State', y='ProfitPAR', data=pueblo)
plt.xlabel('State')
plt.ylabel('Profit per Available Room')
plt.title('Performance by State')

# Show the plot
plt.show()
```

To begin the analysis, we start similarly to our previous task, again by importing the needed libraries into Python. For the purpose of creating a box plot we import the seaborn library in the first line of code as 'sns.' Additionally, in our second line of code we import 'matplotlib.pyplot' as 'plt' for the purpose of customization and displaying the plot. Notice that 'plt' is used in the code as a precursor to indicate specific characteristics of the box plot to be customized, that is, figure size, axis labels, title, etc.

Next, we move to calculating the Profit per Available room (ProfitPAR). To accomplish this, we create a new variable named "ProfitPAR" by dividing the 'Profit' column by the product of the 'number of Rooms' and 365 (number of days in a typical calendar year). This calculation is performed for each row within the DataFrame. Now that we have this new variable, we can create our box plot. To do so we begin by creating a new figure with a specified size using plt.figure(figsize=(10, 6); 10 indicating the divisions, or tics, along the

A Framework for Integrating Python Programming 31

x axis and 6 divisions along the y axis. We then use sns.boxplot to create the box plot, specifying the *x*-axis as "State" and the y-axis as 'ProfitPAR' from the DataFrame 'pueblo.'

Now that the box plot data has been specified, we can make customization options. First, we customize Plot Labels and Title. We use plt.xlabel to label the x-axis as 'State', and plt.ylabel to label the y-axis as "Profit per Available Room." Additionally, we set the plot title using plt.title. Finally, we use plt.show() to display the plot giving us the following output as in Fig. 2.2.

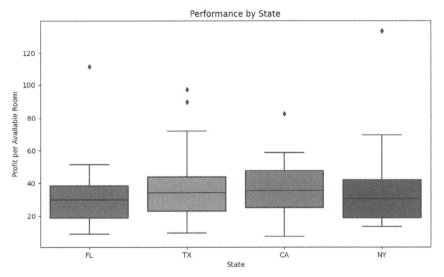

Fig. 2.2. Simple Dataset, Complex Task: Data Visualization.

Complex Dataset

Simple Task

To demonstrate a simple task within a complex dataset, we utilize multiple datasets to create a scatterplot enhanced by an overlaid regression line. Scatterplots are a routine undertaking, and the addition of a regression line is relatively uncomplicated. Because of these factors, we consider this task to be one that can be classified as simple despite the complexity of the dataset utilized. The dataset, adapted from Calderon et al. (2022), attains complexity through the combination of related data found from diverse sources, incorporates nine years of monthly data that has been sourced from four different economy lodging hotels. Additionally, monthly temperature data is procured from the National Weather Service and Consumer Price Index data gathered from the bureau of Labor Statistics. Sample Python code provided below is specifically designed to generate the scatterplot for a single hotel, offering an insight on how these methods can be applied within more complex datasets.

```python
import pandas as pd
import matplotlib.pyplot as plt
import seaborn as sns

# Read data from Excel files
rentals = pd.read_excel("SalesVolumes.xlsx")
costs = pd.read_excel("Cost.xlsx")
cpi = pd.read_excel("cpi.xlsx")
temperature = pd.read_excel("temperaturedata.xlsx")

# Merge the datasets using left joins
df = rentals.merge(costs, on=["City", "Year", "Month"], how="left")
df = df.merge(cpi, on=["Year", "Month"], how="left")
df = df.merge(temperature, on=["City_x", "Year", "Month"], how="left")

# Filter data for the city "Arlington"
df = df[df["City"] = = "Arlington"]

#Find the max cpi and store it
max_cpi = df['CPI'].max()

# Calculate the inflation-adjusted cost
df["adjCost"] = df["Cost"] * max_cpi / df["CPI"]

# Remove unwanted columns
df.drop(["City", "Cost", "CPI"], axis=1, inplace=True)

# Create a scatterplot with regression line
plt.figure(figsize=(10, 6))
sns.scatterplot(data=df,     x="Rooms     rented",
y="adjCost")
plt.xlabel('Rooms Rented')
plt.ylabel('Total Cost')
plt.title('Relationship Between Sales Volume and Cost')
plt.text(300, 4000, 'Costs are inflation-adjusted',
fontsize=10, color='blue')

# Add the regression line
sns.regplot(data=df, x="Rooms rented", y="adjCost",
color='blue', scatter=False)

# Show the plot

plt.show()
```

A Framework for Integrating Python Programming 33

For our first phase of analysis, we begin the process by importing the needed Python libraries. We import 'pandas' for data manipulation, 'matplotlib.pyplot' for plotting, and 'seaborn' for enhancing the plot with a regression line. Our next step involves reading the data from four Excel files using the function pd.read_excel to read data from four Excel files and store them as Pandas DataFrames, each of which corresponding to various aspects of our analysis, more specifically, rentals, costs, cpi (Consumer Price Index), and temperature. Once we have acquired the data required, we then proceed to merging our datasets. We merge the datasets by using left joins on the specified columns ("city," "year," "month") to create the DataFrame 'df.' Our portion of code in these lines, how="left" ensure that all rows from the left DataFrame (in this case, 'rentals') are retained.

To narrow our focus, we can now filter the data to include only rows in which the "city" is identified as "Arlington." This step allows us to concentrate exclusively on the relevant subset of our data. In our next step of analysis, we calculate the inflation-adjusted cost and store it in a new column called "adjCost." In our last bit of data manipulation, we eliminate unwanted columns, in this case "city," "totalCost," and "cpi" using the 'drop' method to pare down our dataset.

Now that our data set has been reduced to only the items required, we can move on to the visualization stage where we will create a scatterplot with a regression line. We create a scatterplot using sns.scatterplot and add axis labels and a title. Additionally, we add a text annotation to indicate that the costs are inflation-adjusted using the function plt.text. We then add the regression line using sns.regplot with the scatter=False argument to suppress the scatter points on top of the line. Finally, we can display the completed plot. This is done by utilizing the function plt.show() which produces, Fig. 2.3's visual

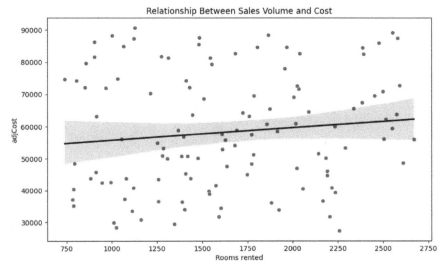

Fig. 2.3. Complex Dataset, Simple Task: Data Visualization.

representation of our scatterplot with regression line, labels, and annotations, providing a comprehensive interpretation of the inflation-adjusted costs within the city of Arlington.

Complex Task – Descriptive Modeling
A more complex undertaking involves estimating a cost function for a single hotel, for the purpose of our analysis we will choose the Arlington hotel. We anticipate that instructors will delve both into the mechanics and semantics of the cost function during their class time while utilizing such analysis. Therefore, this particular exercise may be best suited for courses that include topics such as cost management at a senior graduate level. In the previous example we have already provided code to create the DataFrame, and the following code conducts the regression function and subsequent OLS regression results output.

```
import pandas as pd
import statsmodels.api as sm

# Assuming you have already created and prepared the 'df' DataFrame
# from the previous example

# Define the dependent variable (inflation-adjusted cost) and
# independent variables
y = df['adjCost']
X = df[['Rooms rented', 'Year']]
# You may need to create dummy variables for 'year'
if not already done

# Add a constant to the independent variables (intercept term)
X = sm.add_constant(X)

# Fit a linear regression model
regModel = sm.OLS(y, X).fit()

# Print the regression summary
print(regModel.summary())
```

For this task, we begin by import necessary libraries to Python. Again, we import 'pandas' for data manipulation and 'statsmodels.api' for estimating the linear regression model. Next, we define both our dependent and independent variables. We specify the dependent variable 'y' as 'adjCost' (inflation-adjusted cost) and the independent variables 'X' as room rentals, heating degree days, cooling degree days, and year). You may need to

A Framework for Integrating Python Programming 35

create dummy variables for the 'year' variable if it is not already done in the DataFrame. To ensure the model's accuracy, we add a Constant (Intercept) to the independent variables. We use the function sm.add_constant to add a constant term (intercept) to the independent variables. This is necessary to estimate the intercept in the linear regression model. Next, we fit the linear regression model, to do so we use sm.OLS to specify and fit the linear regression model. This function takes the dependent variable (y) and independent variables (X) as arguments and returns a regression model object encapsulating the models' parameters. Lastly to visualize the regression model summary we use print(regModel.summary()) to display the summary statistics of the linear regression model, which includes coefficients, p-values, R-squared, and other relevant statistics as shown in Table 2.3.

Table 2.3. Complex Dataset, Complex Task – Descriptive Modeling: Linear Regression Model.

OLS Regression Results

Dep. Variable:	adjCost	R-squared:	0.119
Model:	OLS	Adj. R-squared:	0.104
Method:	Least Squares	F-statistic:	7.902
Date:	Mon, 05 Oct 2023	Prob (F-statistic):	0.000604
Time:	12:27:24	Log-Likelihood:	−1337.1
No. Observations:	120	AIC :	2680.
Df Residuals:	117	BIC:	2689.
Df Model:	2		
Covariance Type:	nonrobust		

	coef	std err	t	P>|t|	[0.025	0.975]
const	4.112e+06	1.09e+06	3.789	0.000	1.96e+06	6.26e+06
Rooms rented	3.9671	2.918	1.360	0.177	−1.812	9.746
Year	−2012.3520	537.556	−3.742	0.000	−3077.587	−947.197

Omnibus:	31.106	Durbin-Watson:	1.945
Prob(Omnibus)	0.000	Jarque-Bera (JB):	6.376
Skew:	0.043	Prob(JB):	0.0412
Kurtosis:	1.874	Cond. Ho.	1.84e+06

Notes:
[1] Standard Errors assume that the covariance matrix of the errors is correctly specified.
[2] The condition number is large, 1.84e+06. This might indicate that there are strong multicollinearity or other numerical problems.

Complex Task – Predictive Modeling
Within the following section, we elaborate on a more sophisticated task that leverages complex data to display a time series predictive model. Our approach utilizes the time series data of hotel rentals to generate multiple forecasts for future rentals. The following sample code makes predictions by training and evaluating our data sets and then makes predictions based on the trained model. Additionally, we evaluate the model's performance.

```
# Import Necessary Libraries:
# pandas: Used for handling and manipulating data in
tabular form.
# matplotlib.pyplot: Used for plotting graphs.
#   statsmodels.tsa.holtwinters.ExponentialSmoothing:
Implements the   # Holt-Winters Exponential Smoothing
model for time series forecasting.
# sklearn.metrics.mean_squared_error: Measures the mean
squared error  # between actual and predicted values.
#   sklearn.model_selection.train_test_split:  Splits
the dataset into  # training and testing sets.

import pandas as pd
import matplotlib.pyplot as plt
from        statsmodels.tsa.holtwinters        import
ExponentialSmoothing
from sklearn.metrics import mean_squared_error
from sklearn.model_selection import train_test_split

# Assuming you have already created and prepared the
'df' DataFrame
# from the previous example

# Extract relevant columns
ts_data = df[['adjCost']]

# Convert the 'date' column to datetime format and set
it as the index
# of the DataFrame
ts_data.index = pd.to_datetime(df.index)

# Split the data into training and testing sets
train_size = int(len(ts_data) * 0.8)
train, test = ts_data[:train_size], ts_data[train_size:]

# Fit the Exponential Smoothing model
# "trend='add'" assumes an additive trend
# "seasonal='add' assumes an additive seasonality
# "seasonal_periods=12" assumes a yearly seasonality
pattern based on # 12 months

model   =   ExponentialSmoothing(train,   trend='add',
seasonal='add', seasonal_periods=12)
```

```
result = model.fit()

# Make predictions on the test set using the trained
model
predictions   =   result.predict(start=test.index[0],
end=test.index[-1])

# Evaluate the model
# Calculates the mean squared error between the actual
and predicted # values on the test set, which provides
a measure of how well the
# model performs

mse = mean_squared_error(test, predictions)
print(f'Mean Squared Error: {mse}')

# Plot the training data, testing data and predicted
values for # visualization
# Helps in assessing the model's ability to capture
underlying patterns # in the time series data

plt.figure(figsize=(12, 6))
plt.plot(train.index, train, label='Train')
plt.plot(test.index, test, label='Test')
plt.plot(test.index, predictions, label='Predictions',
color='red')
plt.title('Time Series Forecasting with Exponential
Smoothing')
plt.xlabel('Date')
plt.ylabel('Adjusted Cost')
plt.legend()
plt.show()
```

In Fig. 2.4's example, the Holt-Winters Exponential Smoothing method for times series forecasting was used. The seasonal periods' parameter is set to 12, assuming a yearly seasonality pattern based on monthly data. The parameters may need to be adjusted based on the characteristics of the data. Seasonality may be quarters, particularly in the financial sector. Note that time series forecasting often involves more complex models and considerations, and tuning parameters may be necessary for optimal results. Additionally, there are other models available such as SARIMA, Facebook Prophet, or deep learning techniques depending on the complexity of the data and the patterns that we are attempting to capture.

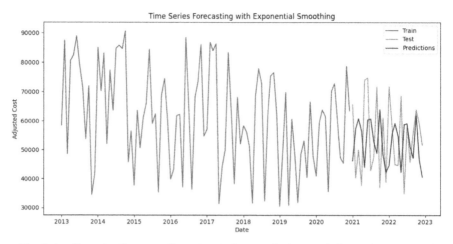

Fig. 2.4. Complex Dataset, Complex Task – Predictive Modeling: Time Series of Hotel Rentals to Create Multiple Rental Forecasts.

EXPANDING THE FRAMEWORK

A (Big) Complex Dataset

In this academic study, we gathered data from the U.S. Bureau of Transportation Statistics database, accessible at transtats.bts.gov. The aviation sector, characterized by its substantial scale, generates an extensive body of operational data that offers valuable insights for managerial, accounting, and financial purposes. The resulting dataset is intricate, given its substantial volume, the necessity to integrate disparate files, and the comprehensive preprocessing efforts required to facilitate the amalgamation of data into a unified flat file suitable for analytical examination. The Airline On-Time Performance Data is used in this study, which compiles data on domestic flights by airlines that surpass 1% of the country's total yearly income from ordinary domestic travel within the United States. The Federal Aviation Administration's (FAA) airplane registration database was downloaded and used to increase the complexity of the dataset.

Our first Complex Dataset analysis is a simple task: Students are tasked to find the ten busiest airports within the large set of data outlined in the collection above. The code required first to import the data, extract it from the zip file and subsequently seek those airports are as follows. Once again, it is important to note that lines beginning with '#' are lines of code for notation purposes only and are meant to guide the user on what the lines of code are executing, they will not execute any function having '#' preceding it.

```
import pandas as pd
import zipfile
```

```
# Extract the data from the ZIP file
with zipfile.ZipFile('flights-2019.zip', 'r') as zip_ref:
  zip_ref.extractall()

# Read the CSV file into a Pandas DataFrame
flights = pd.read_csv('ontime-2019.csv')

# Find the ten busiest airports
busiest_airports = flights['ORIGIN'].value_counts().head(10)

# Display the result
print(busiest_airports)
```

To begin our (big) complex dataset exploration, we start by importing our necessary libraries to python. As we have previously, we import 'pandas' to manage data manipulation and analysis, and 'zipfile' to extract data from the ZIP file. To extract the data from our zip file we utilize the function zipfile.ZipFile to extract the contents of the ZIP file ('flights-2019.zip'), this step allows the accessibility of the contents for further analysis. Subsequently, we read the extracted CSV file ('ontime-2019.csv') into a Pandas DataFrame using the function pd.read_csv. For the purpose of our analysis, we then seek to find the ten busiest airports within our dataset. To do so we use the function value_counts() to count the number of flights originating from each airport and then use head(10) to retrieve the top ten airports with the highest flight frequencies. Once completed, we are then able to display the results using print(busiest_airports) rendering the information shown in Table 2.4.

Now that we have found the busiest airports within the data set, we can seek more specific information. Utilizing the following set of code, we discover the top 10 busiest routes.

Table 2.4. A (Big) Complex Dataset: Busiest Airports by Number of Annual Departures.

ATL	31155
ORD	26216
DFW	23063
CLT	19100
DEN	18507
LAX	17988
PHX	14761
IAH	14598
LGA	13872
SFO	13689

```
import pandas as pd

# Assuming you have already read the 'flights' DataFrame from the
# provided data

# Group the data by pairs of originating and destination airports, and
# count the rows for each group
route_freq=flights.groupby(['ORIGIN', 'DEST']).size().reset_index(name='freq')

# Sort the routes by frequency in descending order
top_10_routes = route_freq.sort_values(by='freq', ascending=False).head(10)

# Display the top 10 busiest routes
print(top_10_routes)
```

To begin our data analysis, we begin once more by importing our necessary libraries into Python. Again, we import 'pandas' to manage data manipulation and analysis. Once imported we can group data and count. We first use `groupby(['ORIGIN', 'DEST']).size().reset_index(name='freq')` to group the data by pairs of originating and destination airports ('ORIGIN' and 'DEST' columns) and count the rows for each group. The result is stored in the 'route_freq' DataFrame with a 'freq' column representing the frequency of each route. To enhance our analysis, we then move to sort routes by frequency. We use `sort_values(by='freq', ascending=False)` to sort the routes by frequency in descending order, so the busiest routes appear at the top. Next, we move to identify the top ten busiest routes. We use `.head(10)` to select the top ten rows (i.e., the top ten busiest routes) from the sorted DataFrame. By doing this, the results are now stored in the 'top_10_routes' DataFrame. To conclude our analysis, we then present the outcome in Table 2.5 by printing the list of our ten busiest flight routes with the function `print(top_10_routes)`, rendering the following outcome.

Big Data – Illustrating Merged Datasets
To examine more complex inquiries, we can task our management accounting students to seek information regarding potential airliner issues that can be uncovered by utilizing a large set of data compiled by merging datasets. Specifically in this example, we will be answering the following questions: First, which aircraft are associated with the most cancellations? Second, what are the taxi times for United Airlines mainline (i.e., non-regional) aircraft at its ten busiest airports? To seek this information, we utilize the following Python code.

A Framework for Integrating Python Programming 41

Table 2.5. A (Big) Complex Dataset: Highest Frequency Routes by Number of Flights.

Origin	Dest	freq
LAX	SFO	1285
SFO	LAX	1283
ORD	LGA	1230
LGA	ORD	1230
LAX	JFK	1064
JFK	LAX	1064
LAX	LAS	1061
LAS	LAX	1059
LGA	BOS	832
BOS	LGA	832

```
import pandas as pd

# Assuming you have already read the 'flights' DataFrame
and other necessary data

# Read the aircraft registrations data and select
relevant columns
tails = pd.read_csv("MASTER.txt")
tails=tails[['N-NUMBER','MFR    MDL    CODE','YEAR
MFR','TYPE ENGINE']]
tails.columns = ['N.NUMBER', 'CODE', 'year', 'engineType']

# Read the aircraft reference data, filter for commer-
cial aircraft, and preprocess the model name
aircraft  =  pd.read_csv('ACFTREF.txt', dtype={'NO-
SEATS': int, 'TYPE-ACFT': int})
aircraft = pd.read_csv("ACFTREF.txt")
aircraft  =  aircraft[(aircraft['NO-SEATS'] > 10) &
(aircraft['TYPE-ACFT'] = = 5)]
aircraft['model'] = aircraft['MODEL'].str.strip()
aircraft  =  aircraft[['CODE',  'MFR',  'model',  'NO-
ENG', 'NO-SEATS']]

# Merge the DataFrames to analyze cancellations
fltStatus = flights[['Cancelled', 'Tail_Number']]
fltStatus['N.NUMBER'] = fltStatus['Tail_Number'].str[1:]
fltStatus  =  fltStatus.merge(tails, left_on='N.NUMBER',
right_on='N.NUMBER', how='left')
fltStatus  =  fltStatus.merge(aircraft, left_on='CODE',
right_on='CODE', how='left')
```

```
# Create a contingency table to count aircraft models
by cancellation status
out     =     pd.crosstab(fltStatus[model],    fltStatus
['CANCELLED'])

# Write the result to a CSV file
out.to_csv("cancellations.csv")

# Calculate cancellation percentage if needed
cancellation_percentage = out[1] / (out[0] + out[1])
```

As with our previous data analysis processes, we begin by importing the necessary Python libraries with the function `import pandas as pd`. Next, we read Aircraft Registrations Data: We read the FAA's master file of aircraft registrations and select the relevant columns. Specifically, we find the N-Number ('N-NUMBER'), manufacturer code ('MFR MDL CODE'), the year manufactured ('YEAR MFR'), and engine type ('TYPE ENGINE'). In the line following we also rename the columns to match the variable names used in the Python code. We then read in our second data set, the FAA's aircraft reference file. Next, we filter it for commercial aircraft, preprocess the model name, and select the relevant columns.

Once both of our DataFrames are read into Python we can merge them to create a consolidated DataFrame (fltStatus) for analysis. Now that the data is merged, we can create a contingency table. A contingency table is a two-dimensional table that can display the frequency distribution of categorical values. These tables are useful when analyzing the relationship between two categorical variables. The cells in our contingency table represent the counts (or frequencies) of observations that fall into specific categories. We use `pd.crosstab` to create a contingency table that counts aircraft models by cancellation status.

Finally, we display our findings in Table 2.6. We utilize the function `to_csv` to write the contingency table to a CSV file. For our analysis, we would like to calculate the cancellation percentage based on the model of airplane engine models and calculate the cancellation percentage.

Table 2.6. A (Big) Complex Dataset – Merged Datasets: Cancellation Rates by Aircraft Type.

Model	
717-200	0.000267
737-700	0.000000
737-705	0.005305
737-71B	0.008351
737-71Q	0.000000
...	...
ERJ 170-200 LL	0.008789
ERJ 170-200 LR	0.012069
ERJ 190-100 IGW	0.017599
MD-88	0.000000
MD-90-30	0.000000

Big data – Taxi-out and Taxi-in Times for Mainline Aircraft at Busiest Airports

Bob Jordan, Southwest's current CEO stated "An airline needs to keep moving. It counts on the aircraft moving, the crews moving, obviously our passengers moving, the bags moving. So, all the pieces and parts need to keep moving" (The Wall Street Journal, 2022). There lies a plethora of issues that can cause a plane to be grounded for longer times that anticipated, ranging from crew shortages, weather, maintenance etc. Therefore, gaining insight into the amount of time planes spend on the ground for taxi-in and taxi-out would be of great interest to airline executives. Utilizing the following Python code, we can examine such figures as displayed in text and via Tables 2.7–2.9.

Table 2.7. A (Big) Complex Dataset – Merged Datasets: Top 10 airports with the most flight originations for United Airlines.

Origin	nrDepartures
ORD	6006
DEN	5797
IAH	5165
EWR	4926
SFO	4446
IAD	2382
LAX	2278
MCO	1130
BOS	1074
LAS	1056

Table 2.8. Combine the Two DataFrames and Remove Missing Values.

Origin	TaxiOut	TaxiIn	nrDepartures
MCO	12.0	4.0	1130
MCO	18.0	3.0	1130
MCO	12.0	4.0	1130
MCO	17.0	6.0	1130
MCO	14.0	7.0	1130
...	...	...	...
BOS	19.0	5.0	1074
BOS	16.0	9.0	1074
BOS	20.0	5.0	1074
BOS	23.0	5.0	1074
BOS	13.0	35.0	1074

Table 2.9. Mean Taxi-out and Taxi-in Times for the Top Ten Airports.

Origin	TaxiOut	TaxiIn
EWR	27.359787	7.524443
ORD	23.006846	7.117048
SFO	22.321598	7.972241
BOS	21.162417	9.988669
LAX	21.062885	8.460862
IAH	20.693470	7.331912
IAD	19.266947	7.898105
LAS	18.337441	9.346919
DEN	17.428349	6.787120
MCO	17.146406	8.859805

```
import pandas as pd

# Assuming you have already read the 'flights' DataFrame
# Identify United Airlines' mainline flights and select relevant
# columns
mainline = flights[(flights['Marketing_Airline_Network'] == "UA") & (flights['Operated_or_Branded_Code_Share_Partners'] == "UA")]
mainline = mainline[['Origin', 'TaxiOut', 'TaxiIn']]

# Identify the top ten airports with the most flight originations for # United Airlines
top10Airports = mainline.groupby('Origin').size().reset_index(name='nrDepartures')
top10Airports = top10Airports.sort_values(by ='nrDepartures', ascending=False).head(10)
print(top10Airports)

# Combine the two DataFrames and remove missing values
result = pd.merge(mainline, top10Airports, on='Origin', how='inner').dropna()
print(result)

# Compute the mean taxi-out and taxi-in times for the top ten airports
result = result.groupby('Origin').agg({'TaxiOut': 'mean', 'TaxiIn': 'mean'}).reset_index()
result = result.sort_values(by='TaxiOut', ascending=False)
print(result)
```

For our final analysis, we begin once more by importing our necessary Libraries. We import 'pandas' to handle data manipulation and analysis. Next, for our specific analytical steps, we look to identify all United Airlines' mainline flights. We filter the 'flights' DataFrame to identify United Airlines' mainline flights where both the marketing carrier and the operating carrier are "UA" (United Airlines). We then select the relevant columns: origin airport ('ORIGIN'), taxi-out time ('TAXI_OUT'), and taxi-in time ('TAXI_IN').

Once all our relevant columns are selected, we then look to Identify the top ten airports. We first group the 'mainline' DataFrame by the origin airport ('ORIGIN') and count the number of observations for each airport using groupby and size(). We then reset the index and rename the count column to 'nrDepartures'. We sort the airports in descending order of departure counts and select the top ten airports. To combine DataFrames and remove missing values, we merge the 'mainline' DataFrame with the 'top10Airports' DataFrame on the 'ORIGIN' column, keeping only the matching rows (inner join). We then drop any rows with missing values (NaN) resulting from airports that are not among United's top ten busiest airports. Lastly, we compute mean taxi-out and taxi-in times. To do this we group the 'result' DataFrame by the origin airport ('ORIGIN') and calculate the mean taxi-out and taxi-in times using the agg function. We reset the index to have a clean DataFrame. Finally, we sort the results by taxi-out time in descending order.

IMPLEMENTATION SUGGESTIONS

In the preceding sections, we outlined the framework for the 2 × 2 design for implementation of Python at various levels of data and task complexity. Because these ideas can be adopted and expanded based on various learning objectives that the professor may need to align with their specific students' abilities, we offer additional suggestions on implementation based on the size of the exercise to be engaged in. For this purpose, we have outlined each of the 2 × 2 dimensions with suggestions on how to implement at the project, module, and course task levels in Table 2.10, panel A. Additionally in Table 2.10, panel B, we provide library requirements and the cases in which such libraries are required, and a brief explanation of the library utilized.

CONCLUSION

While we have seen that many universities have taken up various measures to implement data analytics in their curriculum, higher education has been slow to adopt more advanced programming exercises to implement higher levels of proficiencies outside the standard Excel spreadsheets or Tableau (Andioal et al., 2018; Raschke & Charron, 2021). PWC has even called for reform of the accounting curriculum by adding programming language to their current curricula, Python being their first recommendation (PwC, 2015).

Table 2.10. A Framework for Implementation of Python.

Panel A: 2 × 2 Frame with Varying Levels of Implementation Scope

Simple Task, Simple Dataset:

Project	Analyze a simple dataset containing basic financial data (e.g., revenue, expenses, profit) using pandas and NumPy. Calculate basic statistics, such as mean, median, and standard deviation.
Module	Introduce students to data manipulation and visualization in pandas and Matplotlib using a simple dataset of their choice.
Course Task	Have students create simple visualizations (e.g., bar charts, line plots) of financial data to understand basic trends.

Simple Task, Complex Dataset:

Project	Merge multiple flat files containing financial data from different sources using pandas. Perform basic data cleaning and preparation for analysis.
Module	Teach students how to handle complex datasets using pandas and NumPy. Focus on merging, cleaning, and transforming data.
Course Task	Have students work with a large dataset of financial transactions and perform basic analytics, such as identifying outliers or trends.

Complex Task, Simple Dataset:

Project	Use seaborn and matplotlib to explore hotel profit distribution with data visualization based on a simple dataset of historical financial data.
Module	Introduce students to fundamental machine learning concepts using matplotlib using a simple dataset.
Course Task	Have students find the distribution of hotel profit over multiple variables and visualize using historical financial data and matplotlib.

Complex Task, Complex Dataset:

Project	Use statsmodels, matplotlib and sklearn to build linear regression and predictive models for descriptive analysis of financial news articles. Use a complex dataset containing text and labels.
Module	Teach advanced machine learning concepts using sklearn. Focus on forecasting in time series financial data.
Course Task	Have students work on a project to analyze complex financial datasets using advanced machine learning techniques, such as exponential smoothing or clustering .

Panel B: Library Use Cases

Library	Use Case
NumPy	Basic array operations, statistical calculations
pandas	Data manipulation, merging, cleaning, and analysis of datasets
Matplotlib	Creating simple visualizations like bar charts, line plots
Seaborn	Data visuallization library for creating statistical graphics.
Statsmodels	Module for estimating and testing variety of statistical models
Sklearn	Machine learning that provides tools for data analysis and data mining.

Adapted from Calderon et al. (2022), our framework for integrating Python utilizes two dimensions between: (a) simple and complex data sets and (b) simple and complex tasks. We identify simple data sets as those that are found in small, flat files, which do not require much additional grooming to make ready for data analytics. Conversely, complex data sets are those that are typically large and are comprised of multiple tables which require transformation and modification to get ready for data analytics tasks. We describe simple tasks as those that are more descriptive, while complex tasks are those that are more predictive in nature. This allows instructors to be able to choose from a range of potential levels of each dimension to deploy at varying levels of their academic program.

Python is an excellent choice for implementing data analytics proficiencies to secondary education for many reasons. First, Python can be utilized for a range of programming applications including data science solutions, machine learning frameworks, and web development. In addition, Python is free for students to download, can be run on both mac and windows computers, and requires minimal system requirement to support, making it an ideal choice to implement in the accounting curriculum at both the intermediate and advanced levels. Python was also recently tied as the number one "most wanted programming languages among developers worldwide, as of 2022" listed by statista.com based on a survey ran from May 11 to June 1, 2022, gathering insight from 71,467 software developer respondents, making it a highly marketable skill for freshly minted accounting majors entering the workforce (Statista, 2022).

Python is made even more accessible to students and instructors alike because of new technologies such as ChatGPT which can assist in the code writing process for a variety of accounting course applications. ChatGPT's ability to understand natural language queries and transform those into Python code allows students and faculty to instantly receive assistance while writing script. Allowing students to explore ChatGPT's code writing in tandem with data analysis exercises such as those highlighted in this chapter allows students to apply programming skills directly to real-world accounting scenarios. Further, ChatGPT offers guidance for users for a deeper understanding of both accounting and programming principles.

With the current perception that data analytics is considered the lowest-ranked skill of accounting students by faculty polled at a KPMG national symposium (Ballou, Heitger, & Stoel, 2018), it is clear that empowering students with proficiencies in Python and other data analytics applications will contribute to their successful in the accounting profession. This chapter provides a resource to help accounting faculty incorporate Python into the curriculum.

NOTES

1. See *TIOBE Index for February 2024* at https://www.tiobe.com/tiobe-index/ (Accessed March 7, 2024).

2. Pandas is a popular data manipulation library in Python capable of data manipulation, alignment, handing missing data, time series functionality and input/output tools. Pandas provides easy to use data structures which allows users to efficiently manipulate large data sets.

3. A library is a collection of code for models or functions that makes regular tasks more efficient. They are typically sets of pre-written functions that can be integrated into an individual's code for their own purpose.

REFERENCES

ACCA. (2021). *Coding: As a professional accountant, why you should be interested.* https://www.accaglobal.com/content/dam/ACCA_Global/Technical/tech/PI-CODING-PAPER%20v2.pdf

AICPA. (2015). *Should accounting students learn to code?* https://us.aicpa.org/interestareas/accountingeducation/newsandpublications/should-accounting-students-code

Andiola, L. M., Masters, E., & Norman, C. (2020). Integrating technology and data analytic skills into the accounting curriculum: Accounting department leaders' experiences and insights. *Journal of Accounting Education, 50,* 100655.

Arvind, S., & Yaseen K. (2022). *Internal audit: Key risks and areas of focus 2022.* https://assets.kpmg/content/dam/kpmg/ae/pdf-2022/03/internal-audit-key-risks-and-areas-of-focus-for-2022.pdf

Association to Advance Collegiate Schools of Business. (2018). *Eligibility procedures and accreditation standards for accounting accreditation.* Association to Advance Collegiate Schools of Business.

Augustine, F. K., Jr., Woodside, J., Mendoza, M., & Chambers, V. (2020). Analytics, accounting and big data: enhancing accounting education. *Journal of Management & Engineering Integration, 13*(1), 1–8.

Ballou, B., Heitger, D. L., & Stoel, D. (2018). Data-driven decision-making and its impact on accounting undergraduate curriculum. *Journal of Accounting Education, 44,* 14–24.

Blackmon, S. (2021). *The 10 most in-demand coding and programming languages to learn.* https://www.bestcolleges.com/bootcamps/guides/6-easiest-programming-languages-to-learn/

Calderon, T. G., Hesford, J. W., & Turner, M. J. (2022). A framework for integrating "R" programming into the accounting curriculum. *Advances in Accounting Education: Teaching and Curriculum Innovations, 25,* 209–232.

Cass, S. (2023). *The top programming languages 2023: Python and SQL are on top, but old languages shouldn't be forgotten.* https://spectrum.ieee.org/top-programming-languages/#/index/2021/1/1/1/1/1/50/1/50/1/50/1/30/1/30/1/20/1/20/1/5/1/50/1/100/1/50/

Davenport, T., & Dyche, J. (2013). *Big data in big companies.* International Institute for Analytics. https://www.iqpc.com/media/7863/11710.pdf

Daws, R. (2020). *IEEE Spectrum: Python is the top programming language of 2020.* https://www.developer-tech.com/news/2020/jul/27/ieee-spectrum-Python-top-programming-language-2020/#:~:text=The%20latest%20IEEE%20Spectrum%20shows,artificial%20intelligence%20and%20web%20development

Dow, K. E., Jacknis, N., & Watson, M. W. (2022). A framework and resources to create a data analytics-infused accounting curriculum. *Issues in Accounting Education, 36*(4), 183–205.

Drew, J. (2018). Merging accounting with 'big data' science. *Journal of Accountancy, 226*(1), 48–52.

Dzuranin, A. C., Jones, J. R., & Olvera, R. M. (2018). Infusing data analytics into the accounting curriculum: A framework and insights from faculty. *Journal of Accounting Education, 43,* 24–39.

Goh, C., Kusnadi, Y., & Pan, G. (2022). *The effectiveness of using Python programming approach in teaching financial analytics* (pp. 1–32). https://ink.library.smu.edu.sg/soa_research/2038

Green, K. B., & Green, B. P. (2019). Examining future issues facing internal auditors. *Internal Auditing, 2019,* 6–12.

KPMG. (2019). *Top 10 in 2020: Considerations for impactful internal audit departments.* https://assets.kpmg/content/dam/kpmg/cn/pdf/en/2019/05/top-10-in-2020-considerations-for-impactful-internal-audit-departments.pdf

NASBA. (2022). *Transition policy announced for the 2024 CPA exam under the CPA evolution initiative.* https://nasba.org/blog/2022/02/25/transition-policy/

Press, G. (2016). *Cleaning big data: Most time-consuming, least enjoyable data science task, survey says.* https://www.forbes.com/sites/gilpress/2016/03/23/data-preparation-most-time-consuming-least-enjoyable-data-science-task-survey-says/?sh¼53cb7c6b6f63

PwC. (2015). *Data driven: What students need to succeed in a rapidly changing business world*. https://www.pwc.com/us/en/faculty-resource/assets/PwC-Data-driven-paper-Feb2015.pdf

Ramel, D. (2019). *Popularity index: Python is 2018 'Language of the Year'*. https://adtmag.com/articles/2019/01/08/tiobe-jan-2019.aspx

Raschke, R. L., & Charron, K. F. (2021). Review of data analytic teaching cases, have we covered enough? *Journal of Emerging Technologies in Accounting, 18*(2), 247–255.

Richins, G., Stapleton, A., Stratopoulos, T. C., & Wong, C. (2017). Big data analytics: Opportunity or threat for the accounting profession? *Journal of information systems, 31*(3), 63–79.

Robert Half. (2021). *New research reveals the most lucrative and in-demand digital skills*. https://www.roberthalf.com/au/en/about/press/new-research-reveals-most-lucrative-and-demand-digital-skills

Shein, E. (2015). Python for beginners. *Communications of the ACM, 58*(3), 19–21.

Statista. (2022). *Most wanted programming languages among developers worldwide, as of 2022*. https://www.statista.com/statistics/793631/worldwide-developer-survey-most-wanted-languages/

Vien, C. (2018). *What to know about AACSB Accounting Standard A5*. https://www.journalofaccountancy.com/newsletters/extra-credit/aacsb-accounting-standard-a5.html

The Wall Street Journal. (2022). *The journey of one southwest plane explains the misery of travel now*. https://www.wsj.com/articles/canceled-flights-southwest-airlines-11636493391?mod=wsj_mc_dec21_2

Xu, J., & Frydenberg, M. (2021). Python programming in an IS curriculum: Perceived relevance and outcomes. *Information Systems Education Journal, 19*(4), 37–54.

APPENDIX 1

LIST AND BRIEF DESCRIPTION OF HOTEL DATASET VARIABLES

Property ID = a sequential, numerical code that identifies a particular property.

City = location of the hotel.

State = location of the hotel.

General Manager = name of the hotel's general manager.

Location Type = one of six property types indicating the hotel's market (airport, interstate, resort, small town, suburban and urban).

Number of rooms = the size of the hotel in terms of the number of rooms available for rental each night. Sometimes called "keys" or "beds."

Year Opened = calendar year in which the hotel was opened for business.

Room Rentals = the number of rooms rented during the year.

Revenue = total revenue for a year. This includes revenues from room rentals, Internet access, coin-operated machines (for laundry and vending) and meeting space. Being an economy-lodging hotel, the overwhelming proportion of revenue is derived from room rentals.

Profit = controllable profit at the hotel. This includes all revenues and only those costs that are controllable by the manager. Non-controllable costs (e.g., interest, depreciation and rent) are excluded from the hotel's profit calculation.

Room Rentals, Prior Year = the number of rooms rented during the prior year. This allows calculating the change in rentals.

Revenue, Prior Year = total revenue for the prior year.

Profit, Prior Year = the hotel's controllable profit for the prior year.

Bk>unds = bk>unds provided to guests who had service quality problems at the hotel (e.g., non-working air conditioner, excessive noise and pests).

Bk>unds, Prior Year = bk>unds provided to guests in the prior year.

Compset Rooms Available = the number of rooms available for rent by the hotel's competitive set (compset). The compset is a group of hotels specified by the subject hotel and usually consists of 3–7 competitors that are often within a short distance of the hotel. This information is provided by a third-party benchmarking firm who gathers the information and reports it in aggregate form.

Compset Rentals = the number of rooms rented by hotels in the compset. Combined with *Compset Rooms Available*, hotels can assess the capacity utilization of their competitors.

Compset Revenue = total room revenue by hotels in the compset. Combined with *Compset Rentals*, one can calculate the average price for a room rental at a competitor. This average price is bk>erred to as the Average Daily Rate. When combined with *Compset Rooms Available*, it is possible to compute the Revenue per Available Room (RevPAR), a summary measure of performance that captures both ADR and occupancy (i.e., capacity utilization).

Satisfaction Score = the mean guest satisfaction score obtained from customers completing an online survey. The survey is administered by a third-party consumer research company headquarters in the midwestern United States.

A Framework for Integrating Python Programming 51

Managers are eligible for bonuses based on achieving agreed-upon targets for customer satisfaction.

Guest Complaints = the number of phone calls or letters during the year to corporate headquarters complaining about the guest experience.

Risk Events = any event that occurred at the property that might result in a financial liability or diminution of the company's reputation or image. Examples of risk events include simple thefts of property in a car, assaults, suicides, rapes, and customer and guest injuries.

Internal Audit Score = the property's last internal audit score. The audit includes, among many items, verification that procedures are being followed (e.g., inventory locked in a supply room), regulations adhered to (e.g., government notices on labor rules posted in an area where workers congregate), and guest check-ins are properly completed.

Employees, Front Desk = a count of the number of individuals that worked as front desk staff at a property during the course of the year. Front desk employees consist of the general manager, one or more shift supervisors and guest service representatives that handle guest check-in and check-out, and guest service requests.

Employees, GM = a count of the number of individuals that worked as a general manager (GM) at the property. As turnover in the service industry is high, the median number of persons serving as GM is 2, but 20 properties have had more than 2 GMs in a single year.

Employees, Housekeeping = a count of the number of individuals that worked in the housekeeping department during the year. Staff in this category include room housekeepers, the head housekeeper and laundry room attendants. The median staff size of this department is about 4 employees, yet some properties had as many as 54 individuals working in the department during the year. Staff turnover is highest in housekeeping because it is the lowest average wage rate despite the significant physical demands of the job.

Employees, Maintenance = a count of the number of individuals that worked on maintenance during the year. A typical property will have just one maintenance worker on staff at any given time.

Employees, Other = a count of the number of individuals that worked in any other job classification than those listed above. This is rare.

Hours Worked, Front Desk = the total hours worked by front desk employees (excluding the general manager) during the course of the year.

Hours Worked, GM = the total hours worked by the general manager during the year.

Hours Worked, Housekeeping = the total hours worked by housekeeping staff during the year. Along with the number of rooms rented, it is possible to estimate the mean and median times to clean a room.

Hours Worked, Maintenance = the total number of hours worked by maintenance workers. Most properties are supposed to have a single maintenance worker on staff for a single shift during the week (i.e., Monday – Friday).

Hours Worked, Other = the total number of hours worked by staff not otherwise classified.

Front Desk Turnover (%) = the turnover of the front desk staff during the year, expressed as a percentage. Turnover is defined as the number of terminations divided by the number of year-end employees, multiplied by 100. For example, if 8 employees worked at the front desk last year, and there were 4 employees staffing the front desk on December 31, turnover would be (8/4) × 100 = 200%.

Housekeeping Turnover (%) = the turnover of the housekeep staff during the year, expressed as a percentage. It is computed the same way as the *Front Desk Turnover (%)*.

Year of Last Renovation = the year of the last renovation at the property.

Renovation Type = one of four levels of renovation that was undertaken at the property during the year of last renovation. The four levels are "None," "Basic," "Mid" and "Full." A basic renovation would involve changing "soft goods" such as draperies, bed covers, shower curtains, toilet seats, etc. At the opposite end, a "Full" renovation would include replacing flooring, climate control systems, plumbing fixtures, beds, televisions, etc. in addition to soft goods. A full renovation is likely to include renovation of open areas (e.g., lobby and pool).

Amount, Recent CapEx = the amount of money recently spent (i.e., past three years) for capital expenditures at the specific property.

Total Assets = the total assets reported for the year for the particular property.

GM Tenure (days) = the number of days the GM has been at the particular property.

Survey, Training Provided = the mean score of an employee survey asking employees their perception of the training provided to employees. The score ranges from 1 (minimal or useless) to 10 (extensive and valuable).

Survey, Career Opportunities = the mean score of an employee survey asking employees their perception of the career opportunities available to employees. The score ranges from 1 (none or few) to 10 (many).

Area = the numerical code identifying each of the two areas on which the company is split.

Area Manager = the name of the manager with authority for the specific area.

District = the numerical code identifying a district that the hotel is located in.

District Manager = the name of the manager of a district.

APPENDIX 2

SYNTHETIC DATA CREATION

The synthetic dataset was generated using Python's pandas library and NumPy for numerical simulations. The goal was to simulate a dataset resembling hotel-related financial information, including factors such as room occupancy, revenue, and costs. The synthetic data creation process involved several steps, as detailed below.

We identified key variables relevant to hotel profitability, such as 'RoomsRented,' 'Revenue,' 'Costs,' 'Year,' and 'Month.' These variables were chosen based on their significance in assessing financial performance.

To simulate realistic temporal trends, we created a time series structure with 'Year' and 'Month' as timestamps. This was achieved by generating a sequence of consecutive months spanning multiple years, ensuring the temporal aspect of the dataset.

```
import pandas as pd
import numpy as np
start_date = '2013-01-01'
end_date = '2022-12-01'
date_range = pd.date_range(start=start_date, end=end_date, freq='MS')

# Create synthetic dataset
synthetic_data = pd.DataFrame({'Date': date_range})
```

Synthetic values for 'RoomsRented' and 'Revenue' were generated using random processes to mimic the variability observed in real-world hotel data.

```
# Simulate room occupancy and revenue
synthetic_data['RoomsRented'] = np.random.randint(800, 3000, len(date_range))
synthetic_data['Revenue'] = synthetic_data['RoomsRented'] * np.random.uniform(120, 400, len(date_range))
```

The 'Costs' variable was simulated to represent operational expenses associated with hotel management. For simplicity, we used a linear relationship with 'RoomsRented' to generate costs.

```
# Simulate costs based on a linear relationship with room occupancy
synthetic_data['Costs'] = 0.6 * synthetic_data['RoomsRented'] + np.random.normal(0, 200, len(date_range))
```

The generated data was aggregated to provide a summarized view by grouping data based on 'Year' and 'Month.' This step ensures that the dataset aligns with the analysis requirements outlined in subsequent sections of the chapter.

```
# Group data by year and month
synthetic_data['Year'] = synthetic_data['Date'].dt.year
synthetic_data['Month'] = synthetic_data['Date'].dt.month
synthetic_data_grouped = synthetic_data.groupby(['Year',
'Month']).agg({'RoomsRented':    'sum',    'Revenue':
'sum', 'Costs': 'sum'}).reset_index()
```

The synthetic dataset, generated through the outlined process, serves as a foundational simple dataset for our subsequent analyses of hotel profitability. The code snippets provided demonstrate the transparency and reproducibility of our data generation process.

CHAPTER 3

DATA SCIENCE IN ACCOUNTING: BUDGET ANALYTICS USING MONTE CARLO SIMULATION

Hemantha S. B. Herath and Tejaswini C. Herath

Brock University, Canada

ABSTRACT

Traditional functional budgets are useful for planning under predictable business environments. However, due to increased competition, changes in technology, consumer attitudes, and economic factors affecting supply chains, accountants must understand the characteristics of risk and uncertainty. Additionally, businesses now have access to unprecedented amounts of data pertaining to customers, suppliers, marketing operations, and activities throughout the value chain. Consequently, accountants should be able to harness the computing power, data storage capacity, and availability of analytical tools to analyze and manipulate large data sets to succeed in a data science world. A statistical technique available to accountants to perform predictive and prescriptive analytics is Monte Carlo simulation. This chapter illustrates how to use Monte Carlo simulation in developing a probabilistic cash budget which facilitates better risk assessment, resource allocation, and decision making compared with the traditional deterministic approach.

Keywords: Budgeting; probabilistic cash budgets; Monte Carlo simulation; financial risk analysis; budget analytics; data science

Traditional financial budgets are often based on single-point estimates, which are deterministic in nature. Uncertainty and volatility are inherent in business environments, and hence planning, decision making, and control functions must consider risk and uncertainty. Although Monte Carlo simulation approaches have been suggested for planning and budgeting (Mattessich, 1961), often organizations tend to use sensitivity analysis, decision trees, and scenario planning for dealing with risk and uncertainty. Monte Carlo simulation–based probabilistic budgets or "risked budget models" that would enable high-quality predictions are rarely used in developing financial budgets in organizations and seldom incorporated in management accounting courses at universities (Herath, 2023a).

Posing the question "In what way can future budgeting be improved?" Mattessich (1961, p. 384) first proposed the idea of probabilistic (or stochastic) budgets. His budget model provides an illustration of the mathematical relationships, but Mattessich (1961) does not provide details on how to integrate probability concepts to simulate a financial budget. As discussed in this seminal article, the prerequisite for simulating a financial budget is to translate the traditional budgeting system into algebraic terms. The mathematical formulation of a financial budget in relation to today's competitive business environment has several advantages, as discussed in Mattessich (1961): (1) it is a prerequisite for applying computer-based simulation; (2) it provides the novel mathematical structure of a financial budget; (3) it provides a general and scientific presentation of accounting; (4) it facilitates exploration of new application areas, which furthers the advancement of accounting; and (5) it is more sophisticated, as it integrates accounting with disciplines such as operations research, probability, statistics, and computer science. Coincidentally, the proposed approach to stochastic budgets maps one-to-one with today's data science/business analytics framework.

Monte Carlo simulation techniques have been applied in corporate finance for modeling a project's net present value (NPV) distribution in numerous engineering disciplines, including civil engineering for cost estimation, economic analysis, and project management (Briand & Hill, 2013; Elkjaer, 2000, among others), but the technique has only been sparsely applied in accounting (Lord, 1977, 1979; Mensching et al., 2012). More recently, however, with the recent focus on data science and business analytics, Appelbaum et al. (2017) suggest that techniques such as Monte Carlo simulation and studies may have some appeal to today's CPAs and managers. Developing stochastic budgets using Monte Carlo simulation integrates risk management with budgeting by incorporating multiple sources of input uncertainties affecting a firm's business operations in the budget models. Herath (2023b) uses Excel to illustrate the spreadsheet application of Monte Carlo simulation techniques in accounting, including financial budgeting.

The remainder of this chapter is organized into six sections. Section "Background" discusses the emerging data science/business analytics framework in the context of management accounting. Section "The Monte Carlo Simulation Technique " summarizes the Monte Carlo simulation steps. Section "Simulating a Cash Budget: Hospitality Industry Example " provides a service industry example with data and assumptions and presents the deterministic cash budget.

Section "Traditional Deterministic Cash Budget" illustrates the spreadsheet simulation of the cash budget. Section "Simulation Illustration" discusses simulation results and inferences for risk management. Section "Conclusion" concludes the chapter. In the Appendix, data on occupancy, room rates, and the Excel template (Table A3) with formulas for simulating the ending cash balance are provided.

BACKGROUND

Currently, there is an increasing emphasis on data science in accounting and accounting analytics. According to a novel data science framework proposed by Datar et al. (2022), there are three knowledge domains (in brackets in the context of budgeting) that are required for data science in accounting, as depicted by the intersections of a Venn diagram. They are (1) domain knowledge in management accounting (i.e., traditional budgeting), (2) computer science and data skills (i.e., advanced Excel and R programming), and (3) math and statistics knowledge and inference (i.e., linear algebra models of budgets, basic probability distributions, and statistical inferences).

The chapter is designed with Datar et al.'s (2022) proposed data science framework in mind. That is, first, develop the mathematical representation of the cash budget extending knowledge in developing traditional budgets; second, incorporate uncertainties using probability assumptions required for Monte Carlo sampling; and finally, use Excel with mathematical expressions as the models for spreadsheet simulation. Often, this is the standard approach in Monte Carlo simulation. More to the point, using mathematical expressions as the models allows extending and running budget simulations in Python or R easily. For example, CPA syllabuses in several countries have suggested that accounting students be familiar with R or Python for data scrubbing, statistical modeling, and analysis. (See CPA Canada, 2018, https://www.cpacanada.ca/en/members-area/profession-news/2018/july/adas-practical-learning; CPA Ireland, 2022, https://www.cpaireland.ie/become-a-student/CPA-Qualifications/Data-Analytics-for-Finance.) There are several recent attempts in this direction. Emphasizing the lack of teaching resources, Calderon et al. (2022) propose a two-dimensional framework for incorporating R into the accounting curriculum. In addition, Herath (2023c) illustrates the RStudio application of Monte Carlo simulations, including financial budgeting. Green and Littlejohn (2024) replicate the Calderon et al. (2022) framework to propose incorporation of Python into the accounting curriculum.

Analytics refers to the science of logical analysis (Liberatore & Luo, 2010). Business analytics or, simply put, "business" with "analytics," has been defined in many ways. Davenport and Harris (2007, p. 7) define analytics as "the extensive use of data, statistical and quantitative analysis, explanatory and predictive models, and fact-based management to drive decisions and actions," which Liberatore and Luo (2010, p. 314) articulate as "a process of transforming data into actions through analysis and insights in the context of organizational decision making and problem solving."

Most companies now have access to large amounts of internal and external data, referred to as "big data," that can be characterized by "high volume, high-velocity and/or high-variety" (Janvrin & Watson, 2017). Big data comes from various internal and external sources such as transactions, customer reviews, opinions, competitor information, market information, and much more. These data can be structured or unstructured. Analytics leverages big data sets and uses better data analytic and visualization software (Janvrin & Watson, 2017). Richins et al. (2017) argue that big data can transform accounting in several ways. For instance, rather than relying on traditional sampling techniques to perform tests of details, automated processes could examine entire populations for unusual patterns and anomalies. Visualization can enhance accounting tasks to obtain audit evidence and complete financial statement audits. However, the primary goal of management accounting has not changed from creating and providing information to internal and external decision makers (Janvrin & Watson, 2017).

Analysis can be directed in many different orientations or outlooks. Descriptive analytics is the use of data to understand past and current business performance to respond to queries such as, What happened? and What is happening? Descriptive statistical measures such as means and standard deviations, probability distributions, visualizations, or charts as well as Key Performance Indicators or dashboards can aid in this kind of analysis (Janvrin & Watson, 2017). Predictive analytics answers the question, What will happen? and Why will it happen? It is characterized by predictive and forecasting models to predict the future by examining historical data, detecting patterns or relationships in these data, and then extrapolating these relationships forward in time. The last category of analysis is prescriptive analytics, which attempts to answer the question, What should be done? and uses various optimization techniques.

Data analytics can be leveraged in many aspects of management accounting (Appelbaum et al., 2017). In cost accounting, where the focus is on using internal data to generate financial reports, descriptive analytics helps to summarize and describe the financial situation of a business. Performance measurement focuses on the assessment of efficiency and effectiveness of programs, initiatives, processes, or functions within an organization. Internal data along with external data such as industry benchmarks can be used to understand the performance and to predict future performance. These insights can further be used in planning and decision making. Accountants often make predictions and make decisions under uncertainty and risk. More to the point, business analytics or data science tools are therefore useful for accountants in conducting prescriptive analysis to help decision makers navigate uncertainties. A statistical technique that has been suggested to accountants in predictive and prescriptive analytics is Monte Carlo studies/simulation (Appelbaum et al., 2017, pp. 33, 38).

In a recent accounting educational article, Burkert et al. (2022) introduce Monte Carlo simulation analysis as an advanced tool for assessing uncertainty. More specifically, the case study illustrates capital budgeting in the hospitality sector where the decision involves selecting between competing alternatives to renovate an existing hotel when funds are limited. An important pedagogical component in the case is that students are required to identify suitable probability distributions for several uncertain parameters, such as rooms rented, room rate, and project expenses, for performing the Monte Carlo simulations. In our chapter, the probability distributions are assumed, since the primary focus is on model development and running the simulations in Excel. However, unlike the proposed chapter, the article by Burkert et al. (2022) does not use the native simulation tools in Excel.

THE MONTE CARLO SIMULATION TECHNIQUE

Monte Carlo simulation is a powerful analytical tool for developing probabilistic budgets. More specifically, it allows estimating the probability of different outcomes driven by key budget drivers and allows an organization to adopt and modify strategies based on the organization's risk tolerance. Monte Carlo simulation is based on random sampling where values are generated from given input probability distributions. The simulations are run on a computer using random numbers or pseudo random numbers. Thereafter, statistical analysis is performed to determine the likelihood of an uncertain outcome of interest. The basic steps in carrying out Monte Carlo simulations are model definition, identifying and assignment of a probability distribution, running the simulations, and analyzing the simulation output. Details on Monte Carlo simulation steps in many decision settings in cost and management accounting are explained in Burkert et al. (2022), Herath (2023b, 2023c), and Herath and Sharman (2017, 2019).

Defining the Model

A model must be first defined in order to carry out the simulations. More specifically, Monte Carlo simulation uses a mathematical model to mimic the real-world situation. When simulating a cash budget, its mathematical representation can be used as a model. For simple simulations, the models can also be set up directly on a spreadsheet, but this is not often recommended when a million or more simulation runs are performed to increase accuracy. The mathematical model is an algebraic expression of a budget or a component of a budget linking both the unknown uncertain random variables and the known parameters describing their relationship to the output of interest.

Identification and Assignment of Input Probability Distributions

Once the unknown input parameters or random variables have been identified based on budget assumptions, probability distributions must be assigned to each one of them. Here, the accountant may use objective probabilities for demand, product prices, market share and growth rates, etc., or may use subjective probabilities based on expert opinion and estimates (e.g., marketing experts and economists). When we perform Monte Carlo simulations using spreadsheets, many built-in functions can be directly used. For example, the RAND() function in MS Excel generates a random number between 0 and 1. In order to sample from an input probability distribution, the general approach is to use the *"inverse transformation method."* In Excel, the inversion can be carried out simply by using built-in Excel functions. For example, the built-in functions such as LOGNORM.INV(*probability, mean, standard deviation*), NORM.INV(*probability, mean, standard deviation*), and RANDBETWEEN(L,H) can be directly used to sample from a lognormal, normal, and uniform distribution. In a uniform distribution, L and H specify the distribution's lower and upper bounds.

Running the Simulations

Large numbers of simulation runs are carried out by generating random numbers, sampling from each input distribution, and computing output values given by the mathematical model (algebraic expression). In this step, a large sample of possible outcomes is generated. In MS Excel, once the mathematical model is expressed as an Excel equation, it can be copied and pasted to generate many simulations. Excel *Data Tables* can also be used, but they may be cumbersome to set up for complex budget models and when millions of replications are required. Graphical displays such as histograms, scatter plots, box plots, and fitted distributions allow comparing risks and understanding how risks aggregate with multiple uncertain random inputs in budget analysis.

Analyzing the Simulation Output

The simulation output provides valuable insights for budget analysis and managing risks. As part of the analysis, descriptive statistics such as the mean, mode, median, percentiles, and standard deviation can be computed. In MS Excel, the *Data, Data Analysis, Descriptive Statistics* option in the dropdown menu directly computes the required descriptive statistics. In order to assess risks, however, probability distributions such as a normal distribution or a lognormal distribution may be fitted to the simulation output. These fitted output distributions allow computing, among other risk measures, 68%, 90%, and 99% confidence limits, the probability of the output values being less than, more than, or between certain thresholds to gauge risks through computed probabilities.

SIMULATING A CASH BUDGET: HOSPITALITY INDUSTRY EXAMPLE

The main purpose of this generic example[1] is to illustrate how to set up and carry out a Monte Carlo simulation of a cash budget in Excel. Hence, all probability distributions for uncertain parameters (e.g., occupancy rates, room rates, and fixed and variable costs) are assumed for simplicity. A hypothetical data set is used. For example, the means and variances are computed and used as the means and variances for the assumed normal and lognormal distributions. Similarly, for the assumed uniform distributions, computed maximum and minimum values are either directly used as their lower and upper bounds or simply assumed, as in the case of other fixed costs and variable costs per night. However, in practice, deriving those variables and associated probability distributions could be challenging (Burkert et al., 2022). These assumptions are discussed as limitations of this chapter in the conclusion section.

Data and Assumptions

Marina Royale owns a high-end resort in the Caribbean. The resort has 300 rooms. Seventy percent (210 rooms) are on average allocated for corporate clients (CC), and the remaining 30% (90 rooms) are allocated for individual customers (IC). In the hospitality industry, corporate clients have longer-term relationships and receive specialized services and personalized attention. For these reasons, Marina Royale can charge higher room rates for its corporate clientele. Individual customers, on the other hand, are typically onetime infrequent individuals, companies, or organizations, and they are charged lower room rates than corporate clients. The full room capacity for a year is $365 \times 300 = 109{,}500$ room nights. The occupancy rates are estimated based on the days of the week. For the purpose of this illustration, it is assumed that the 365 days of the year are made up of 53 Sundays and 52 days Saturday through Friday of the week: $53 + 6 \times 52 = 365$.

In the hospitality industry, the occupancy rate, which is the ratio of number of occupied rooms to total rooms available, indicates availability of rooms. Generally, the hotel industry is volatile, and hence it is difficult to predict occupancy rates. Consequently, accountants in Marina Royale have decided to consider the occupancy rates pertaining to both corporate clients and individual customers as uncertain random variables. The input probability distributions assumed for these occupancy rates are based on historic averages adjusted for the current year. Typically, occupancy rates vary according to room rates, but this dependency is not modeled in this example, Table A1 in the Appendix provides the estimated occupancy rates for both corporate clients and individual customers, the assumed probability distributions, and parameter values. The weekend days, Saturday and Sunday, are holidays (non-working days) and denoted by H, while the five remaining weekdays are denoted by W.

The occupancy rate for corporate clients during weekend holidays is modeled as a random variable O_{CCH} for the 105 Saturdays and Sundays of the year. For the remaining 260 weekdays of the year, uncertain corporate client occupancy rate is modeled as a random variable given by O_{CCW}. Similarly, the random variables for the individual customers occupancy rate for the 105 Saturday and Sunday weekend holidays is labeled O_{ICH} and for the 260 weekdays is labeled O_{ICW}. Using these random variables, the number of occupied rooms used by corporate clients during the year 20X1 is computed as $210(105 O_{CCH} + 260 O_{CCW}) = 22050 O_{CCH} + 54600 O_{CCW}$. The number of occupied rooms used by individual customers during the year 20X1 is computed as $90(105 O_{ICH} + 260 O_{ICW}) = 9450 O_{ICH} + 23400 O_{ICW}$.

Room rates are considered uncertain random variables. More specifically, the room rates for corporate clients during the weekend holidays and weekdays are assumed to be the same. Different room rates for weekend holidays and weekdays are assumed for individual customers. In addition, the variable cost per occupied room and other fixed costs are also considered as uncertain random variables in the budget model. Thus, the nine unknown parameters (random variables) considered in the simulation of Marina Royale's cash budget are the following:

- O_{CCH}: Occupancy rate for corporate clients on weekend holidays.
- O_{CCW}: Occupancy rate for corporate clients on weekdays.
- O_{ICH}: Occupancy rate for individual customers on weekend holidays.
- O_{ICW}: Occupancy rate for individual customers on weekdays.
- R_{CC}: Average room rate for corporate clients for both holiday weekends and weekdays.
- R_{ICH}: Average room rate for individual customers on holiday weekends.
- R_{ICW}: Average room rate for individual customers on weekdays.
- F: Budgeted other fixed overhead.
- v: Variable cost per occupied room per night.

The distribution and the parameter values for the nine random variables in the Marina Royale example are summarized as follows:

- O_{CCH} follows a normal distribution with a mean of 75.58% and a standard deviation of 5.20%, $O_{CCH}\sim$ Normal(75.58%, 5.20%^{2}).
- O_{CCW} follows a uniform distribution with a lower bound of 90% and an upper bound of 100%, $O_{CCW}\sim$ Uniform(90%, 100%).
- O_{ICH} follows a uniform distribution with a lower bound of 88% and an upper bound of 100%, $O_{ICH}\sim$ Uniform(88%, 100%).
- O_{ICW} follows a normal distribution with a mean of 65.57% and a standard deviation of 10.68%, $O_{ICW}\sim$Normal(65.57%, 10.68%^{2}).
- R_{CC} is lognormal with a log mean of 5.6610 and log standard deviation of 0.0058, $R_{CC}\sim$Lognormal(5.6610, 0.0058).
- R_{ICH} is lognormal with a log mean of 5.4454 and log standard deviation of 0.0219, $R_{ICH}\sim$Lognormal(5.4454, 0.0219).
- R_{ICW} is lognormal with a log mean of 5.0451 and log standard deviation of 0.1180, $R_{ICW}\sim$Lognormal(5.0451, 0.1180).
- Budgeted other fixed cost follows a uniform distribution with a lower bound of $1,440,000 and an upper bound of $1,920,000, $F\sim$Uniform(1440000, 1920000).
- Variable cost per occupied room follows a uniform distribution with a lower bound of $30 and an upper bound of $40, $v\sim$Uniform(30, 40).

Additional assumptions and known parameter values for 20X1 are given as follows:

- The December 31, 20X0 balance in the cash account is $1,500,000.
- All sales are on account for corporate clients. The total sales revenue for 20X0 is $24,000,000. For corporate clients, out of the 70% allocated room nights, on average, 80% of the sales are collected in the year of sales and the remaining

Data Science in Accounting 63

20% are collected in the coming year. In the case of the 30% allocated room nights for individual customers, all sales (cash, credit card, and debit) are collected in the year of sales.
- Fixed salaries (including benefits) are estimated to be $400,000 per month, totaling $4,800,000 for the year.
- Other fixed operating expenses and variable costs are uncertain and paid in cash in the year they are incurred.
- Interest charges to be paid in 20X1 are estimated to be $7,200,000 for the year.

Mathematical Expressions

In carrying out a Monte Carlo simulation of a probabilistic cash budget, the first step is to develop a model that takes the form of a mathematical expression of the traditional cash budget. The mathematical expressions are derived using the nine unknown random variables, which are economic value drivers that are assumed to be uncertain. Table 3.1 shows the derivation of the mathematical expressions or simulation models for Marina Royale's probabilistic cash budget.

The mathematical expression for simulating total cash available for 20X1 is

$$4.86 + 22050(0.80)R_{cc}O_{CCH} + 54600(0.80)R_{cc}O_{CCW} + 9450R_{ICH}O_{ICH} + 23400R_{ICW}O_{ICW}.$$

Similarly, the mathematical models for simulating the total cash disbursements is

$$22050vO_{CCH} + 54600vO_{CCW} + 9450vO_{ICH} + 23400vO_{ICW} + F + 12.$$

The ending cash balance of Marina Royale as at 31 December 20X1 is given by

$$22050(0.8R_{cc}O_{CCH} - vO_{CCH}) + 54600(0.8R_{cc}O_{CCW} - vO_{CCW}) + 9450(R_{ICH}O_{CCH} - vO_{ICH}) + 23400(R_{ICW}O_{CCW} - vO_{ICW}) - F - 7.14.$$

Table 3.1. Probabilistic Cash Budget for Marina Royale for 20X1 ($million).

Beginning Cash Balance (1/1/20X1)	1.5
Received on account from room occupancy	
Corporate Clients	
Year 20X0 (20% ×0.70 ×24)	3.36
Year 20X1 (80%) of sales revenue	$0.80(22050R_{cc}O_{CCH} + 54600\,R_{cc}O_{CCW})$
Individual Customers	
Year 20X1 (100%) of sales revenue	$9450R_{ICH}O_{ICH} + 23400R_{ICW}O_{ICW}$
Total cash available	$4.86 + 22050(0.80)\,R_{cc}O_{CCH} + 54600(0.80)R_{cc}O_{CCW}$
	$+ 9450R_{ICH}O_{ICH} + 23400R_{ICW}O_{ICW}$
Disbursements	
Variable costs	$v[(22050O_{CCH} + 54600O_{CCW}) + (9450O_{ICH} + 23400O_{ICW})]$
Fixed salaries	4.8
Other fixed costs	F
Interest	7.2
Total disbursements	$22050vO_{CCH} + 54600vO_{CCW} + 9450vO_{ICH} + 23400vO_{ICW} + F + 12$
Ending cash balance (31/12/20X1)	$22050(0.8R_{cc}O_{CCH} - vO_{CCH}) + 54600(0.8R_{cc}O_{CCW}$
	$- vO_{CCW}) + 9450(R_{ICH}O_{CCH} - vO_{ICH}) + 23400(R_{ICW}\,O_{CCW}$
	$- vO_{ICW}) - F - 7.14$

It is the net difference of total cash available and total cash disbursements. A probabilistic cash budget allows disaggregating uncertainty in ending cash balance into uncertainty in the total cash available and uncertainty in total cash payments. Assessment of risks by components is one of the main advantages of a probability budget and is extremely useful from the treasury function. Such risk assessment is not available in a traditional deterministic cash budget.

TRADITIONAL DETERMINISTIC CASH BUDGET

The traditional deterministic cash budget of Marina Royale for the year 20X1 is presented in Table 3.2. Notice that a deterministic cash budget is based on averages of the numbers and does not consider uncertainties. Based on the data in Tables A1 and A2 in the Appendix, the expected average occupancy rates are 75% for corporate clients on weekends, 95% for corporate clients on weekdays, 95% for individual customers on weekends, and 65% for individual customers on weekdays. The expected average room rates are $287 for corporate clients on weekends and weekdays, $232 for individual customers on weekends, and $156 for individual customers on weekdays. The total cash available for 20X1 is 25.021 million and includes the following: beginning cash balance of $1.5 million, 20X0 collections from corporate clients amounting to $3.36 million, 20X1 cash sales from corporate clients amounting to $15.706 million, and 20X1 cash sales from individual customers amounting to $4.456 million.

The total disbursements, which amount to $16.921 million, consist of the following cash payments:

- 20X1 variable room expenses amounting to $3.241 million.
- Fixed salaries for 20X1 amounting to $4.8 million.

Table 3.2. Deterministic Cash Budget: Marina Royale for 20X1.

	$
Beginning Cash Balance	1,500,000
Received on Account from Room Occupancy	
Corporate Clients	
Year 20X0	3,360,000
Year 20X1	15,706,362
Individual Customers	
Year 20X0	–
Year 20X1	4,455,540
Total Cash Available	**25,021,902**
Disbursements	
Variable Costs	3,240,825
Fixed Salaries	4,800,000
Other Fixed Costs	1,680,000
Interest	7,200,000
Total Cash Disbursements	**16,920,825**
Ending Cash Balance	**8,101,077**

- Other fixed costs amounting to $1.68 million, which is the average of (1.44+1.92)/2.
- Interest expenses for 20X1 amounting to $7.2 million.

The ending cash balance based on traditional budgeting amounts to a surplus of $8.1 million.

SIMULATION ILLUSTRATION

The Monte Carlo simulation of the main components of Marina Royale's cash budget for 20X1 is illustrated in the following subsections.

Simulating Total Cash Available

The model for simulating the probabilistic total cash available for 20X1 is $4.86 + 22050(0.80)R_{CC}O_{CCH} + 54600(0.80)R_{CC}O_{CCW} + 9450R_{ICH}O_{ICH} + 23400R_{ICW}O_{ICW}$.

Notice that the seven random variables that drive uncertainty in total cash available are corporate client weekend occupancy rates given by O_{CCH}~Normal(75.58%, 5.20%²), corporate client weekday occupancy rate given by O_{CCW}~Uniform(90%,100%), individual customer weekend occupancy rate given by O_{ICH}~Uniform(88%,100%), individual customer weekday occupancy rate given by O_{ICW}~Normal(65.57%, 10.68%²), corporate client room rate given by R_{CC}~Lognormal(5.6610, 0.0058), individual customer weekend room rate given by R_{ICH}~Lognormal(5.4454, 0.0219), and individual customer weekday room rates are given by R_{ICW}~Lognormal(5.0451, 0.1180).

Using the built-in Excel functions = NORM.INV(RAND(),0.7558,0.520) for O_{CCH}, = RANDBETWEEN(90,100) for O_{CCW}, = RANDBETWEEN(88,100) for O_{ICH}, = NORM.INV(RAND(),0.6557,0.1068) for O_{ICW}, = LOGNORM.INV(RAND(),5.6610,0.0058) for R_{CC}, = LOGNORM.INV(RAND(),5.4454,0.0219) for R_{ICH}, and = LOGNORM.INV(RAND(),5.0451,0.1180) for R_{ICW}, a particular value for total cash available is computed per the mathematical expression $4.86 + 22050(0.80)R_{CC}O_{CCH} + 54600(0.80)R_{CC}O_{CCW} + 9450R_{ICH}O_{ICH} + 23400R_{ICW}O_{ICW}$. In order to generate a probability distribution for total cash available in 20X1 for Marina Royale, 2,000 values are sampled, and a relative frequency distribution is prepared along with descriptive statistics computed using the Excel Data Analysis tool. The descriptive statistics fitted normal probability distribution, and relative frequency distribution for the simulated total cash available are shown in Fig. 3.1. A visual analysis indicates a reasonable normal distribution fit for the simulated total cash available.

The simulated values for total cash available in 20X1 follow a probability distribution with a mean of $25,192,788 and a standard deviation of $711,428. The standard deviation is not zero, indicating that actual cash available in 20X1 is not deterministic but varies given uncertainties in occupancy and room rates. Per traditional budgeting, the total cash available in 20X1 is $25,021,902,

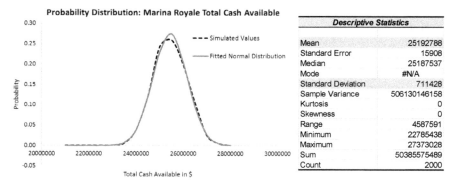

Fig. 3.1. Probabilistic Total Cash Available and Descriptive Statistics for 20X1.

which is quite close to the average value of simulated cash available for the year (i.e., $25,192,788). Notice the standard deviation of the simulated cash available amount is only 3% of the average cash availability.

Simulating Total Cash Payments in 20X1

The model for simulating probabilistic total cash disbursed for 20X1 is $22050vO_{CCH} + 54600vO_{CCW} + 9450vO_{ICH} + 23400vO_{ICW} + F + 12$. Notice that there are six random variables driving the value of disbursements. They include O_{CCH}, O_{CCW}, O_{ICH}, O_{ICW}, other fixed cost F~Uniform(1440000, 1920000), and variable cost v~Uniform(30, 40). Using the built-in Excel function =RANDBETWEEN (1440000, 1920000) and =RANDBETWEEN (30, 40) for the budgeted fixed and variable expenses, the total cash disbursed in 20X1 can be computed using the formula $22050vO_{CCH} + 54600vO_{CCW} + 9450vO_{ICH} + 23400vO_{ICW} + F + 12$. In order to generate a probability distribution for total cash disbursed during the year, 2,000 values are sampled, and a relative frequency distribution along with a fitted normal distribution and descriptive statistics are prepared as shown in Fig. 3.2. A visual analysis indicates a weak normal distribution fit for the simulated total cash disbursements, as it appears to follow a bimodal distribution.

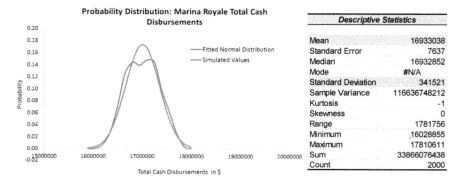

Fig. 3.2. Probabilistic Total Cash Disbursed and Descriptive Statistics for 20X1.

Per traditional budgeting, the total cash disbursed is $16,920,825 and is closer to the average value of simulated cash disbursements amounting to $16,933,038. Notice, however, that the standard deviation of the simulated amount is only $341,521 or 2%, indicating a very low degree of volatility in the cash payments. The reason for both total cash available and total cash disbursed to have low volatility is because the mean occupancy and room rates were used. If the accountant's rate estimates were not the same as the distributional means, then these volatilities would be higher, which would be what is most likely to occur.

Simulating the Ending Cash Balance

The model for simulating the ending cash balance for 20X1 is $22050(0.8R_{CC} O_{CCH} - vO_{CCH}) + 54600(0.8R_{CC}O_{CCW} - vO_{CCW}) + 9450(R_{ICH}\ O_{CCH} - vO_{ICH}) + 23400(R_{ICW}O_{CCW} - vO_{ICW}) - F - 7.14$. In modeling the ending cash balance, all nine random variables are included in the model. They are corporate client weekend occupancy rates given by $O_{CC}H \sim \text{Normal}(75.58\%, 5.20\%^2)$, corporate client weekday occupancy rate given by $O_{CCW} \sim \text{Uniform}(90\%, 100\%)$, individual customer weekend occupancy rate given by $O_{ICH} \sim \text{Uniform}(88\%, 100\%)$, individual customer weekday occupancy rate given by $O_{ICW} \sim \text{Normal}(65.57\%, 10.68\%^2)$, corporate client room rate given by $R_{CC} \sim \text{Lognormal}(5.6610, 0.0058)$, individual customer weekend room rate given by $R_{ICH} \sim \text{Lognormal}(5.4454, 0.0219)$, and individual customer weekday room rates given by $R_{ICW} \sim \text{Lognormal}(5.0451, 0.1180)$, other fixed cost $F \sim \text{Uniform}(1440000, 1920000)$, and variable cost $v \sim \text{Uniform}(30, 40)$.

The ending cash balance for 20X1 can be computed using the formula $22050(0.8R_{CC}O_{CCH} - vO_{CCH}) + 54600(0.8R_{CC}O_{CCW} - vO_{CCW}) + 9450(R_{ICH}O_{CCH} - vO_{ICH}) + 23400(R_{ICW}O_{CCW} - vO_{ICW}) - F - 7.14$. In order to generate a probability distribution for ending cash balance, 2,000 values are sampled, and a relative frequency distribution and the descriptive statistics are prepared as shown in Fig. 3.3. Alternatively, the simulated values can also be obtained by taking the difference between the 2,000 previously simulated values for total cash available and the total cash disbursements. A visual analysis indicates a reasonable normal distribution fit for the simulated ending cash balance, as it is symmetrical. Interestingly, the

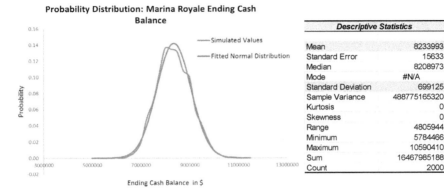

Fig. 3.3. Probabilistic Ending Cash Balance and Descriptive Statistics for 20X1.

normal distribution fit allows making several useful statistical inferences, which is not available in the traditional deterministic budgeting approach.

Per traditional budgeting, the ending cash balance in 20X1 amounts to $8,101,077. In contrast, the ending cash balance per the Monte Carlo simulations is on average $8,233,993 with a standard deviation of $699,125. The volatility in the ending cash balance for Marina Royale is 9%, which is high, indicating that uncertainties pertaining to cash availability and disbursements have an aggregating effect on the ending cash balance. In traditional deterministic budgets, these uncertainties are ignored. Taking uncertainties into consideration provides valuable information for managing financial risks, including estimating working capital requirements.

Statistical Inferences

The fitted normal distribution for ending cash balance has a mean $\mu = \$8,233,993$ and a standard deviation $\sigma = \$699,125$ and provides an opportunity to perform a detailed risk analysis regarding Marina Royale's financial position in 20X1. A quick analysis that provides risk insights includes the symmetric intervals for the ending cash balance distribution. They are the following:

- There is a 68% chance that ending cash balance (ω) will lie in the interval ($\mu - \sigma \leq \omega \leq \mu + \sigma$). More to the point, with 68% confidence, the accountant can be assured that the ending cash balance will be in the range ($\$7,534,868 \leq \omega \leq \$8,933,117$).
- There is a 95% chance that ending cash balance, (ω), will lie in the interval ($\mu - 2\sigma \leq \omega \leq \mu + 2\sigma$). There is a 95% confidence level that the ending cash balance will be in the range ($\$6,835,743 \leq \omega \leq \$9,632,242$).
- Similarly, there is a 99% chance that ending cash balance, (ω), will lie in the interval ($\mu - 3\sigma \leq \omega \leq \mu + 3\sigma$). More specifically, there is a 99% confidence level that the ending cash balance will be in the range ($\$6,136,619 \leq \omega \leq \$10,331,366$).

Other probability assessments regarding Marina Royale's cash budget useful for assessing risks may include the following:

(a) *What is the probability of total cash available being less than the forecast deterministic budget estimate of $25,192,788?*

It can be computed using the Excel built-in function =NORM. DIST(25021902, μ, σ, TRUE), where $\mu = 25{,}192{,}788$ and $\sigma = 711{,}428$ equal to 41%. More specifically, there is a 59% chance that the forecast total cash availability exceeds the deterministic estimate.

(b) *What is the probability of total cash disbursements to exceed $16,500,000?*

Using the function =NORM.DIST(16500000, μ, σ, TRUE) where $\mu = 16{,}933{,}038$ and $\sigma = 341{,}521$, first compute the probability that the cash payments will be less than $16.5 million, which is 10.2%. Then, by taking 1–10.2%, the estimated cash payments to exceed $16.5 million are approximately determined as a 90% chance.

(c) *What is the probability of the ending cash balance being less than the forecast deterministic budget estimate of $8,101,077?*

Using the function =NORM.DIST(8101077, μ, σ, TRUE), where $\mu = 8,233,933$ and $\sigma = 699,125$, the probability is found to be 42.5%. More specifically, there is a 57.5% chance that the forecast ending cash balance exceeds the deterministic estimate.

Consequently, such information can be used by Marina Royale's accountants for planning cash and fund management. In addition to the above statistical inferences, accountants may also analyze the simulation results for data visualization, as in descriptive analytics. For example, in Fig. 3.4, components of the cash budget scaled in log values are shown to assess how uncertainties aggregate. As shown, the combination of uncertainties pertaining to cash availability and disbursements, though individually low, indicated by the narrower spreads, results in larger uncertainty for the ending cash balance, as observed by the wider spread of its normal distribution.

Why are such insights important for risk management and budgeting? Insights from simulation output are useful for Marina Royale's management because, with these visuals and statistical inferences, management can better assess what to expect in 20X1 with respect to generating and spending cash to provide a positive experience to guests. Basically, budget simulations allow accountants

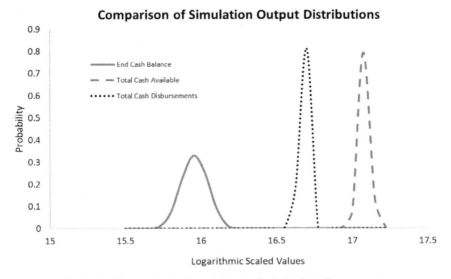

Fig. 3.4. Uncertainties Pertaining to Cash Budget Components.

to anticipate and plan for future funding contingencies that will affect business operations, especially if downside risks increase with lower-than-expected future room/occupancy rates, increase in variable room expenses due to labor shortages, and increase in other fixed costs due to inflation, supply chain disruptions, etc.

CONCLUSION

In this chapter, the Monte Carlo simulation technique is applied to cash budgeting using a step-by-step approach in Microsoft Excel. Risk management and budgeting are related concepts that ideally should be integrated. Unfortunately, traditional budgeting does not provide a seamless mechanism to integrate these two concepts. As this chapter demonstrates, Monte Carlo simulation, which is recommended as a predictive and prescriptive analytic tool, allows this seamless integration by using the budget itself as a simulation model. On the other hand, in scenario planning, only a few future events are assumed, compared with simulation, where unlimited scenarios are simultaneously considered. Sensitivity analysis or what-if analysis only tells how a budget changes for a selected change in input variable values. More to the point, as accounting analytics is gaining traction, with Monte Carlo simulation, uncertainties and the likelihood of different types of risks can be quantified to guide planning and budgeting in organizations.

One of the main limitations that should be addressed in future research is modeling input variables and their distributions, which would enhance the simulation. Burkert et al. (2022) seeks to address this issue by providing students and instructors with guidance on how to select input distribution such as the triangular and BetaPERT and calibrate with minimum, maximum, and most likely (mode) values from the data. Alternatively, where actual data are available, students can use distributional fitting software to identify the variables and their associated probability distributions. In the case where historic data are not available, instructors can demonstrate how students may use expert opinion to elicit a distribution. For example, for a normal distribution, one half of the area (50%) would lie between 2/3 standard deviation of the mean. Consequently, instructors may make their applications of simulation in the classroom more nuanced by requiring students to justify their choices of variables used in the simulation and their distributions. Finally, the Excel-based simulation approach discussed in this chapter can be used to develop probabilistic operating budgets and in other areas of management accounting such as probabilistic cost-volume-profit analysis, capacity planning, and other managerial and cost decision models.

NOTE

1 The idea for this exercise was motivated by Horngren et al. (2011). In that example, no uncertainty is considered. Consequently, our example is entirely different, since probability distributions are assumed for model variables.

REFERENCES

Appelbaum, D., Kogan, A., Vasarhelyi, M., & Yan, Z. (2017). Impact of business analytics and enterprise systems on managerial accounting. *International Journal of Accounting Information Systems, 25,* 29–44.

Briand, G., & Hill, R. C. (2013). Teaching basic econometric concepts using Monte Carlo simulations in Excel. *International Review of Economics Education, 12,* 60–79.

Burkert, M., Calderon, T., Hesford, J. W., & Turner, M. J. (2022). Azure Lodging, Inc.: A case study on capital budgeting with capital rationing in a service industry context. *Issues in Accounting Education, 37*(2), 67–89.

Calderon, T. G., Hesford, J. W., & Turner, M. J. (2022). A framework for integrating R Programming into the accounting curriculum. In T. G. Calderon (Ed.), *Advances in accounting education* (Vol. 26, pp. 209–232). Emerald Publishing Limited.

CPA Canada. (2018, July 18). Basic audit data analytics with R. https://www.cpacanada.ca/en/members-area/profession-news/2018/july/adas-practical-learning

CPA Ireland. (2022, June 15). Data analytics for finance. https://www.cpaireland.ie/become-a-student/CPA-Qualifications/Data-Analytics-for-Finance

Datar, S. M., Rajan, M. V., Beaubien, L., & Janz, S. (2022). *Horngren's cost accounting: A managerial emphasis.* Pearson Canada.

Davenport, T. H., & Harris, J. G. (2007). *Competing on analytics: The new science of winning.* Harvard Business Review Press.

Elkjaer, M. (2000). Stochastic budget simulation. *International Journal of Project Management, 18*(2), 139–147.

Green, K., & Littlejohn, A. (2024). A framework for integrating Python programming into the accounting curricula. *Advances in Accounting Education, 28* (forthcoming).

Herath, H. S. B. (2023a). Technology enhanced learning: Monte Carlo simulation of a cash budget. *International Journal of Intelligent Computing Research, 14*(1), ISSN: 2042 4655 (Online). https://infonomics-society.org/ijicr/

Herath, H. S. B. (2023b). *Predictive analytics – A self study guide: Monte Carlo Simulation with applications to managerial and cost accounting, Part 1: Excel.* Independently published. https://www.amazon.ca/dp/B0CN3C8287/ref=sr_1_20?crid=38KR8FT366YXE&keywords=predictive+analytics&qid=1699636196&s=digital-text&sprefix=%2Cdigital-text%2C91&sr=1-20

Herath, H. S. B. (2023c). *Predictive analytics – A self study guide: Monte Carlo Simulation with applications to managerial and cost accounting, Part 2: Modeling with R.* Independently published. https://www.amazon.ca/gp/product/B0CP2Z9Z81?ref_=dbs_m_mng_rwt_calw_tkin_1&storeType=ebooks

Herath, H. S. B., & Sharman, P. A. (2017). Activity idle capacity cost estimation via Monte Carlo simulation. *Journal of Cost Management, 31*(2), 30–40.

Herath, H. S. B., & Sharman, P. A. (2019). Stochastic cost-volume-profit (CVP) analysis – Modeling multiple random variables. *Journal of Cost Management* (September/October), 33–45.

Horngren, C. T., Sundem, G. L., Stratton, W. O., & Beaulieu, P. (2011). *Management Accounting* (sixth Canadianed.). Pearson Canada.

Janvrin, D. J., & Watson, M. W. (2017). "Big Data": A new twist to accounting. *Journal of Accounting Education, 38,* 3–8.

Liberatore, M. J., & Luo, W. (2010). The analytics movement: Implications for operations research. *Interfaces, 40*(4), 313–324.

Lord, R. J. (1977). Probabilistic budgeting: One practical experience. *WSC '77: Proceedings of the 9th Conference on Winter Simulation, 2,* 608–616.

Lord, R. J. (1979). Coping with future uncertainties through probabilistic budgeting. *Insights into Experiential Pedagogy, 6,* 86–89.

Mattessich, R. (1961). Budgeting model and system simulation. *The Accounting Review, 36*(3), 384–397.

Mensching, J., Adams, S. J., Gardiner, L., & Jones, N. (2012). Modeling the budgeting process: Enriching the learning environment using Monte Carlo simulations. *AIS Educator Journal, 7*(1), 53–67.

Richins, G., Stapleton, A., Stratopoulos, T. C., & Wong, C. (2017). Big data analytics: Opportunity or threat for the accounting profession? *Journal of Information Systems, 31*(3), 63–79.

APPENDIX

Table A1. Data and Distributional Assumptions on Occupancy Rates.

OCC-H: Average Monthly Occupancy – Corporate Clients (Holidays)

	Jan.	Feb.	Mar.	Apr.	May	Jun.	Jul.	Aug.	Sep.	Oct.	Nov.	Dec.	Normal Mean	Stdev
Saturday	74%	78%	85%	82%	81%	82%	74%	84%	72%	80%	71%	72%	75.58%	5.20%
Sunday	72%	79%	67%	78%	73%	76%	74%	75%	67%	70%	79%	69%		

OCC-W: Average Monthly Occupancy – Corporate Clients (Weekdays)

	Jan.	Feb.	Mar.	Apr.	May	Jun.	Jul.	Aug.	Sep.	Oct.	Nov.	Dec.	Uniform Min	Max
Monday	96%	99%	92%	96%	100%	93%	99%	98%	96%	99%	100%	98%	90.00%	100.00%
Tuesday	95%	91%	90%	92%	94%	94%	96%	94%	92%	93%	93%	91%	Mean	
Wednesday	100%	95%	93%	100%	95%	92%	98%	95%	95%	95%	97%	96%	95%	
Thursday	99%	98%	95%	97%	98%	95%	94%	96%	99%	94%	94%	93%		
Friday	93%	93%	92%	96%	98%	96%	99%	100%	99%	96%	94%	94%		

OIC-H: Average Monthly Occupancy – Individual Customers (Holidays)

	Jan.	Feb.	Mar.	Apr.	May	Jun.	Jul.	Aug.	Sep.	Oct.	Nov.	Dec.	Uniform Min	Max
Saturday	92%	96%	100%	99%	95%	93%	95%	100%	100%	96%	91%	96%	88.00%	100.00%
Sunday	97%	97%	88%	97%	99%	97%	91%	92%	93%	97%	99%	93%		

OIC-W: Average Monthly Occupancy – Individual Customers (Weekdays)

	Jan.	Feb.	Mar.	Apr.	May	Jun.	Jul.	Aug.	Sep.	Oct.	Nov.	Dec.	Normal Mean	Stdev
Monday	57%	58%	60%	52%	59%	54%	46%	52%	47%	58%	45%	48%	65.57%	10.68%
Tuesday	61%	55%	53%	62%	55%	59%	69%	49%	58%	65%	75%	74%		
Wednesday	72%	50%	73%	67%	51%	52%	65%	60%	62%	72%	56%	67%		
Thursday	70%	75%	74%	77%	74%	75%	72%	70%	77%	77%	77%	72%		
Friday	79%	77%	80%	78%	76%	75%	75%	80%	78%	76%	73%	79%		

Data Science in Accounting 73

Table A2. Data and Distributional Assumptions on Room Rates.

RCC: Average Room Rates – Corporate Clients (Weekdays and Weekends)

	Jan.	Feb.	Mar.	Apr.	May	Jun.	Jul.	Aug.	Sep.	Oct.	Nov.	Dec.	Mean
Saturday	285	286	285	288	287	288	288	285	288	285	290	286	287
Sunday	287	287	285	285	286	287	289	288	290	290	290	288	
Monday	290	286	285	289	288	289	290	290	289	286	289	290	
Tuesday	289	286	288	288	285	288	286	288	287	285	286	288	
Wednesday	287	289	288	287	285	288	289	287	287	290	287	290	
Thursday	286	287	289	286	288	286	287	288	289	286	289	285	
Friday	285	287	285	290	290	285	287	290	286	288	287	286	

Converted to Logarithmic

	Jan.	Feb.	Mar.	Apr.	May	Jun.	Jul.	Aug.	Sep.	Oct.	Nov.	Dec.	Lognormal
													Mean Stdev
Saturday	5.6525	5.6560	5.6525	5.6630	5.6595	5.6630	5.6630	5.6525	5.6630	5.6525	5.6699	5.6560	5.6610 0.0058
Sunday	5.6595	5.6595	5.6525	5.6525	5.6560	5.6595	5.6664	5.6630	5.6699	5.6699	5.6699	5.6630	
Monday	5.6699	5.6560	5.6525	5.6664	5.6630	5.6664	5.6699	5.6699	5.6664	5.6560	5.6664	5.6699	
Tuesday	5.6664	5.6560	5.6630	5.6630	5.6525	5.6630	5.6560	5.6630	5.6595	5.6525	5.6560	5.6630	
Wednesday	5.6595	5.6664	5.6630	5.6595	5.6525	5.6630	5.6664	5.6595	5.6595	5.6699	5.6595	5.6699	
Thursday	5.6560	5.6595	5.6664	5.6560	5.6630	5.6560	5.6595	5.6630	5.6664	5.6560	5.6664	5.6525	
Friday	5.6525	5.6595	5.6525	5.6699	5.6699	5.6525	5.6595	5.6699	5.6560	5.6630	5.6595	5.6560	

R-ICH: Average Room Rates – Individual Customers (Holidays)

	Jan.	Feb.	Mar.	Apr.	May	Jun.	Jul.	Aug.	Sep.	Oct.	Nov.	Dec.	Mean
Saturday	232	225	228	233	233	235	225	238	228	231	236	228	232
Sunday	237	230	240	239	230	227	226	226	240	239	227	229	

Converted to Logarithmic

	Jan.	Feb.	Mar.	Apr.	May	Jun.	Jul.	Aug.	Sep.	Oct.	Nov.	Dec.	Lognormal
													Mean Stdev
Saturday	5.4467	5.4161	5.4293	5.4510	5.4510	5.4596	5.4161	5.4723	5.4293	5.4424	5.4638	5.4293	5.4454 0.0219
Sunday	5.4681	5.4381	5.4806	5.4765	5.4381	5.4250	5.4205	5.4205	5.4806	5.4765	5.4250	5.4337	

R-ICW: Average Room Rates – Individual Customers (Weekdays)

	Jan.	Feb.	Mar.	Apr.	May	Jun.	Jul.	Aug.	Sep.	Oct.	Nov.	Dec.	Mean
Monday	166	126	135	136	175	129	181	154	160	132	127	148	156

(Continued)

Table A2. (*Continued*)

	Jan.	Feb.	Mar.	Apr.	May	Jun.	Jul.	Aug.	Sep.	Oct.	Nov.	Dec.
Tuesday	141	142	153	170	145	152	140	150	174	164	147	134
Wednesday	143	166	151	170	169	152	188	155	172	165	133	168
Thursday	138	126	187	169	171	179	187	183	184	171	146	154
Friday	128	141	181	153	151	152	133	161	183	176	175	137

Converted to Logarithmic

	Jan.	Feb.	Mar.	Apr.	May	Jun.	Jul.	Aug.	Sep.	Oct.	Nov.	Dec.	Lognormal Mean	Stdev
Monday	5.1120	4.8363	4.9053	4.9127	5.1648	4.8598	5.1985	5.0370	5.0752	4.8828	4.8442	4.9972	5.0451	0.1180
Tuesday	4.9488	4.9558	5.0304	5.1358	4.9767	5.0239	4.9416	5.0106	5.1591	5.0999	4.9904	4.8978		
Wednesday	4.9628	5.1120	5.0173	5.1358	5.1299	5.0239	5.2364	5.0434	5.1475	5.1059	4.8903	5.1240		
Thursday	4.9273	4.8363	5.2311	5.1299	5.1417	5.1874	5.2311	5.2095	5.2149	5.1417	4.9836	5.0370		
Friday	4.8520	4.9488	5.1985	5.0304	5.0173	5.0239	4.8903	5.0814	5.2095	5.1705	5.1648	4.9200		

Note: Room rates are converted to natural logarithmic values using the LN() function, since log-normal distributions are assumed.

Table A3. Excel Template for Simulating the Ending Cash Balance.

THEME 2
INNOVATIVE TEACHING CASES IN TAXATION

CHAPTER 4

ALBERT'S FAMILY PET STORE: A CASE EXPLORING GUARANTEED PAYMENTS, BOOK TO TAX DIFFERENCES, AND FORM 1065

Jodi Olson[a] and Brian Huels[b]

[a]Winona State University, USA
[b]University of Wisconsin – Whitewater, USA

ABSTRACT

Partnership and limited liability company (LLC) entity types are commonplace in the business world. Unfortunately, in many tax classrooms, individual and corporate taxation topics tend to dominate the syllabus. In alignment with the CPA Evolution Model Curriculum, referencing the importance of teaching partnership returns in accounting education, this case helps fill this gap by offering an engaging, hands-on activity that allows students to prepare a partnership tax return based on a flow of information that would be commonplace in practice. Students are presented with book financial statements, a partnership agreement, and other real-world information to bridge the gap from textbook to practice. Specifically, students go from start to finish in the preparation of Albert's Family Pet Store partnership tax return for the most recent tax year. Data gathered from pre- and post-surveys support the usage of this activity. Results show that this activity is viewed as a valuable learning experience that provides a unique platform for students to build confidence in their ability to prepare and understand Form 1065, Form K-1, and Form 4562 while simulating the use of trial balance software to make the book and federal tax journal entries.

Keywords: Partnerships; accounting; taxation; guaranteed payments; book financial statements; tax return

In 2020, a total of over 4.28 million partnership and limited liability company (LLC) partnership tax returns (Form 1065) were filed with the Internal Revenue Service (2022). This number represents a 27.4% increase from the previous decade (Internal Revenue Service, 2020). In comparison, over the same ten-year period, the filing of C-corporation returns (Form 1120) decreased by 22.8% while S-corporation returns (Form 1120-S) increased by 11.9%, respectively – far less than the increase experienced by partnership filings (Internal Revenue Service 2020). This large change in the filing of partnership returns is partly attributable to the expansion of partnership variations, particularly LLCs, which became increasingly popular in the United States in the mid-1990s (Riles & Whitlock, 2003). LLCs now account for over 70% of partnership returns (Decarlo et al., 2020).

From the practitioner's side, the filing of partnership returns can be quite complex. One reason for this complexity is that partners of a partnership do not receive wages. Instead, owners are compensated through guaranteed payments, a topic that has seen much historical ambiguity (Steinberg, 2004). Also, partners are taxed on the partnership's income, resulting in the calculation of self-employment tax at the individual level. Furthermore, partnerships and LLCs can create complex operating agreements that allow for special allocations of items between partners. Income, deductions, credits, and the like all can be specially allocated to partners. Compared to other business entities where allocations are typically proportional to ownership percentages, the less stringent and more flexible allocation can make the filing of partnership returns more complex (Maloney et al., 2020).

In the classroom, tax form preparation tends to start with complete business data and pushes the students' focus to the task of completing a tax return. Unfortunately, this tends to oversimplify the tax return preparation process. In reality, the preparation of a business entity tax return involves a process that requires a significant amount of critical thinking. For example, client data must be gathered, trial balance information prepared and/or reviewed, adjusting entries posted, book/tax differences identified, tax work papers generated, and finally, a tax return is prepared for review. Throughout all of this, in practice, the partnership agreement needs to be consulted as allocations will very often not be proportionate to partnership ownership percentages. Although partnership agreements are discussed in the classroom, it is typically done in a business law or a foundation level chapter of tax. Coverage in this manner, removed from the actual tax return preparation process, strips students of the ability to see the importance of how all the pieces interact. Furthermore, research continuously shows the need for students to develop a greater level of critical thinking ability

(Wolcott & Sargent, 2021) and that experiential learning activities including case studies and practical applications (similar to this activity) can help increase skills such as problem solving and critical thinking (Gittings et al., 2020).

Acknowledging the significant amount of partnership tax returns that are filed as well as the need for students to be able to actively engage in the preparation of said returns in practice, this activity provides a bridge to help students get the best of both worlds – tax knowledge and practical experience. In addition, most accounting courses, except tax, are heavily oriented around journal entries that reference a trial balance. This activity lets students see that financial and tax accounting are not two different worlds – but rather critical pieces of the puzzle that allow for a complete tax return to be prepared.

While the literature has well established that using journal entries to teach business taxation is effective (Bayer et al., 1989; Fisher & Hageman, 2012; Fry & Fry, 1988) and some research utilizes a trial balance worksheet (Bayer et al., 1989; Fry & Fry, 1988; Sonnier, 2010) the literature lacks a clear simulation of the entire process students may experience with most partnership returns in practice. This case fills that gap by letting students start with a client's unadjusted financial statements while finishing with a complete tax return. Also, the CPA Evolution Model Curriculum clearly lays out several learning objectives (e.g., calculate ordinary business income, distinguish book depreciation and accelerated MACRS depreciation, identify nondeductible expenses, determine what constitutes non-separately stated items, analyze components of partnership income/deductions) that are important to Partnerships, which this case also addresses (AICPA & NASBA, 2021).

Finally, a review of extant teaching cases highlights the need for additional activities within the tax area (Fogarty, 2022). A search of the Meyer and Meyer (2014) accounting case database yields only two cases that cover partnership accounting (Drnevich & Sternburg, 2017; Fisher & Hageman, 2012). The scarcity of partnership tax cases is further supported by the findings of Adams et al. (2022) who discovered only three teaching cases related to partnerships looking at the time period from 2003 to 2021.

Looking at the demands of the field, demands within the classroom, and the current lack of resources to meet such demands – this case is both timely and relevant.

THE ACTIVITY

This activity introduces students to the process of taking book information and transforming it into a tax return. A process that tends to be oversimplified in many accounting textbooks, this activity provides students with the pieces needed to complete the puzzle of the creation of Form 1065 and related forms. Specifically, this activity provides students with a partnership agreement and a set of unadjusted book financial statements. Students are then asked to go through the full cycle of preparing a tax return accomplishing several specific learning objectives of this activity along the way. First, students update the book financial statements through the creation of an adjusted trial balance (Learning Objective 1). From there, students determine any necessary book to tax differences (Schedule M-1 items) and update their supporting work papers accordingly with federal tax journal entries (Learning Objective 2). Finally, students are asked to prepare Form 1065 and supporting tax forms for the partnership (Learning Objectives 3 and 4). All of these steps are supported by students consulting the partnership agreement of the entity. The activity provides students with the opportunity to engage in critical thinking to pull all of the pieces together.

Details of the activity are provided next. The chapter concludes with a summary of activity assessments based on past usage.

Partnership Agreement

Related to partnership accounting, book or tax, the partnership agreement is one of the first things that should be obtained and reviewed when dealing with a new client. Typically, in the workplace, this document can be found in the permanent file of the client. In the classroom, the importance of a partnership agreement is typically discussed; however, students do not usually get the ability to read through a partnership agreement and apply said agreement to the preparation of book or tax financial statements. To help bridge this gap and provide a more real-world application experience, this activity is based on students pulling information from a provided partnership agreement (see Appendix 1).

Unadjusted Book Financial Statements

Students are also provided with a set of comparative unadjusted book financial statements (income statement, statement of partners' capital, and balance sheet) for the two most recent years ended (see Appendix 2). A review of these financial statements should help students understand the importance of looking through documents to try to gauge the believability and completeness of client information. In combination, students should also be able to verify that the partnership is operating in accordance with the guidelines established by the partnership agreement.

Other Information

Trying to mirror what students will see in practice, this activity also provides an invoice of a current year fixed-asset purchase and a loan amortization schedule (see Appendix 3). Both of these items are needed to accurately complete the activity and are provided in a manner that makes students think about why the information is being provided to them. Being able to critically think and identify issues such as current versus long-term classification, if current year depreciation is accurately reflected, as well as getting a gut feel for the completeness of financial statements are very useful skills. All too often, students are provided with the exact information they need to answer a question. This activity tries to remove these crutches by providing students with the information in raw form so that they can sift through and determine how the information is relevant to the task

Albert's Family Pet Store

at hand. In this context, the generation of an accurate Form 1065 and supporting documents. Also, the fixed-asset purchase invoice allows instructors the freedom to talk about topics such as sales and use tax, if applicable.

Student Instructions

As mentioned, students are given the pieces needed to prepare the end deliverable, a partnership tax return for Albert's Family Pet Store. Student instructions are left intentionally brief to mirror practice. Basically, here is a bunch of stuff – look through it and prepare a tax return. The respective deliverables that instructors ask students for may vary; however, three recommended deliverables for this activity are listed below. Each of these deliverables is mapped to the learning objectives which are presented in the subsequent section of this chapter.

1. Prepare an adjusted book trial balance. This should include but is not limited to any needed adjustments for book depreciation and current versus long-term notes payable (see Learning Objective 1).
2. Determine if any book to tax adjustments need to be made (see Learning Objectives 2).
3. Prepare a US Return of Partnership Income (Form 1065), including all needed supporting forms (e.g., Form 4562, K-1s, etc.) (see Learning Objectives 3 and 4).

LEARNING OBJECTIVES AND IMPLEMENTATION GUIDANCE

Learning Objectives

The learning objectives of this activity are driven by the motivation behind this case and are in alignment with the CPA Evolution Model Curriculum for Partnerships. Details related to the CPA Evolution Model are shown in Fig. 4.1.

Module 9: Partnerships		
Topic 1: Determination of ordinary business income (loss) and separately stated items		
Summary	Estimated Hours	Suggested course(s)
Identify and calculate ordinary business income (loss) and separately stated items for a partnership using appropriate tax preparer technology.	1-1.5	TAX

Fig. 4.1. Excerpt from the CPA Evolution Model Curriculum (AICPA & NASBA, 2021, p. 49).

After completion of this case, students should be able to:

1. Take raw client information, review it to gain an understanding of the business, make decisions about said information's completeness and prepare an adjusted book trial balance to address any shortcomings (Learning Objective 1).

2. Review client provided information and identify any relevant book-versus-tax differences (Schedule M-1 items) (Learning Objective 2).
3. Demonstrate knowledge of the proper calculation and reporting of guaranteed payments (both related to capital and services provided) (Learning Objective 3).
4. Assemble and migrate information from work papers into a completed Form 1065 and related forms (Form 4562, K-1, etc.) (Learning Objective 4).

Implementation Information and Guidance

To facilitate the implementation of this activity, all needed materials are included in the appendices, with electronic versions of all materials and answer keys available from the authors upon request.

Authors experience with administering the activity leads us to provide the following implementation suggestions for instructors. First, a period of two weeks is recommended between the date assigned and the due date of the project. Second, a check figure is suggested for taxable income to provide the student's guidance on whether they are on the right track after completing the trial balance. Third, we recommend the activity be assigned after relevant content to the assignment has been covered in the classroom. In addition, providing references for prior learning for Form 4562 and MACRS depreciation may prove useful, as in our experience, some students struggled to retain this information as it was not a recent topic within the assigned course. And finally, if your curriculum is focused on corporations in financial accounting classes and students have not yet taken advanced financial accounting, where partnerships are typically discussed in greater detail, do a review of capital accounts, as the concept may be new to them.

Classroom Validation

The activity was implemented across four classes during the fall 2020 and fall 2021 semesters. Two classes were comprised of students pursuing an associate's degree at a two-year college. And, the other two classes were students pursuing master's degrees at a midwestern US state university. In total, fifty (50) students participated in the activity and provided feedback from both a subjective and objective perspective. Table 4.1A summarizes the results of pre and post-subjective questions presented to students. Table 4.1A is presented showing all students that were assessed related to this activity. Table 4.1B, includes the same summary, however results are further broken down by degree type (e.g., Associates; Masters). Table 4.2 provides a summary of additional student feedback completed post activity. Tables 4.1A, 4.1B and 4.2 summarize the reported means using a scale of 1 (strongly disagree) to 5 (strongly agree). Finally, Table 4.3 provides a summary of an objective question presented to students related to their ability to properly identify common book versus tax differences. The numbers reported within Table 4.3 identify the number of students that were able to correctly identify the book versus tax treatment difference for each respective item.

Students perceived that the activity helped increase their understanding of guaranteed payments and the treatment for both book (pre = 3.28; post = 3.88,

Table 4.1A. Pre/Post-Activity Questionnaire Results – Combined.

Student Experiential Feedback (n = 50) (1 = Strongly Disagree; 5 Strongly Agree)	Learning Objective Mapping	Mean (Std. Dev) Pre	Mean (Std. Dev) Post	Difference (Pre/Post)
I understand how guaranteed payments are treated for "book" purposes	1, 3	3.28 (0.88)	3.88 (0.80)	0.60**
I understand how guaranteed payments are treated for "tax" purposes	3	3.36 (0.87)	3.86 (0.87)	0.49*
I understand the tax law contained in I.R.C. Sec. 707(c) – transactions between partner and partnership	3	3.16 (0.88)	3.38 (0.84)	0.21
I am aware of the differences between compensation paid to a partner versus compensation paid to an employee of a partnership	3	3.80 (0.76)	3.98 (0.84)	0.18
I am confident in my ability to prepare Form 1065 (US Return of Partnership Tax Return).	2, 4	3.44 (0.76)	3.82 (0.90)	0.38*
I am confident in my ability to understand Form 1065 (US Return of Partnership Tax Return).	2, 4	3.51 (0.77)	3.94 (0.87)	0.43*
I am confident in my ability to prepare Form K-1 (Partner's Share of Income, Deductions, Credits, etc.)	3, 4	3.44 (0.81)	3.70 (0.95)	0.26
I am confident in my ability to understand Form K-1	3, 4	3.45 (0.83)	3.84 (0.91)	0.39*
I am confident in my ability to prepare Form 4562 (Depreciation and Amortization)	4	3.29 (0.83)	3.78 (0.93)	0.49*
I am confident in my ability to understand Form 4562 (Depreciation and Amortization)	4	3.42 (0.83)	3.90 (0.97)	0.48*

*Indicates significant differences in the pre-case and post-case t-statistics ($p < 0.05$).
**Indicates significant differences in the pre-case and post-case t-statistics ($p < 0.001$).

$p < 0.001$) and tax purposes (pre = 3.36; post = 3.86, $p < 0.05$). Students also indicated an increase in confidence related to the preparation (pre = 3.44; post = 3.82, $p < 0.05$) and understanding (pre = 3.51; post = 3.94, $p < 0.01$) of Form 1065 – US Return of Partnership Income. Finally, students also indicated a significant gain in confidence related to their ability to prepare (pre = 3.44; post = 3.82, $p < 0.05$) and understand Form K-1 (pre = 3.45; post = 3.84, $p < 0.05$) and their ability to prepare (pre = 3.29; post = 3.78, $p < 0.05$) and understand Form 4562 (pre = 3.31; post = 3.84, $p < 0.05$). Table 1B provides added analysis by degree level (e.g., Associates Level or Masters Level) showing similar findings to the combined sample displayed in Table 1A.

Table 4.2 presents a summary results of students' responses regarding the activity experience itself. For analysis purposes, means and standard deviations are provided for the entire sample as well as by class (associate and master degree levels).

Students found the activity interesting (4.04) and a good mechanism to increase their tax knowledge (4.34). Also, students admitted that the activity was challenging (4.44) and also brought forward the complexity involved in the preparation of a partnership tax return (4.52). Student feedback at both the Associate's and Master's degree level provides a strong level of support for using this activity in the classroom.

Table 4.1B. Pre-/Post-Activity Questionnaire Results – By Degree Level.

Student Experiential Feedback (1 = Strongly Disagree; 5 Strongly Agree)	Associates Level Mean (Std. Dev) (n = 23) Pre	Post	Difference (Pre/Post)	Masters Level Mean (Std. Dev) (n = 27) Pre	Post	Difference (Pre/Post)
I understand how guaranteed payments are treated for "book" purposes	3.33 (0.88)	3.78 (1.00)	0.45*	3.22 (0.89)	3.96 (0.59)	0.74**
I understand how guaranteed payments are treated for "tax" purposes	3.39 (0.92)	3.83 (0.98)	0.43	3.33 (0.83)	3.88 (0.77)	0.55*
I understand the tax law contained in I.R.C. Sec. 707(c) – transactions between partner and partnership	3.07 (0.90)	3.29 (0.85)	0.22	3.26 (0.86)	3.44 (0.85)	0.18
I am aware of the differences between compensation paid to a partner versus compensation paid to an employee of a partnership	3.82 (0.82)	3.87 (0.97)	0.05	3.78 (0.70)	4.07 (0.73)	0.29
I am confident in my ability to prepare Form 1065 (US Return of Partnership Tax Return)	3.46 (0.69)	3.70 (1.11)	0.24	3.41 (0.84)	3.93 (0.68)	0.52*
I am confident in my ability to understand Form 1065 (US Return of Partnership Tax Return)	3.46 (0.69)	3.91 (1.00)	0.45*	3.56 (0.85)	3.96 (0.76)	0.40*
I am confident in my ability to prepare Form K-1 (Partner's Share of Income, Deductions, Credits, etc.)	3.46 (0.79)	3.70 (1.02)	0.24	3.41 (0.84)	3.70 (0.91)	0.29
I am confident in my ability to understand Form K-1	3.43 (0.84)	3.83 (0.89)	0.40*	3.48 (0.85)	3.85 (0.95)	0.37
I am confident in my ability to prepare Form 4562 (Depreciation and Amortization)	3.50 (0.79)	3.74 (1.05)	0.24	3.07 (0.83)	3.81 (0.83)	0.74**
I am confident in my ability to understand Form 4562 (Depreciation and Amortization)	3.61 (0.83)	3.91 (1.08)	0.30	3.22 (0.80)	3.89 (0.89)	0.67*

*Indicates significant differences in the pre-case and post-case *t*-statistics ($p < 0.05$).
**Indicates significant differences in the pre-case and post-case *t*-statistics ($p < 0.001$).

Albert's Family Pet Store   85

Table 4.2. Post-activity Questionnaire Results.

	Statement (1 = Strongly Disagree; 5 Strongly Agree)	Assoc (n = 23)	Master (n = 27)	All (n = 50)
1	This activity increased my ability to prepare Form 1065	4.13 (0.69)	4.30 (0.61)	4.22 (0.65)
2	This activity increased my ability to prepare Form K-1	3.91 (0.95)	4.26 (0.66)	4.10 (0.81)
3	This activity increased my ability to prepare Form 4562	3.87 (0.92)	4.22 (0.58)	4.06 (0.77)
4	This activity increased my understanding of Form 1065	3.91 (0.95)	4.30 (0.47)	4.12 (0.75)
5	This activity increased my understanding of Form K-1	3.83 (1.11)	4.22 (0.58)	4.04 (0.88)
6	This activity increased my understanding of Form 4562	3.78 (1.04)	4.19 (0.68)	4.00 (0.88)
7	I found this assignment interesting	3.70 (1.15)	4.33 (0.73)	4.04 (0.99)
8	The assignment provided an opportunity to increase my tax knowledge	4.26 (0.92)	4.41 (0.57)	4.34 (0.75)
9	The activity was challenging	4.30 (0.97)	4.56 (0.58)	4.44 (0.79)
10	The activity helped me better realize the complexity of preparing a partnership tax return	4.22 (1.04)	4.78 (0.42)	4.52 (0.81)
11	The amount of time allowed to complete the case was reasonable	4.04 (1.15)	4.56 (0.64)	4.32 (0.94)
12	Compared to a traditional short-problem assignment, this assignment helped me learn tax rules in context	3.61 (1.20)	4.30 (0.61)	3.98 (0.98)
13	I feel that the case was a valuable learning experience	4.04 (0.98)	4.48 (0.51)	4.28 (0.78)
14	The Trial Balance Software (Excel) enhanced my understanding of business tax preparation procedures in the real world	4.00 (0.95)	4.33 (0.55)	4.18 (0.77)

Table 4.3. Pre-/Post-Activity Objective Question Results.

Question (n = 19)	Pre	Post	Difference (Pre/Post) (n = 19)
Which of the following book expenses are typically treated different for tax purposes?			
Meals[a]	14	18	4
Entertainment	12	13	1
Office Supplies	0	0	–
Partner compensation	9	10	1
Penalties	4	15	11
Advertising	1	0	(1)
Utilities	0	0	–
Interest on partner capital balances	9	13	4
Depreciation	13	13	0
Average # of Correct Responses (max = 6)	*53.5%*	*72.0%*	*+18.5%*

Note: This objective question was added to the fall 2021 administration of this activity. 19 students, all associate's level, in total responded to this question pre-/post-activity.
[b]The activity was administered using 2019 and 2020 tax years during which meals were only 50% deductible. If used during 2021 or 2022, business-related meals would be 100% deductible. As of 2023, the majority of business meals have returned to being 50% deductible for tax purposes.

Objectively speaking, the activity also enhances students' understanding of tax law. As seen in Table 4.3, students were asked to identify which expenses are typically treated differently for book and tax purposes. Students showed a large increase in their understanding of how meals, interest on partner capital balances, and penalties differ for tax purposes. Pre-activity, on average, students identified 53.5% of the provided book versus tax differences. Post-activity students correctly identified 72.0% of the differences. This 18.5% increase is impressive as the activity was completed after students had already received teaching related to tax law.

CONCLUSION

In conclusion, this project provides much needed preparatory skills to students for a very complex area of business taxation with the aid of the framework that they are accustomed to using in their other accounting courses. Moreover, the case provides an opportunity for instructors to both prepare students for the CPA exam and help them bridge the gap between the classroom and practice by having them replicate the activities necessary to prepare the partnership return from client data.

The fact pattern presented by this activity provides students with a very real-world situation where they can move through the entire tax return preparation process via review of a partnership agreement, source documents, and client provided financial statements. An analysis of pre-post activity data shows significant benefits that student stakeholders receive from the assignment of this activity. Furthermore, with the CPA exam undergoing significant changes students further benefit from an activity that allows them to apply concepts that will be covered on future CPA exams. In addition, this activity benefits instructors as it provides an outlet for them to assess student learning in a more complex manner than what might typically be used in a classroom setting (e.g., quizzes or exams).

We also believe that this activity benefits the profession as it should give students some confidence of what they may see in the workplace. The sooner students can start seeing and working through real-world type engagements the quicker they will be able to grow within the profession. In summary, the usage of this activity creates a win–win situation for all stakeholders involved.

REFERENCES

Adams, M. T., Inger, K. K., & Meckfessel, M. D. (2022). Educational tax cases: An annotated bibliography. *Advances in Accounting Education: Teaching and Curriculum Innovations*, 26, 191–206.

AICPA & NASBA. (2021, November). *CPA evolution model curriculum*. https://nasba.org/wp-content/uploads/2021/06/Model-curriculum_web_6.11.21.pdf

Bayer, F. A., Hopkins, D. M., & Pierce, B. J. (1989). Integrating tax concepts and financial accounting concepts into the partnership accounting curriculum. *Journal of Accounting Education*, 7(2), 195–216.

Decarlo, R., Ozer-Gurbuz, T., & Shumofsky, N. (2020). *Partnership returns, tax year 2018*. Statistics and Income Bulletin Fall 2020. https://www.irs.gov/pub/irs-pdf/p1136.pdf#page=58

Drnevich, D., & Sternburg, T. J. (2017). Taxes and organizational form: An activity in partnership and corporate entities. *Issues in Accounting Education*, 32(2), 1–12.

Fisher, D. G., & Hageman, A. M. (2012). Using journal entries to teach partnership tax: An illustrative case. *Journal of Accounting Education*, 30(1), 100–130.

Fogarty, T. (2022). A review of published tax cases: Contents, value-added and constraints. *Advances in Accounting Education: Teaching and Curriculum Innovations*, 26, 175–190.

Fry, N. E., & Fry, E. H. (1988). How journal entries are used to teach taxation. *Journal of Accounting Education*, 6(1), 149–157.
Gittings, L., Taplin, R., & Kerr, R. (2020). Experiential learning activities in university accounting education: A systematic literature review. *Journal of Accounting Education*, 52, 100680.
Internal Revenue Service. (2020). *SOI tax stats – Numbers of returns filed by type of return – IRS data book (Table 2)*. https://www.irs.gov/statistics/soi-tax-stats-all-years-irs-data-books
Internal Revenue Service. (2022). *SOI tax stats – Partnership statistics by entity type*. https://www.irs.gov/statistics/soi-tax-stats-partnership-statistics-by-entity-type
Maloney, D. M., Young, J. C., Nellen, A., & Persellin, M. (2020). *South-Western Federal taxation 2021: Comprehensive* (44th ed.). Cengage.
Meyer, M. J., & Meyer, T. S. (2014). Accounting case search: A web-based search tool for finding published accounting cases. *Journal of Accounting Education*, 32(4), 16–23.
Riles, J., & Whitlock, B. (2003). The ABCs of LLCs. *National Public Accountant*, p. 16.
Sonnier, B. (2010). Utopia Home Health, Inc.: A case study on c corporation taxation from Cradle to Grave. *Issues in Accounting Education*, 25(4), 755–774.
Steinberg, L. R. (2004). Fun and games with guaranteed payments. *Tax Lawyer*, 57(2), 533–570.
Wolcott, S. K., & Sargent, M. J. (2021). Critical thinking in accounting education: Status and call to action. *Journal of Accounting Education*, 56, 100731.

APPENDIX 1 – PARTNERSHIP AGREEMENT

ALBERT'S FAMILY PET STORE

PARTNERSHIP AGREEMENT

THIS PARTNERSHIP AGREEMENT is made on January 1, X1. **BETWEEN.**

Partner Name	Address
Rex Albert	22 Pretend Street	Pretend, FL 12345
Kelly Albert	33 Pretend Street	Pretend, FL 12345

NAME AND BUSINESS. The parties hereby form a partnership under the name Albert's Family Pet Store which will operate a store front location that will engage in the selling of pet supplies. The principal office of the business shall be located at 999 Pretend Street | Pretend, FL 12345.

TERM. The partnership shall begin on January 1, X1, and shall continue until agreed by unanimous consent of the Partners.

INITIAL CAPITAL CONTRIBUTIONS. Each of the Partners has contributed to the capital of the Partnership, in cash, as listed below. All partners will contribute their respective Capital Contributions fully and on time.

Partner Name	Agreed Value
Rex Albert	$100,000
Kelly Albert	30,000
Total	$130,000

COMPENSATION FOR SERVICES RENDERED: As of the signing of this Partnership Agreement, the Partners agree that Kelly Albert will be paid the following compensation for services rendered over the first two years of the Partnership's existence (X1 and X2), as listed. Additional compensation for services rendered, by both Partners, as from time to time may be agreed upon by unanimous consent of the Partners.

Kelly Albert – Compensation	
X1	$10,000
X2	$50,000

INTEREST ON CAPITAL: Each partner will be paid on an annual basis an amount of interest based on their initial capital contributions (as shown above). The rate used for interest payments will be 2%. In the event of future drawings that are deemed a return of initial capital contributions the base number used for the calculation of interest will be reduced. As of the signing of this Partnership Agreement, the interest amounts to be paid are as follows:

Partner Name	Agreed Value
Rex Albert	$2,000
Kelly Albert	600
Total	$2,600

PROFIT AND LOSS ALLOCATION. Subject to the other provisions of this Agreement (Compensation and Interest on Capital), the net profits and losses of the Partnership, for both accounting and tax purposes, will accrue to and be borne by the Partners according to the following schedule. Any and all profit and loss allocation should be performed after the allocation of compensation for services rendered (if any):

Partner Name	Profit and Loss %
Rex Albert	75%
Kelly Albert	25%

MANAGEMENT DUTIES AND RESTRICTIONS. The partners shall have equal rights in the management of the partnership business, and each partner shall devote his entire time to the conduct of the business. Without the consent of the other partner neither partner shall on behalf of the partnership borrow or lend money, or make, deliver, or accept any commercial paper, or execute any mortgage, security agreement, bond, or lease, or purchase or contract to purchase, or sell or contract to sell any property for or of the partnership other than the type of property bought and sold in the regular course of its business.

BANKING. All funds of the partnership shall be deposited in its name in such checking account or accounts as shall be designated by the partners. All withdrawals are to be made upon checks signed by either partner.

BOOKS. The partnership books shall be maintained at the principal office of the partnership, and each partner shall at all times have access thereto. The books shall be kept on a calendar year (ending on December 31st of each year).

VOLUNTARY TERMINATION. The partnership may be dissolved at any time by agreement of the partners, in which event the partners shall proceed with reasonable promptness to liquidate the business of the partnership. The partnership name shall be sold with the other assets of the business. The assets of the partnership business shall be used and distributed in the following order: (a) to pay or provide for the payment of all partnership liabilities and liquidating expenses and obligations; (b) to equalize the income accounts of the partners; (c) to discharge the balance of the income accounts of the partners; (d) to equalize the capital accounts of the partners; and (e) to discharge the balance of the capital accounts of the partners.

DEATH. Upon the death of either partner, the surviving partner shall have the right either to purchase the interest of the decedent in the partnership or to terminate and liquidate the partnership business. If the surviving partner elects to purchase the decedent's interest, he shall serve notice in writing of such election, within three months after the death of the decedent, upon the executor or administrator of the decedent, or, if at the time of such election no legal representative has been appointed, upon any one of the known legal heirs of the decedent at the last-known address of such heir. (a) If the surviving partner elects to purchase the interest of the decedent in the partnership, the purchase price shall be equal to the decedent's capital account as at the date of his death plus the decedent's income account as at the end of the prior fiscal year, increased by his share of partnership profits or decreased by his share of partnership losses for the period from the beginning of the fiscal year in which his death occurred until the end of the calendar month in which his death occurred, and decreased by withdrawals charged to his income account during such period. No allowance shall be made for goodwill, trade name, patents, or other intangible assets, except as those assets have been reflected on the partnership books immediately prior to the decedent's death; but the survivor shall nevertheless be entitled to use the trade name of the partnership. (b) Except as herein otherwise stated, the procedure as to liquidation and distribution of the assets of the partnership business shall be the same as stated in paragraph 10 with reference to voluntary termination.

ARBITRATION. Any controversy or claim arising out of or relating to this Agreement, or the breach hereof, shall be settled by arbitration in accordance with the rules, then obtaining, of the American Arbitration Association, and judgment upon the award rendered may be entered in any court having jurisdiction thereof.

Executed this 1st day of January, X1.

Rex Albert

Printed: Rex Albert

Kelly Albert

Printed: Kelly Albert

APPENDIX 2 – UNADJUSTED FINANCIAL STATEMENTS

Albert's Family Pet Store Partnership
Income Statement
For the Years Ended December 31, X1 and December 31, X2

	X2	X1
Sales	$ 1,000,000	$ 500,000
Less: Cost of Goods Sold	719,404	373,222
Gross Profit	**$ 280,596**	**$ 126,778**
Operating Expenses		
Employee Wages	$ 60,000	$ 31,200
Payroll Tax Expense	4,800	2,496
Depreciation Expense	10,400	10,000
Insurance Expense	12,000	12,000
Rent Expense	25,200	24,000
Guaranteed Payment - Compensation	50,000	10,000
Utilities Expense	5,000	4,603
Telephone Expense	2,500	2,400
Meals - Business	3,000	3,000
Entertainment - Business	2,000	2,000
Penalties	50	50
Charitable Donations (Cash)	2,000	1,000
Total Operating Expenses	**$ 176,950**	**$ 102,749**
Income from Operations	**$ 103,646**	**$ 24,029**
Nonoperating Items		
Guaranteed Payment - Interest	$ (2,600)	$ (2,600)
Interest Expense - Bank	(1,046)	(1,429)
Net Income	**$ 100,000**	**$ 20,000**

Albert's Family Pet Store Partnership
Balance Sheet
December 31, X1 and December 31, X2

	12/31/X2	12/31/X1
Assets		
Cash	$ 130,703	$ 90,893
Accounts Receivable	50,000	10,000
Inventories	100,000	50,000
Prepaid Insurance	1,000	1,000
Store Fixtures	70,000	70,000
Computer	2,000	-
Accumulated Depreciation	(20,400)	(10,000)
Total Assets	**$ 333,303**	**$ 211,893**
Liabilities		
Accounts Payable	$ 60,000	$ 30,000
Wages Payable	2,500	1,300
Notes Payable (see amortization schedule)	20,803	30,593
Total Liabilities	**$ 83,303**	**$ 61,893**
Capital		
Rex Albert, Capital	$ 190,000	$ 115,000
Kelly Albert, Capital	60,000	35,000
Total Capital	**$ 250,000**	**$ 150,000**
Total Liabilities and Capital	**$ 333,303**	**$ 211,893**

Albert's Family Pet Store Partnership
Statement of Partner's Capital
For the Years Ended December 31, X1 and December 31, X2

	Kelly Albert	Rex Albert	Total
Capital, 1/1/X1	$ 30,000	$ 100,000	$ 130,000
Remaining Income - X1	5,000	15,000	20,000
Capital, 12/31/X1	$ 35,000	$ 115,000	$ 150,000
Capital, 1/1/X2	$ 35,000	$ 115,000	$ 150,000
Remaining Income - X2	25,000	75,000	100,000
Capital, 12/31/X2	$ 60,000	$ 190,000	$ 250,000

APPENDIX 3 – OTHER WORK PAPERS

ALBERT'S FAMILY PETE STORE PARTNERSHIP
NOTE PAYABLE - LOAN AMORTIZATION

LOAN AMOUNT	40,000	LENGTH OF LOAN	4 YEARS	INTEREST RATE	4.00%

PERIOD	BEG. BALANCES	PAYMENT	INTEREST	PRINCIPAL	ENDING BALANCE
1	40,000	903	133	770	39,230
2	39,230	903	131	772	38,458
3	38,458	903	128	775	37,683
4	37,683	903	126	777	36,906
5	36,906	903	123	780	36,126
6	36,126	903	120	783	35,343
7	35,343	903	118	785	34,558
8	34,558	903	115	788	33,770
9	33,770	903	113	790	32,980
10	32,980	903	110	793	32,187
11	32,187	903	107	796	31,391
12	31,391	903	105	798	30,593
13	30,593	903	102	801	29,792
14	29,792	903	99	804	28,988
15	28,988	903	97	806	28,182
16	28,182	903	94	809	27,373
17	27,373	903	91	812	26,561
18	26,561	903	89	814	25,747
19	25,747	903	86	817	24,930
20	24,930	903	83	820	24,110
21	24,110	903	80	823	23,287
22	23,287	903	78	825	22,462
23	22,462	903	75	828	21,634
24	21,634	903	72	831	20,803
25	20,803	903	69	834	19,969
26	19,969	903	67	836	19,133
27	19,133	903	64	839	18,294
28	18,294	903	61	842	17,452
29	17,452	903	58	845	16,607
30	16,607	903	55	848	15,759
31	15,759	903	53	850	14,909
32	14,909	903	50	853	14,056
33	14,056	903	47	856	13,200
34	13,200	903	44	859	12,341
35	12,341	903	41	862	11,479
36	11,479	903	38	865	10,614
37	10,614	903	35	868	9,746
38	9,746	903	32	871	8,875
39	8,875	903	30	873	8,002
40	8,002	903	27	876	7,126
41	7,126	903	24	879	6,247
42	6,247	903	21	882	5,365
43	5,365	903	18	885	4,480
44	4,480	903	15	888	3,592
45	3,592	903	12	891	2,701
46	2,701	903	9	894	1,807
47	1,807	903	6	897	910
48	900	903	3	900	-

Albert's Family Pet Store

Invoice

Computers R' Us

Date: 1/1/X2
Number: 9001

Sold to: Albert's Family Pet Store Partnership

PAID - CHECK NUMBER 2019

Qty	Item #	Description	Unit Price	Line Total
1.00	P1234	Computer (New - In Box)	$ 1,904.76	$ 1,904.76

Total (pre-tax) $ 1,904.76
Sales Tax (5%) 95.24
Total (pre-tax) $ 2,000.00

CHAPTER 5

VETERANS GOLF AND SOCIAL CLUB: AN INSTRUCTIONAL CASE FOR NOT FOR PROFITS

Mitchell Franklin

Le Moyne College, USA

ABSTRACT

This case examines the tax implications of various not-for-profit statuses available to an organization. Students are presented with a case that considers whether the organization currently classified as a 501(c)(7) organization is properly classified, or should be classified as a 501(c)(3) organization, which would allow its members to take contributions as a tax deductible contribution. This allows students to gain a more complete understanding of the impact classification of a not for profit may have on the organization and taxpayer. The case provides an opportunity for an instructor to teach and evaluate students in tax research at an appropriate level for the course. The case can be adapted to use in undergraduate and graduate courses for individual taxation, or tax research. Student responses indicate they find the case interesting and beneficial. Reviews by other non-author faculty and professional CPAs in practice also concur that this case is beneficial and valuable to student growth.

Keywords: Not for profit; 501(c)(3); 501(c)(7); tax research; charitable contributions; charitable deductions; religious organization; social club

The prior literature, as well as the authors' own teaching experience, shows that there is a deficiency of pedagogical research in tax (Adams et al., 2022; Fogarty, 2022; Franklin, 2015, 2017, 2018). This is particularly true for pedagogical research that instructors may bring to the classroom to discuss critical issues in the taxation of not-for-profit organizations. This study adds an innovative case to the literature, which fills some of that void. Students are presented with a case that requires them to consider whether the current classification of an entity as a 501(c)(7) organization is appropriate, or whether the classification should be a 501(c)(3) organization, which would allow its members to take contributions as a tax deductible contribution.

The motivation for this exercise is to develop writing, research and communication skills using a traditional tax research assignment to reflect a current topic that a student might encounter in a professional setting through the use of current events that impact a tax professional. Specifically, students are asked to look at a not-for-profit organization and determine what the proper classification should be using a very unique fact pattern that requires critical thought and analysis of primary source material to reach a conclusion. From the required analysis, students can develop research skills, critical thinking skills, written communication skills for multiple stakeholders in addition to other professional skills that the profession deems necessary within an accounting curriculum. The use of the not-for-profit organization has been a consistent item in the news over the past several years, as highlighted in this exercise. Specifically, how the Tax Cuts and Jobs Act has targeted the deductibility of contributions to organizations such as colleges and universities in exchange for seating rights, how municipalities have explored the establishment of charities to collect tax revenues as a means to avoid the SALT cap and various other areas of debate. More directly to this exercise, recent tax law research shows how organizations have attempted to modify their operational models to fit into the IRS classification as a "church" to allow the deductibility of contributions. This case presents an organization that shares the traits of a country club, that is highly restricted as to deductibility of dues and is considering its ability to be classified as a church so that member contributions can be deducted.

THE CASE

Veterans' Golf and Country Club is an exclusive private club located in the Catskills area of New York State. The club was founded in the 1950s by a group of 50 Jewish War Veterans following World War II.

When the club was founded, it was located in a farmhouse on an inactive farm that the group of veterans purchased at a bankruptcy auction. The members purchased the farm with the intent that the farmhouse would be used as a recreation area for the members, and they would hold the surrounding land for investment purposes to develop at a later date. The farm was purchased in the title of a corporation that the veterans formed to make the purchase. The corporation was approved and compliant for Section 501(c)(7) status by the IRS.

The veterans and their families would use the farmhouse as a place to gather and spend time together. As families, the farmhouse would on some days be used to host parties, while on some evenings the men would gather to play poker, and on other evenings the women would play bridge (a card game often played by Jewish women). Friday nights, the evening of the Jewish Sabbath, many of the families would gather and hold their own prayer and dinner. On all major Jewish holidays, the members would meet in the farmhouse to pray and celebrate together. Members would bring their own food prepared at home, or use a small kitchen to prepare their own meals.

This pattern continued with little change for about 10 years. Over this 10-year period, each of the families that used the farm deposited money into a bank account established by the founders who purchased the farm on a weekly basis. Half of the money deposited weekly was used to maintain the property, and the other half was set aside as savings to fund the future development of the property. The membership also grew over this 10-year period from the initial 50 Veterans who purchased the land to approximately 75 families, all who were Jewish Veterans affiliated with the war. As these 25 additional members joined they paid an "initiation fee" to represent their share of membership in the farmhouse. By this point, to ensure management of the property was efficient, the membership formed a five-person board of directors who managed the entity and made operational decisions. The by-laws stated that board membership would rotate on 2-year terms, and any blood relative of a founding member, older than 21 years old can serve on the board.

The Catskills area of New York has always been an area of resorts and had a very heavy Jewish population. By the late 1960s, the families who shared this farmhouse as their recreational and religious home decided it was time to invest in the farmhouse, to upgrade it to something nicer, and develop the acreage of land surrounding it. As Catskill residents, they always could use the resorts but used the farmhouse as a place to relax and have fun while not having to mix with tourists at the resorts. Many of these members, though Jewish were not formal members of another Temple and would use the farmhouse to celebrate and practice religious prayer and custom independently. Members would call it their "temple."

The decision was made by the 75 families to significantly upgrade the farmhouse and have amenities of their own formal social club. Each family contributed additional funds, in addition to the savings accumulated since founding from the weekly contributions and built an Olympic sized swimming pool on the property, with a separate pool house building.

The owners also decided to share the pool and renovated farmhouse with other residents who were not relatives of the founding Veterans, but live in the area. The organization maintained its Section 501(c)(7) tax exemption from the IRS to be tax exempt as a social club and developed a process of member recruitment and sponsorship compliant with regulations. As the membership was going to become open to more than just families of the Jewish veterans and not restrict membership to any religion or race, they decided to create a second membership class, called "associate members" that do not get voting or control rights as members. The two membership classes and rights of each class are summarized in Table 5.1A.

Table 5.1A. Summary of Membership Requirements Comparing Full and Associate Members of the Organization.

Full Member	Associate Member
Must be a blood relative of one of the Jewish Veterans who founded the organization and purchased the property. Veterans who do not have a blood relationship with an initial founder are not eligible for this class of membership	Open to any individual/family. Businesses may not join under a corporate membership. To join, one must be sponsored and invited to join by two "full members" and receive approval by a membership committee of "full members" appointed by the board of directors. Associate members do not have to be Jewish, but are encouraged to take part in the religious activities, as they typically are part of fun and casual social events. It is encouraged that all members not of Jewish faith use the activities to learn about the faith, and see how beliefs may integrate to their own faith practice
Pay annual dues and make an "initiation contribution." The "initiation contribution" is deposited into the account referenced as used for investment and expansion of the property. The annual dues cover operating expenses of the organization. Full members take zero profits made for themselves. If the organization liquidates, the members have legally agreed within the corporate charter that any proceeds will be donated to an IRS recognized not for profit veterans organization as determined by the board at liquidation	New associate members are billed an up front "initiation contribution." The dollar amount is the same as what full members contribute. Associate members are awarded no operational interest, but the initiation contribution is deposited into the same established savings account for investment and expansion as the full members. Annual dues paid cover the operating budget. Associate members pay the same dues as full members
Full members have voting rights. They vote for other full members to sit on the board of directors and run the organization	Associate members have no voting rights. They cannot sit on the board of directors nor are they part of any management decisions. Associate members can elect one Associate member to represent the membership at Board meetings and to committees on an "ad hoc" basis to provide opinions and make suggestions, but lack any power to vote or govern
As full members are all blood relatives of Jewish founders, they are assumed to all be of Jewish faith	Members can be any religion. Non Jewish members are expected to take part in at least one "faith based event" per year. Near 100% of non-Jewish members comply with this, as all social events typically have some religious theme tied to it
Full members have unlimited access to all club resources	Associate members have full club access, no restrictions. They just lack ownership interest and governance

As the farmhouse was renovated and the pool opened, the number of associate members grew quickly. In addition to housing social activities, the renovated farmhouse had a commercial grade, modern kitchen. They added a daily lunch and dinner menu, hired a restaurant management team, and added a bar where members could come in for meals and drinks. Members would also utilize the facility for special family occasions, such as weddings and Bar/Bat Mitzvahs when children reach their teenage years. At this point, the club was named "Catskill Veterans' Pool and Social Club."

It was important to the founding Veterans and families who took over leadership in succession that as the club expanded it also retained its founding religious identity. The original charter of the organization requires that events have a religious identity. To ensure the religious identity was maintained, the pool would be used for religious events at least once per month. Some weeks over the summer, they would have special events such as "swim and sabbath."[1] Religious services would be available to members who could participate while in the pool. The intent was to make religious events fun and keep children engaged in the religion.

The club did not have its own rabbi, but other members would lead the ordinary services,[2] and occasional guest rabbis could come in to lead services or perform rituals that only a rabbi can perform.

As the 1970s and 1980s passed, the club became very successful and expanded. The most notable expansions were the addition of four tennis courts, the expansion of the farmhouse to a full "clubhouse" facility tripling its square footage, and the addition of a 18 hole regulation golf course. Membership expanded to approximately 500 families in the "associate member" class, and 250 families in the "full member" class. The golf course was acclaimed as a top private course in the area, and the tennis courts were always busy, fielding a highly competitive interclub tennis team with other tennis clubs in the area. The Organization was renamed "Catskill Veterans' Golf and Social Club." The golf course and tennis club maintained a religious identity and they were both used for religious rituals throughout the year as the weather permitted. Every Sunday morning, on the golf and tennis courts, one could have a "blessing of the balls" performed prior to the start of a match. Over 90% of the associate member class at any time was of Jewish faith. Of the 10% not of Jewish faith, a vast majority of these members did take part in select religious Jewish rituals throughout the year and were always welcome and fully included.

To the present day, the club continues to expand and flourish, despite cyclical membership dips during periods of economic downturn. Very little changed as to how the club operated or membership structured. The club has also developed a policy within the last year that no events will be hosted on premises that support a political organization, due to the highly polarized political environment to prevent member conflict in response to requests to hold such events, and to ensure compliance with established tax-exempt status.

It is now July of the current year, and the Board of Directors receives an email from an associate member, Yakkov Pearlman, a member of the club and local medical doctor. The email reads as follows:

Dear Board,

I am being audited by the IRS and very confused. Since joining the club ten years ago, I have always deducted my membership dues on my tax return. This is my temple, as is for many members. We attended services here, and celebrated our kids' Bar/Bat Mitzvah here. Myself, and other members have been deducting our dues as religious contributions because this is our "temple," not just a golf and social club. We assumed our dues were tax deductible.

Golf and tennis are activities we do within our temple. All temples offer social activities. If I lose the audit, this will cost myself, and other members who take the same deduction a lot of money. With my state income tax deduction now limited to only $10,000 per year, charitable deductions such as this are even more important to me.

Why are we not classified as a religious organization for the IRS so we can deduct our dues? I thought we were classified as a religious organization? Other members may get mad and blame the club if they get billed by the IRS for taking a bad tax deduction. The Board better correct this now.

Thank you.

Yakkov"

The board forwards the above email to both its legal council and CPA firm. You are the CPA representing the club and need to address this matter for the board so that they can properly counsel the membership, and coordinate with the attorneys to prevent any legal issues that might come from this misunderstanding with members.

Write a professional memo to the file that addresses the following before you consult with the client:

1. What is the difference between not for profit status as a social club versus a religious organization?
2. Could this club have been previously classified as a religious not for profit, so that members could have deducted dues paid?
3. Is there a legal precedent to reclassify this club as a religious organization so that members can take a tax deduction for dues paid in the future? If there is not any legal precedent that applies here, based on your understanding and analysis of the rules, and facts that describe the clubs specific operations, could the club reclassify legally as a religious organization?
4. Does the club have any risk of liability to members who have been deducting their dues in prior years such as Yakkov? The club has not been marketing in any way that member dues are tax deductible, nor has been following any IRS regulations required of a religious organization that allows dues to have been deducted. If the club can be re-classified as a religious organization, what IRS requirements would they have for the membership as to deductibility?

CASE LEARNING OBJECTIVES AND IMPLEMENTATION GUIDANCE

Motivation for the Case

As shown in prior research, there is a deficiency of pedagogical research in tax compared to that of other areas within accounting education (Adams et al., 2022; Fogarty, 2022; Franklin, 2015, 2017, 2018). This case builds on the need for additional pedagogical research by adding a tool that can be utilized in the classroom to enhance the educational experience consistent with other areas of accounting education, build on communication skills, as well as critical thinking skills required in all areas of accounting education.

There has also been considerable research and debate professionally as to the role not-for-profits play in tax policy and business decisions, specifically use of the "church" to provide the most significant tax advantaged status for an organization and donor with intent of making a donation. Camp et al. (2022) provide an example to illustrate the current significance of the topic. Specifically, the authors discuss how an organization may reconfigure their mission and organizational structure to meet the requirements to be classified as a church. Camp et al. (2022) specifically relate to this exercise as a member of the organization in question is requesting to leadership that the specific organization be examined to determine if it meets the litmus test to be classified as a church and consider reclassification to a church for member tax benefit.

Following the passage of the Tax Cuts and Jobs Act, there was also considerable debate on how taxes and other expenses could be recharacterized as deductible charitable contribution to negate the negative tax impacts of the $10,000 SALT cap (Colinvaux, 2018). The rules of deductibility have also impacted colleges and universities as they can no longer solicit tax deductible contributions in exchange for purchase rights of preferred seats to athletic events.[3]

Utilization of cases to teach tax research concepts using case studies helps to close expectation gaps that exist between the profession and the classroom, CPA exam requirements, and employer expectations of minimum skills expected of a new hire (Lawson et al., 2014). The ability to research, review and evaluate primary source material and synthesize various primary sources to advise clients on specific tax issues develops research and critical thinking skills, as deemed important by Larkins (2008), and enhances key skills that are routinely tested on the CPA exam (Franklin & Morrow, 2017). Not only has it been clearly demonstrated that writing and communication skills are key for accounting graduates, Noga and Rupert (2017) demonstrated that writing assignments create significant stress on college students. To support prior research, a tax research case with a significant written component requirement can provide the necessary reinforcement of these skills to reduce anxiety. The skills developed within this assignment are also consistent with the findings from Baril et al. (1998) and would meet the concept of critical thinking presented by them. Baril et al. (1998) show that students entering the accounting profession require enhanced critical thinking skills and enter the profession lacking key skills. The ability to conduct and analyze research in a manner that this assignment requires enhances these key skills referenced by Baril et al. as enhancements in curricular needs. As this case links professional writing skill development to taxation, it also addresses a key call to improve critical thinking skills as defined by Wolcott and Sargent (2021), and a call for faculty to link subjects across disciplines to teach critical thinking. Increased use of writing assignments in class, combined with proper instruction and feedback to improve writing skills should increase student comfort, and confidence and reduce the stress that Noga and Rupert (2017) note students face.

Based upon a review of other cases published in primary accounting education journals, there are no other cases currently published that focus on an analysis of this subject area in this manner.[4] Stone and Erickson (2017) examine the not for profit status of a church, and now decision-making strategy is utilized to expand but does not touch on the specific fact pattern that govern this case, so is not considered to conflict with this case. It is mentioned herein as it is another case that relates to the not for profit of an established church, while this case explores whether an organization should have been classified as a church.

Case Development

After the initial version of the case was developed and administered, the author conducted a small test of the assignment in an undergraduate taxation course at a private university in the Northeast USA. In this 15-week course, students are required to research and write approximately one case every 2 weeks, beginning with the second week of class. The cases were typically assigned from the textbook utilized within the class, which is Rupert et al. (2022).

This was assigned at the end of the semester as a comprehensive research assignment with its own stand-alone grade weight of 20% of a course grade, so students had received feedback on previous research assignments and were familiar with instructor expectations of writing quality and the Facts, Issues, Rules, Analysis, Conclusion (FIRAC) methodology commonly used (and required in that course) for tax research memos. The textbook Appendix A provides detailed coverage of writing in this format (Rupert et al., 2022).

Overall, students performed well on the assignment, which the instructor attributes to the assignment of previous cases to get students accustomed to the preparation of professional memos, as well as class introduction to different types of not for profit entities and tax differences. Students mostly focused exactly on the type of mistakes and issues that they had seen the instructor provide feedback on for their own previous memos, indicating that students were learning from the feedback and attempting to integrate it into future attempts. Student impressions of this assignment are discussed within the efficacy section of this chapter. In addition to efficacy from student use of this assignment prior to development as a formal case, additional efficacy was collected from other taxation faculty at different institutions during the case development. Other faculty members from institutions who teach taxation at both the undergraduate and graduate level reviewed this case for classroom applicability. In each case, the instructor indicated favorably that they would indeed utilize this case within their course and the resources provided within the teaching notes[5] are sufficient to implement the case. Feedback to improve the case was also provided by the instructors and has been integrated into the case. Feedback involved addition of additional facts in the storyboard to better guide students to make the case more realistic, and removal of the client letter as a requirement to emphasize the professional memo. It was suggested that the requirement of the memo and letter may be too long for the assignment and detract focus from the other technical learning objectives, specifically if students had experience preparing letters and memos on shorter assignments throughout the term on assignments that were shorter and less technical in nature. Faculty who wish to require a letter as an addition to the memo, or in place of it could modify the assignment to reflect this change. The teaching notes only reflect the assignment in its current form with the requirement of the professional memo for the work papers.

A senior tax partner at a regional CPA firm in the northeast also reviewed the case. The partner felt that for a college student at the undergraduate or graduate level if time constraints existed, a student would gain more benefit from writing the work paper memo instead of the client letter. The partner also commented that the topic of this case is highly relevant for students as firms have been tackling many issues with the use of charitable contributions as a manner to maximize itemized deductions for clients in lieu of the $10,000 SALT tax limit, and disallowance of charitable deductions that historically have been permitted, such as donations to academic institutions for benefits such as season athletics ticket rights as well as other changes.[6,7]

Learning Objectives

This case requires students to:

1. Review an email provided to a client.
2. Integrate the email from the client with prior knowledge of how the client has historically operated.
3. Research primary source material to learn about a topic that is of current interest to the tax profession.
4. Search for legal precedence and based on analysis make and defend a suggestion based on documents reviewed.
5. Communicate findings in the same way typically expected of a professional to a work paper file.

The specific fact pattern of this case has not been litigated to the knowledge of the authors, but requires the student to make a judgment. Specific student learning objectives for the case are:

LO1: Compare and contrast the different types of not-for-profit tax-exempt organizations allowed by congress.

This case is designed to be used within an undergraduate or graduate taxation course, as described previously. For students with no prior tax experience, this case would be assigned after basic taxation research skills were introduced, and after coverage of itemized deductions. Typically, as the charitable contribution is covered as an itemized deduction, part of the discussion would be that not all not-for-profits allow the charitable deduction and would provide a brief discussion of examples. The case would expand on the class discussion, and expand to research skills that review primary source material related to the topic. Part of this discussion also should involve a discussion of the Tax Cuts and Jobs Act, specifically how this act impacted the deductibility of charitable contributions, and how some organizations, specifically states explored the utilization of a "charity" as a means to allow the deductibility of school tax payments in lieu of the $10,000 SALT deduction limit (Colinvaux, 2018).

LO2: Discuss the criteria of a regulatory determined tax-exempt religious organization and how it differs from other tax-exempt organizations allowed.

Of the various types of not for profit organizations, religious organizations have unique traits that allow the deduction of contribution, not allowed for other types of not-for-profit. It is important for this assignment, specifically when used on undergraduate students with limited tax experience to discuss this briefly and create awareness of the differences and traits.[8] For graduate students with tax experience, there is considerable tax research on the matter, and case law that examines criteria, and provides examples of cases where the status of the church as a charitable organization is addressed. The most recent publication that experienced students can be directed to is Camp et al. (2022).

LO3: Apply tax research skills, using primary source material to build a case that supports a determination on a unique fact pattern.

Tax research is considered a critical skill and a topic that is introduced at the undergraduate tax level, and emphasized at the graduate tax level. Tax research is introduced in main market tax textbooks such as Spilker et al. (2022) and Rupert et al. (2022). This case provides an opportunity to apply the research skills covered in these main-market books, but is more in-depth than the cases often covered within these books. Instructors can use this case to test these skills, and do so as a higher stake research project within their course if desired.

LO4: Prepare professional documentation to demonstrate an understanding of the applicability of technical tax rules to a specific client scenario and communicate these results to stakeholders.

As documented within the deliverables, students will create a professionally written tax research memo that analyzes and relates tax rules to the actual client fact pattern, complete with properly cited sources. An example of a well prepared submission is included as part of the teaching notes. Instructors also have the opportunity to request students write a professional client letter as an addition to the memo, or in place of the memo as assigned.

Table 5.2 provides a map of the learning objectives for the specific case requirements.

Implementation Guidance

This case is designed for use in either an undergraduate or graduate tax research course or an individual taxation course. The case would ideally be completed by students on an individual basis, but it is easily adaptable to a group assignment. As a matter of instructor preference, it was assigned as an individual project to ensure all members of the class could do the necessary work at all levels independently, both research and writing. It can be assigned as a group project but should be accompanied by a peer evaluation form to ensure that all students played a material role in the completion of the assignment. As the primary objective of the case is to build and reinforce tax research skills, instructors may wish to assign this case at a point later in the semester when students have had experience with tax research doing more basic research assignments. For students with no prior

Table 5.2. Map of Learning Objectives to Case Requirements.

Case Requirement	Learning Objective(s)
Part 1: What is the difference between not for profit status as a social club versus a religious organization	LO1
Part 2: Could this club have been previously classified as a religious not for profit, so that members could have deducted dues paid?	LO1 LO2
Part 3: Is there a legal precedent to reclassify this club as a religious organization so that members can take a tax deduction for dues paid in the future? If there is not any legal precedent that applies here, based on your understanding and analysis of the rules, and facts that describe the clubs specific operations, could the club reclassify legally to a religious organization?	LO1 LO2 LO3
Part 4: Does the club have any risk of liability to members who have been deducting their dues in prior years such as Yakkov? The club has not been marketing in any way that member dues are tax deductible, nor has been following any IRS regulations required of a religious organization that allows dues to have been deducted. If the club is able to be re-classified as a religious organization, what IRS requirements would they have to the membership as to deductibility?	LO2 LO3
Part 5: Write a professional memo to the file, that addresses the following before you consult with the client	LO1 LO2 LO3 LO4

tax exposure, it is suggested that this case not be used until there has been a discussion of itemized deductions, specifically the individual charitable contribution as well as tax research. Based on feedback from students, colleagues and reviewers as previously discussed, this case was substantially revised to address the feedback received.

During the implementation of this case in an undergraduate setting, instructors typically assigned the case later in the semester, after the subject of itemized deductions, specifically discussion of the charitable deduction. Instructors assigned the case after other tax research assignments were completed and graded so students would have the benefit of learning and increased comfort in the type of writing expected. In all situations where the case was implemented, students were first exposed to (either through discussion or assignment) how to use tax research software, specifically Checkpoint, how to locate and evaluate tax authority and how to prepare professional communication. Students were asked to read textbook coverage of tax research and communication as covered in their textbook, and other supplements that instructors may provide.

Specifically, when the assignment was assigned to undergraduates, students were in the final segment of the semester and had already completed three short research assignments during the semester. The prior assignments completed were assignments from the Rupert et al. (2022) textbook at the end of chapters titled as "tax research problems" available at the end of each chapter of the book. At the beginning of the semester, before the first assignment was completed, the chapter in the same book on tax research was covered with a detailed discussion of

Appendix A in the same book which covers the structure of a tax research memorandum as well as a client letter. As this was done as part of standard chapter coverage on tax research, roughly 20 minutes were spent in class, and students were directed to read the appendix as an assignment prior to class. By the time this assignment was administered students had significant experience conducting basic tax research and using the memo and letter formats as provided. There had been previous discussion in class on itemized deductions and the role of the charitable contribution as a deduction, as well as homework assignments via the online homework tool as part of standard chapter coverage. The discussion followed the textbook content with no outside materials provided. The assignment was released on the course management system and was accompanied by a 15-minute video recorded by the course instructor discussing the requirements of the assignment. This 15-minute video would be the same as a 15-minute class time presentation. The instructor elected to use a video so that students could use it for reference as they completed the assignment. The video covered all assignment requirements, and also referenced the students to the IRS website and Publication 1128 as a starting point to obtain background on the different types of not for profit organizations available. It was also emphasized that secondary sources like this are not to be cited in final submissions, and the textbook chapter on tax research is to be used as a guide. Very little time was spent within the video discussing these organizations as it felt that part of the learning process should be to learn the concept through independent research using the materials referenced.

Students were given 3 weeks to complete the assignment, which was 1 week longer than prior research assignments administered over the semester. Advanced graduate students would likely be able to complete this assignment in less time. As different institutions have such variations of student skill levels within their programs, it is suggested that instructors use their best judgment on how much time to allow based on the relative difficulty of this assignment compared to other assignments assigned over the course of the semester and significance of final course grade allocated to the assignment. Each instructor will have their own variation based on the readiness of their own students.

Approximately 1 week prior to the assignment being due, the instructor ended class approximately 20 minutes early and remained in the classroom to answer any specific questions students may have had on the assignment so there was additional availability outside of office hours with no student conflicts. Some students had general questions, but no questions to show that there were any difficulties with the assignment beyond what an instructor would expect when students are working through a new and unique problem independently. Most questions involved confirming the quality of sources they searched and verifying general expectations provided in the introductory video.

The tax course in which this case was used covers content using a research focus as opposed to the traditional form and compliance focus used in many undergraduate introductory courses. Based on the nature of research and writing in this assignment, this case likely would not be suitable for a course that has a low research focus. In many institutions that utilize this focus, instructors may consider using this exercise in a second tax course that often introduces tax research, or at the graduate level where tax courses offered traditionally have a heavier research focus. In a class that has a predominant graduate audience, completion of this case should be manageable to the student without the volume of smaller cases assigned prior to the instance where this case was utilized. As the emphasis of this case is tax research, an experienced student should be able to complete this assignment regardless of in class coverage on itemized deductions or charitable contribution deductions. These are topics that a student should be able to self-familiarize with as they conduct research and from personal experiences.

This case was developed and utilized in class during the time when the changes to several itemized deductions were put into place by the TCJA 2017. Tax law is ever changing – and will continue to be – so it is important for students to develop the research skills not just to analyze current tax law but to ensure conclusions are made using the most current tax laws. In the event the TCJA changes or sunsets in 2025 the concepts will still apply, and this case is expected to remain valid.

EVIDENCE OF EFFICACY, GRADING AND STUDENT FEEDBACK

The overarching goal of the case is to expand tax research through the application of a taxation topic that the profession deems as highly relevant. The goals for students, as laid out in the learning objectives in the previous section, can be evaluated by asking the following questions when reviewing student deliverables:

1. Did the student provide clear and actionable comments for the questions requested?
2. Did the student define and clarify key differences between of a religious organization and a social club (501(c)(3) versus 501(b)(7)) organization?
3. Did the student critically analyze proper primary research sources relative to both types of organization?
4. Did the student properly apply appropriate primary source material to the client scenario in the case?
5. Did the student provide a clear and specific recommendation to the client on proper IRS classification the organization should be?
6. Did the student write and format the tax research memo as instructed?

Table 5.1B maps these questions to the learning objectives evaluated. For purposes of grading, the teaching notes contain a sample answer, as well as discussion of elements a student should have in their answer. Recognition and communication of writing style errors is one way to improve a common significant weakness for students in professional writing skills, as found by Noga and Rupert (2017). This feedback should also be constructive and, to a certain extent, kind rather than punitive.

This case has been implemented by an instructor at their respective institution. This case was administered as a formal course activity. The author did collect student feedback as part of the standard end of semester course evaluation process,

Table 5.1B. Evaluation of Learning Objectives.

Performance Evaluated	Learning Objective(s) Measured
Did the student provide clear and actionable comments for the questions requested?	LO4
Did the student define and clarify key differences between of a religious organization and social club (501(c)(3) vs 501(b)(7)) organization?	LO1 LO4
Did the student critically analyze proper primary research sources relative to both types of organization?	LO2 LO4
Did the student properly apply appropriate primary source material to the client scenario in the case?	LO2 LO3 LO4
Did the student provide a clear and specific recommendation to the client on proper IRS classification the organization should be?	LO3 LO4
Did the student write and format the tax research memo as instructed?	LO1 LO2 LO3 LO4

as standard practice for all major classroom deliverables for continual improvement purposes in the course. This collection of feedback was not a formal testing and data collection.

The author of this case also had a discussion with a senior tax partner from a large regional CPA firm on the relevance of the case. The CPA reviewer, who has several social clubs such as current clients conferred that the fact pattern of the case, topic and deliverables are realistic and of value for a college student to be exposed to in a classroom project. Additionally, younger entry level public accountants were asked to provide feedback.

Practitioner Reaction

Practitioners who reviewed this case at all levels thought it was very well prepared. Those at the senior and partner level affirmed that the case does a good job of making students aware of what professional tax research is, and to critically think about a situation that does not necessarily have one direct solution. The professionals at the senior and partner levels also affirmed that the format and expectation of deliverables are appropriate and what would be expected of a professional within the firm charged with a task such as this case. The format students were asked to follow is consistent with what the firms involved utilize.

Staff at lower levels also were very impressed with the assignment quality. It was reported that the expectation within this assignment is consistent with work that has been expected of them, and also based around a realistic fact pattern that is of interest. One reviewer in particular noted that he has spent a considerable amount of time working with clients to determine new avenues to create charitable contribution deductions in response to the restrictions in place on current SALT deduction limits.

Faculty Reaction

This case has been reviewed by non-author faculty at different stages in its development process. Reactions have been positive and state that the deliverables are clear, and that the expectations are clear to the learning objectives, and that the objectives are highly relevant. The faculty reviewer described this case as turnkey, and simple to integrate with the resources provided, and also one that the students found very interesting.

The faculty reviewer has provided the following feedback:

> This was a very useful case and led to a very interesting discussion with the class. Not only was this a great assignment to discuss the benefits of the itemized deduction, but also led to a super discussion of tax policy, and the purpose to allow deductions such as this, which really presents no cause other than socialization of the club members. Students seem to understand why taxpayers are permitted to deduct contributions to traditional charities and religious organizations, but one question raised was "how is allowing a club that only serves a social purpose a benefit to society in any way that it should be tax exempt?" This led to a very interesting discussion of important tax policy issues, which is an area of my research. This case can be used with both graduate and undergraduate students, though with undergraduate students it may be useful to provide students with some guidance to start their research.

Student Reaction

Students completed this exercise as a standard in-class assignment. The instructors, as part of end of semester teaching evaluations, routinely request students to reflect on all graded deliverables during the semester. This evaluation includes the quality of general homework assignments as well as projects and cases assigned. The instructor uses comments received to continually improve the course and quality of assignments administered. The end of semester teaching evaluation response rate for the term this assignment was used in the present form was 73%. Of those conducting the evaluation, all students had very positive feedback on this assignment. Some specific applicable quotes are:

> Great assignment. Thought provoking.

> Showed the assignment to a partner at my tax internship. Told me that it is a great assignment, do what it asks and actually share it with me once complete as it looks so interesting. Getting to do the assignment and share it with my supervisor shows it is a very respected assignment.

Constructive criticism of the assignment was the lack of one specific answer, and that guidance should have been provided of a case to locate and analyze to "start the research" as put by one student. The author feels that this may be a useful suggestion when using this case with an undergraduate population, but for a graduate population who has tax research experience they should not need guidance once they begin a search reading Sections 501(c)(3) and 501(c)(7) as provided, and have a comfort level to navigate related searches to those sections using any common tax research database. Students using this case were asked to use RIA Checkpoint to conduct research, as provided within the institution library.

This assignment was also used by an author to measure mastery of the programs' AACSB Assurance of Learning assessment that pertains to written communication skills. From that evaluation, using the rubric specific to the AOL objectives, 84% of students satisfied the learning goals assessed.

CONCLUSION

This exercise examined the tax implications of two not for profit statuses available to an organization. Students were presented with a case that considered whether the organization currently classified as a 501(c)(7) organization is properly classified, or should be classified as a 501(c)(3) organization, which would allow its members to take payments to the organization as a tax deductible contribution. Through completion of this exercise, students gain a more complete understanding of the impact that classification of a not for profit may have on the organization and taxpayer. The case also provided an opportunity for the instructor to teach and evaluate students in tax research to an appropriate level at an undergraduate or graduate level. Student responses indicated that the case was interesting and beneficial. Review by other non-author faculty and professional CPA's in practice also concurred that this case is beneficial and valuable to student growth. Not only is this exercise a positive learning exercise to demonstrate the use of not-for-profit status of the organization, but teaches and reinforces key skills of tax research and professional communication.

NOTES

1. Sabbath is defined as the weekly Jewish prayer service to observe Shabbat every Friday night/Saturday morning.

2. In many classes of Jewish faith, a rabbi is not needed to lead a prayer service. Any individual of Jewish faith can lead a typical daily prayer service. Rabbis' are needed for certain rituals, such as a Jewish marriage, Bar/Bat Mitzvah or "naming" of a new baby.

3. https://answerconnect.cch.com/document/arp109fc87418cc7c4e8c922122a0e6a38eb6/federal/irc/explanation/tickets-to-athletic-events-or-booster-club-dues-for-colleges-or-universities

4. Accounting education journals reviewed were: *Issues in Accounting Education, Journal of Accounting Education, Advances in Accounting Education,* and *Accounting Education and The Accounting Educators' Journal.* These journals were searched over the period 2010–2022. The authors also reviewed Adams et al. (2022), which also confirms no like cases exist in the subject matter published in any primary accounting journal.

5. Readers who wish to adopt the case for teaching purposes may obtain the teaching notes by contacting the authors directly.

6. https://www.taxpolicycenter.org/briefing-book/how-did-tcja-affect-incentives-charitable-giving

7. https://www.gordonfischerlawfirm.com/tax-talk-deductibility-of-college-sports-ticket-rights/

8. One may elect to utilize this website from the IRS as a reference, or as part of class discussion: https://www.irs.gov/charities-non-profits/churches-religious-organizations/churches-defined#:~:text=Distinct%20legal%20existence,code%20of%20doctrine%20and%20discipline and also https://www.irs.gov/charities-non-profits/other-non-profits/social-clubs.

REFERENCES

Adams, M. T., Inger, K. K., & Meckfessel, M. D. (2022). Educational tax cases: An annotated bibliography. In T. G .Calderon (Ed.), *Advances in accounting education: Teaching and curriculum innovations* (Vol. 26, pp. 191–206). Emerald Publishing Limited.

Baril, C. P., Cunningham, B. M., Fordham, D. R., Gardner, R. L., & Wolcott, S. K. (1998). Critical thinking in the public accounting profession: Aptitudes and attitudes. *Journal of Accounting Education, 16*(3–4), 381–406.

Camp, J., Masselli, J., & Yurko, A. J. (2022). Religion versus politics: An age-old question with continued importance to the US nonprofit classification system. *The ATA Journal of Legal Tax Research, 21*(1), 1–21.

Colinvaux, R. (2018). Failed charity: Taking state tax benefits into account for purposes of the charitable deduction. *Buffalo Law Review, 66*, 779.

Fogarty, T. (2022). A review of published tax cases: Contents, value-added and constraints. *Advances in Accounting Education: Teaching and Curriculum Innovations, 26*, 175–190.

Franklin, M. (2015). A best practice approach to engage students to increase interest in tax as a profession. *Journal of Business and Accounting, 2015*, 160–170.

Franklin, M. (2017). Accounting education literature from 2015 and its implications. *Journal of Accounting and Finance, 15*(5), 98–113.

Franklin, M. (2018). Research in tax education: 2010–2017. *Journal of Business and Accounting, 11*(1), 97–116.

Franklin, M., & Morrow, M. (2017). Changes to the 2017 CPA exam: An opportunity to further students' professional success. *The Tax Adviser, 48*(2), 130–132.

Larkins, E. R. (2008). Learning to interpret and reconcile tax authority. In B. N. Schwartz & A. N. Catanach, Jr (Eds.), *Advances in accounting education* (Vol. 9, pp. 95–113). Emerald Group Publishing Limited.

Lawson, R. A., Blocher, E. J., Brewer, P. C., Cokins, G., Sorensen, J. E., Stout, D. E., Sundem, G. L., Wolcott, S. K., & Wouters, M. J. (2014). Focusing accounting curricula on students' long-run careers: Recommendations for an integrated competency-based framework for accounting education. *Issues in Accounting Education, 29*(2), 295–317.

Noga, T., & Rupert, T. (2017). Reducing written communication apprehension for students in tax classes. In T. G. Calderon (Ed.), *Advances in accounting education: Teaching and curriculum innovations* (Vol. 22, pp. 57–97). Emerald Publishing Limited.

Rupert, T., Anderson, K., Hulse, D., & Franklin, M. (2022). *Pearson's Federal taxation 2023 individuals*. Pearson.

Stone, M. F., & Erickson, S. L. (2017). Hometown community church: Opportunities and challenges of continued growth. *Issues in Accounting Education, 32*(3), 129–136.

Spilker, B., Ayers, B. C., Barrick, J. A., Lewis, T., Robinson, J., Weaver, C., & Worsham, R. G. (2022). *McGraw Hill's taxation of individuals and business entities: 2022 Edition*. McGraw Hill.

Wolcott, S. K., & Sargent, M. J. (2021). Critical thinking in accounting education: Status and call to action. *Journal of Accounting Education, 56*, 100731.

THEME 3
PIPELINE ISSUES AND THE CPA EXAM

CHAPTER 6

WHY GRADUATE ACCOUNTING STUDENTS DO NOT SIT FOR THE CPA EXAM: PERCEPTIONS OF THE CPA CREDENTIAL

Deirdre Collier[a], Hannah Rozen[a] and Alexander J. Sannella[b]

[a]Fairleigh Dickinson University, USA
[b]Rutgers, The State University of New Jersey, USA

ABSTRACT

Despite the high demand for certified public accountants, the supply of professionals produced by colleges and universities is insufficient. Contributing to the inadequate supply, which the profession refers to as a "pipeline challenge," are students who major in accounting but do not sit for the CPA exam. We shed light on this issue by studying students' perceptions about the content of the CPA exam and the value of earning a CPA credential based on a survey of graduate accounting students at two East Coast universities. Overall, we find that students who do not plan to take the CPA underestimate the value of the CPA credential. We find that students cite various reasons for avoiding the exam including the difficulty of the exam, difficulty in preparation time and cost. We contend that until students perceive the true value of the credential, initiatives to increase the pipeline may not fully succeed. We suggest several potential interventions to educate students about the importance of the exam and encourage them to reconsider taking it.

Keywords: Pipeline challenge; CPA exam; CPA value proposition; avoiding the exam; graduate students; supply of accounting professionals

The shortage of licensed accounting professionals, described as a pipeline shortage, is a major concern among accounting firms, educators, and professional organizations. Close to 75% of current accountants are at or near retirement age according to the AICPA Trends report of 2023 (CPA Practice Advisor, 2023). The number of CPA exam candidates has fallen more than 32% since 2016, and the year 2022 saw the lowest number of CPA exam takers since 2006 (New York State Society of Certified Public Accountants (NYSSCPA), 2023). Furthermore, the number of bachelor's degrees awarded has fallen 17% since 2016, while master's degrees in accounting have declined 21.2%.

The profession is seeking to reverse the situation and has become focused on increasing the accounting pipeline. To that end, the AICPA, in consultation with stakeholders including state CPA societies, accounting firms, academics, the Center for Audit Quality (CAQ), state boards of accountancy and NASBA has commenced various initiatives to pursue and retain accounting talent, aiming to reach students while still in high school and support them through successful completion of the CPA exam (Strickland, 2023).

The pipeline issue persists despite the high demand for certified public accountants. Contributing to the inadequate supply are students who pursue accounting degrees but do not sit for the CPA exam. We shed light on this issue by studying students' perceptions about the content of the CPA exam and the value of earning a CPA credential based on a survey of graduate accounting students at two East Coast universities. Graduate accounting students would normally have both the prerequisite hours and the relevant coursework to sit the exam. Understanding why this captive segment of the accounting student body does not pursue the CPA credential could help the profession tailor creative strategies to encourage those students to become CPAs and partially alleviate the pipeline challenges. Overall, we find that roughly 20% of graduate accounting students in our sample do not plan to sit for the CPA exam and their dominant reason is underestimating the value of the CPA credential. Aside from not valuing the credential, we find that students cite various reasons for avoiding the exam, including the difficulty of the exam, the challenge of preparing, and the associated costs. Based on our results, we offer various ideas that the profession may explore to increase the number of students who choose to sit for the exam. A major area of focus must be strategies to change the perceived value proposition of the CPA credential.

The next section of this chapter presents a brief background that discusses how the profession characterizes the pipeline challenge and how it seeks to address it. It includes a short review of relevant published studies. Next, we present the research question and our methodology. A description and discussion of the results follows. We end with a conclusion that summarizes the results and presents implications for the profession.

BACKGROUND

The AICPA Pipeline Acceleration Plan, built upon dialogue with all stakeholders, is composed of six parts: (1) raise awareness; (2) improve perceptions; (3) training and education; (4) firm culture and business models; (5) diversity, equity, and inclusion; and (6) partnering with educational institutions to develop necessary skills (AICPA & CIMA, 2023). A National Pipeline Advisory Group has focused primarily on points 1–3, which are relevant to students before and during a degree-seeking program (Waggoner, 2023). Taylor (2023) discusses various aspects of the pipeline acceleration plan that are of particular interest to academics, including the Experience, Learn and Earn (ELE) Pilot which intends to provide a pathway for students who have earned a bachelor's degree in accounting but who are without the means or a plan to earn the additional 30 credits required for licensing. Contrary to earlier works (Gabre et al., 2017; Trout & Blazer, 2017) which found that the 150-hour requirement did not significantly influence the decision to sit for the exam, recently, Burke and Polimeni (2023) and Castonguay (2023) using data from the Center for Audit Quality (CAQ) find that the 150-hour requirement is among the top reasons keeping students away from majoring in accounting. These authors, as well as others (e.g., Dawkins & Dugan, 2022; Dawkins et al., 2020; Hood, 2023), feel that the ELE initiative falls woefully short of alleviating that barrier.

Taylor (2023) also highlights the AICPA's various high school and college initiatives including lobbying for STEM recognition, focusing funding on students who plan to pursue CPA licensure, supporting NASBA's expansion of the 18-month window, and aiming to create positive awareness of the profession among middle and high school students. Brink et al. (2023) and Comunale et al. (2023) reinforce the importance of proactively engaging students at an early stage of career selection, and Bandla (2023) suggests mentors are a powerful recruitment tool.

While these initiatives are no doubt important, the CPA exam itself, with its associated costs, remains a major hurdle to increasing the number of licensed CPAs (Burke & Polimeni, 2023; Cardona et al., 2021; Coe, 2016; Comunale et al., 2023; Crowley & Cadotte, 2023; Dawkins & Dugan, 2022; Dickins et al., 2022; Hood, 2023; Illinois CPA Society (ICPAS), 2021; Pitstick, 2022; Udeh, 2022; Wen et al., 2015). According to a recent Illinois Society of CPA (ICPAS) report, fewer than half of all accounting graduates ever sit for the CPA exam – and even fewer eventually pass it (ICPAS, 2021). Previous research has attempted to identify factors that contribute to students' intention to sit for the CPA exam, and our research contributes to this effort.

Calderon and Nagy (2020) conducted a comprehensive review of the academic research related to the CPA. They describe several research streams related to exam success including educational requirements (Bline et al., 2021; Dickins et al., 2021); institutional characteristics, such as accreditation (Morgan et al., 2012); faculty characteristics (Bates, 2018; Bergner et al., 2020; Bline et al., 2016; Smith & Emerson, 2017); candidate characteristics such as age, time since graduation (Udeh, 2022); number of exam attempts, GPA, SAT score, graduate education, gender (Trout & Blazer, 2017; Wen et al., 2015); work experience (Mustapha & Hassan, 2012; Wen et al., 2015); family support (Charron & Lowe, 2009; Coe, 2016; Trout & Blazer, 2017); and race (Cardona et al., 2021).

One factor not considered in this research stream is the perceived value proposition of the CPA credential itself. While the AICPA and others are aware that there are misperceptions about the accounting field (Comunale et al., 2023;

Dawkins & Dugan, 2022; Pitstick, 2022) and list improving perceptions of the profession as a primary focus of the pipeline evolution project, there is at least an implied presumption that those pursuing an accounting degree value the CPA credential. Several recent papers suggest that this may not be the case. Hood (2023) finds, in a small survey, that approximately 20% of students perceive the CPA exam as somewhat valuable or not valuable. Udeh (2022) urges the accounting profession, educators, and employers to promote the value of the CPA license in order to motivate students to sit for the exam shortly after graduation. She conjectures that students do not value their credentials enough. However, she offers no survey or other evidence to support her belief.

The ICPAS surveyed a broad spectrum of accounting students and offer interesting insight into their intent to take the exam as well as their perceived value proposition of the CPA credential (ICPAS, 2021). The Society received 2,500 responses from both those who do not plan to become CPAs and those who do. Of the respondents who do not plan to become CPAs, 32% said they do not see how the CPA credential adds value or relevance to their careers. Other reasons students offered for not pursuing the credential include not seeing the return on investment (28%), not being required by employers (28%), and a preference to obtain other credentials (28%). Those who planned to sit the CPA exam valued their credentials. Their main obstacles to its pursuit were the workload time commitment (63%), personal time commitment (41%), fear of failure (51%), and difficulty of the CPA exam (54%).

Our study extends the extant literature by focusing on why graduate accounting students do not take the CPA exam. Typically, these students have both the prerequisite credit hours and the minimum required coursework to sit for the exam. Thus, one might presume that they will pursue the exam. Not pursuing the CPA exam accentuates the pipeline problem and accordingly challenges the profession to find innovative ways to encourage that segment of the accounting student population to pursue careers as CPAs.

RESEARCH QUESTION AND METHOD

Our primary *research question* is to determine the reasons students give when they indicate that they have no intention to pursue the CPA exam. It is possible that these students have misperceptions about either the value of the CPA designation or the difficulty in passing the exam and prematurely preclude any attempt to sit for the exam. We also investigate differences among subgroups of those not planning to take the exam to see whether these differences suggest unique policy implications for these populations. Identification of differences was conducted using either Chi-squared tests or *t*-tests (2-tailed), as appropriate. By identifying factors which may discourage students from taking the CPA exam, we hope to provide insight that may help to design focused strategies to at least partially mitigate the pipeline challenge.

Our sample consisted of 336 graduate accounting students at two East Coast universities. The sample included both students who planned to sit for the CPA exam and those who did not. The a priori distribution of those two sets of students was unknown at the time of the survey so we were not able to stratify the sample into two equal subgroups, which might possibly enhance the power of our analysis. We administered the survey, which officially received IRB exemptions from both universities, to 446 students over the fall and spring semesters of 2019–2021 in the students' introductory graduate accounting course, and approximately 75% of the students returned the survey. The survey instrument, which was evaluated for validity and reliability, is available by contacting the authors.

RESULTS

Of the 336 respondents, 80% planned on taking the CPA exam, and 20% either were unsure whether they would take the exam or did not plan to sit for it (hereafter, non-test takers). Once the respondents were classified as either test takers or non-test takers, we focused on the non-test taking respondents. Table 6.1 provides descriptive demographic statistics for all respondents.

Respondents were 52% female and 48% male. Eighty percent of respondents were between 19 and 29 years of age; 46% attended a private versus a public

Table 6.1. Demographics of Survey Participants.

	Number[a]	Percentage
Panel A: Gender		
Female	174	51.94
Male	161	48.06
Sum	**335**	**100.00**
Panel B: Age of participants		
Up to age 29 – (1)	265	80.8
Between 30 and 39 – (2)	51	15.5
40 and over – (3)	12	3.7
Sum	**328**	**100.00**
Panel C: Public versus private		
Private (1)	149	45.0
Public (2)	182	55.0
Sum	**331**	**100.00**
Panel D: Number of years work experience		
Less than 1 year – (1)	140	42.3
1–3 years – (2)	127	38.3
4–6 years – (3)	30	9.1
7–10 years – (4)	22	6.65
More than 10 years – (5)	12	3.65
Sum	**331**	**100.00**
Panel E: English as a Second Language		
Yes – (1)	55	16.47
NO – (2)	279	85.63
Sum	**334**	**100.00**

[a]There are 336 total observations. Some panel observations are less than this amount, because not all participants answered each question.

school; 80% had 3 years or less of work experience, while 20% had more than 3 years of experience.

We used four demographic groupings (gender, age, school type and work experience) in Table 6.2 to describe test takers (Panel A) and non-test takers (Panel B). Test takers were compared with non-test takers to see if they differed significantly in any of the four groupings. Unlike Trout and Blazer (2017) and Wen et al. (2015) who found no differences between the genders as far as intention to sit for the exam, our survey revealed that males were significantly more likely to express an intention to take the exam. Chi-squared tests revealed that females were more likely to be non-test takers than males (p-value = 0.0002) and those with more work experience were more likely to plan to be test-takers than those with less experience (p-value = 0.034).

Table 6.2. Demographics of Those Planning Versus *Not* Planning to Take CPA Exam.

	Number Responses	Percentage of Total[a]
Panel A: Students planning to take exam		
Female	124	37.0
Male	141	42.1
Sum	**265**	**79.1**
Age of participants		
Up to age 29	210	64.0
Age 30 and over	51	15.5
Sum	**261**	**79.5**
Public versus private		
Private	113	34.1
Public	151	45.6
Sum	**264**	**79.7**
Number of years work experience		
3 years or less	206	62.2
More than 3 years	58	17.5
Sum	**264**	**79.7**
Panel B: Students not planning/unsure about exam		
Female	50	14.9
Male	20	6.0
Sum	**70**	**20.9**
Age of participants		
Up to age 29	55	16.8
Age 30 and over	12	3.7
Sum	**67**	**20.5**
Public versus private		
Private	36	10.8
Public	31	9.4
Sum	**67**	**20.2**
Number of years work experience		
3 years or less	60	18.1
More than 3 years	5	2.1
Sum	**65**	**20.2**

[a]Add panels A and B to reach 100%; rounding errors cause some totals to > < 100%.

Table 6.3 focuses on student perceptions of the value proposition of the CPA credential. As in Table 6.2, this table provides information on the four demographic groupings in two panels: test-takers (Panel A) and non-test takers (Panel B).[1] For these questions, students could select multiple responses; percentages were calculated based on the number of respondents, either test takers or non-test takers. Differences between populations were examined using two-tailed t-tests. Interestingly, we observe that regardless of intention to sit for the exam, students perceived the most important value of the CPA to be its prestige, closely followed by its practicality, and then the higher earning power of professionals with the CPA designation. We observe no statistically significant (p-value = 0.116) differences between the views of takers and non-test takers in terms of their relative rankings of the most important value of the exam using a Chi-squared tests. However, the populations did differ in the number of reasons students identified as important to take the exam. The 264 students planning on taking the exam gave 726 reasons to take the exam or 2.75 reasons per student. The 67 non-test takers gave only 96 reasons they felt the exam was important, less than 1.5 reasons per student.

Table 6.3. Perceptions of Those Planning Versus *Not* Planning to Take CPA Exam.

	Number of Responses[a]	Percentage of Students Giving as Reason[b]
Panel A: Perceptions of students planning to take exam, N = 264		
Perceived value of the CPA license		
Practical	259	98.1[c]
Prestige	269	98.9[c]
Earnings power	201	76.1[c]
Other	5	1.9
Panel B: Perceptions of students not planning to take exam N = 67		
Perceived value of the CPA license		
Practical	30	44.8[c]
Prestige	38	56.7[c]
Earnings power	25	37.3[c]
Other	3	4.5
Reason for not taking exam		
Exam is unnecessary	29	43.3
Too difficult to find the time	20	30.0
Exam will be too difficult	16	23.9
Other	10	14.9
Factors impacting reconsideration of exam		
Receiving time/support from employers	37	55.2
Gaining confidence in ability to pass exam	10	14.9
Job requirement	10	14.9
Other	8	11.9

[a]Students were allowed to select as many reasons as they wished.
[b]Percentage is of either test taker respondents or non-test taker respondents.
[c]Chi-squared tests showed significant differences (p-value < 0.01) between test takers and non-test takers.

Chi-squared tests showed that the two groups differed in the percentage of times each reason was selected (*p*-value 0.0001). Clearly, the non-test takers recognized fewer benefits of the exam than the non-test takers.

We asked the next question – reasons not to take the exam – of only non-test takers. The primary reasons students chose not to sit for the CPA exam were thinking the CPA credential was unnecessary (43.3%), difficulty in finding time to study for the exam (30.0%), and perceived exam difficulty (23.9%). Though test-takers and non-test takers agree on the relative ranking of reasons to take the exam, non-test takers believe the test conferred fewer benefits overall. These students may be difficult to convert to test-takers, but a potential opportunity may exist if they recognize more fully the test's potential benefits.

We asked non-test takers to indicate what factors might cause them to reconsider sitting the exam. Our results in Table 6.3 show that receiving employer support is the most salient factor by a wide margin (selected 55.2% of the time). Gaining confidence in taking the exam or having the exam as a job requirement would each induce 14.9% to reconsider. Though no significant differences were found among those who would reconsider the exam if it were a job requirement, this was not true of gaining confidence. Non-test taking men were more likely to say that they would be more likely to take the exam if they gained confidence, 25.9%, versus female non-test takers, 7.9% (two-tailed *t*-test, *p*-value 0.012). When the differences were looked at by age, only 9.3% of those 29 and younger felt that gaining confidence would make them reconsider the exam versus 45% of those older than 29 (*p*-value 0.001).

Table 6.4 provides statistics used to determine if these perceptions differed when we divided the results into the four demographic subgroups. The results were reported using a two-tailed *t*-test to determine if there were significant differences between the groups in their perceptions of the exam, and *p*-values are shown.

When looking at perceptions of exam takers (Table 6.4, Panel A), males and females did not significantly differ in believing that the exam would be practical and prestigious. However, 30.6% of females versus 24.9% of males indicated that they believed the exam would increase their earnings (*p*-value 0.022). We observed no statistically significant differences between perceptions of the exam's usefulness when test takers were divided by either age or work experience. On the other hand, the differences between students at the private versus the public university were statistically significant. Close to 37% of students at the public university felt the exam was practical versus 33.3% of students at the private universities (*p*-value 0.082). Almost 40% of the public university students believed that the exam was prestigious versus 31.3% of the private university students (*p*-value 0.007). Students at the private university were much more likely (34.1%) to believe the exam would enhance their earning power compared to 23.4% of public university students (*p*-value < 0.0001).

Turning to Panel B (Table 6.4), we only observed four statistically significant differences at the 10% level and none at the 5% or 1% level for the perceived value of the exam among the non-test takers based on their demographics.[2] Significant differences emerged, however, when comparing the reasons for not taking the

Table 6.4. Comparing Perceptions within Groups (All Percentages Based on Full Sample).

	Gender		Work Experience		Age		School Type	
	Male	Female	≤3 Years	>3 Years	≤29 Years	≥30 Years	Public	Private
Panel A: Students Planning on Taking Exam								
Percent of group	87.6%	71.3%	77.4%	89.2%	79.3%	81.0%	83.0%	75.8%
	0.000***		0.008**		0.191		0.027*	
Perceived value of exam								
Practical	36.8%	33.3%	35.1%	36.4%	35.6%	33.3%	36.8%	33.3%
	0.081		0.200		0.175		0.082*	
Prestigious	38.1%	34.9%	36.1%	40.0%	36.6%	37.7%	39.2%	31.3%
	0.094		0.107		0.213		0.007**	
Earnings power	24.9%	30.6%	28.2%	22.7%	27.2%	27.5%	23.4%	34.1%
	0.022**		0.059		0.238		0.000***	
Other	0.2%	1.2%	0.6%	0.9%	0.6%	1.5%	0.6%	1.2%
	0.026*		0.188		0.105		0.079	
Panel B: Students Not Planning on Taking Exam								
Percent of group	12.4%	28.7%	22.7%	10.8%	20.7%	19.0%	17.0%	24.2%
	0.000***		0.008**		0.191		0.027*	
Perceived value of exam								
Practical	38.5%	28.6%	29.9%	36.8%	31.0%	33.3%	23.8%	34.2%
	0.088		0.139		0.222		0.091	
Prestigious	30.8%	42.9%	41.5%	31.6%	39.1%	44.5%	47.6%	36.9%
	0.071		0.106		0.189		0.093	
Earnings power	26.9%	25.7%	26.0%	26.3%	26.4%	22.2%	23.8%	26.3%
	0.226		0.244		0.196		0.204	
Other	3.8%	2.8%	2.6%	5.3%	3.5%	0%	4.8%	2.6%
	0.201		0.138		0.143		0.154	

(*Continued*)

Table 6.4. (Continued)

	Gender		Work Experience		Age		School Type	
	Male	Female	≤3 Years	>3 Years	≤29 Years	≥30 Years	Public	Private
Reason for not taking exam								
Unnecessary	37.5%	39.2%	40.9%	18.2%	39.7%	28.6%	36.1%	32.7%
	0.222		*0.037**		*0.109*		*0.185*	
Too difficult	29.2%	17.7%	18.2%	54.5%	17.4%	50.0%	36.1%	18.4%
	0.064		*0.002****		*0.002****		*0.016***	
Time constraints	20.8%	29.4%	27.3%	18.2%	27.0%	21.4%	19.4%	30.6%
	0.108		*0.131*		*0.167*		*0.061*	
Other	12.5%	13.7%	13.6%	9.1%	15.9%	0%	8.3%	18.4%
	0.021		*0.170*		*0.027**		*0.047**	
Reason to reconsider exam								
Receive time/support	48.2%	63.2%	58.2%	50.0%	59.3%	45.5%	66.7%	53.3%
	0.057		*0.158*		*0.100*		*0.077*	
Gain confidence in ability to pass	25.9%	7.9%	14.6%	20.0%	9.3%	45.5%	19.0%	13.3%
	*0.012***		*0.165*		*0.001****		*0.137*	
Job requirement	14.8%	15.8%	14.6%	20.0%	16.7%	9.1%	4.8%	20.0%
	0.229		*0.165*		*0.131*		*0.027**	
Other	11.1%	13.1%	12.7%	10.0%	14.8%	0%	9.5%	13.3%
	0.201		*0.202*		*0.043**		*0.165*	

Note: Numbers in *italics* are *p*-values for two-tailed *t*-tests of the differences between the two groups.
*Significant at 10% level. **Significant at 5% level. ***Significant at 1% level.

exam. Students with more work experience appear to be more certain of their plans with regard to pursuing or not pursuing the CPA exam. Almost 90% of the more experienced students plan to pursue the exam (see Table 6.4, Panel A). Of those not planning to pursue the exam, nearly 55% cited the exam's difficulty as their reason. Students with less work experience seem less aware of the value of the CPA as expressed by nearly 41% saying the exam was unnecessary (compared to 18% of students with more than three years' work experience, p-value 0.037). This is consistent with results reported previously by Wen et al. (2015) for ESL students with at least three years of experience.

The exam's difficulty was cited as a reason for its avoidance by only 18.2% of those with less work experience compared to 54.5% of those with more work experience (p-value 0.002). Similarly, 50% of those older than 29 versus only 17.4% of those 29 or below cited exam difficulty as a reason for not taking the exam. By contrast, only 29.2% of males and 17.7% of females cited difficulty level as an inhibitor in taking the exams. Interestingly only 18.4% of students attending the private university versus 36.1% of those from the public university cited difficulty level. In general, it appears that years of work experience and age play dominant roles in the perceptions of exam difficulty as an inhibitor to pursuing the CPA credential.

Differences also emerged when looking at factors that might influence reconsideration of the exam. Interestingly, 25.9% of males said that gaining confidence would cause them to reconsider versus only 7.9% of females (p-value 0.012); confidence was cited by 45.5% of those older than 29 and only 9.3% of those under 30 (p-value 0.0001). Having a job requirement as a reason to reconsider varied significantly (p-value 0.027) only among school types with 4.8% and 20% of students from the public and private universities, respectively, giving this as a reason. One factor that stands out is the relatively high proportion of non-test takers across all groups who would reconsider the exam if they received time off and support from their employers to pursue the exam. While most non-test takers would be motivated by this factor, it appears that those who might be most highly motivated to reconsider are females, those with three or fewer years of experience, those 28 or younger, and those who attend public universities.

DISCUSSION AND IMPLICATIONS

Our research study examined differences between those planning to take the CPA exam and those not planning to take it. Although qualified to sit for the exam, over 20% of our respondents were either planning not to take the exam or unsure whether they would take it (collectively, non-test takers). Several demographic characteristics were associated with non-test takers. Significantly fewer women (71.3%) than men (87.6%) plan to pursue the exam (p-value $<$ 0.0001). We also found that experience matters: those with less work experience were significantly less motivated to pursue the CPA license (p-value 0.008).

The most striking findings of our study relate to perceptions regarding the CPA exam's value proposition. For test takers, both practicality and prestige were selected by almost 100% of our sample as reasons to take the exam; 75% of the respondents thought earnings power to be an important reason. The perceptions of non-test takers sharply differed. Only 56.7% of this group perceived the exam to be prestigious, 44.8% felt it was practical and only 37.3% felt it would increase earnings. At best, non-test takers could be described as less than enthusiastic regarding the value of the CPA license.

Non-test takers offered various reasons for not taking the exam and factors that would nudge them toward its reconsideration. The primary reasons students did not choose to sit for the CPA exam were thinking the CPA credential was unnecessary (43.3%), the difficulty in finding time to study for the exam (30.0%), and perceived exam difficulty (23.9%). Finding the time to study showed no variation when the results were examined by group. Overall, the high (43.3%) proportion of students who view the CPA credential as unnecessary is intriguing, but it is also important to note that 56.7% of those who do not plan to take the exam did not indicate that the test is unnecessary. This means that if other reasons could be changed – primarily finding time to study and increasing confidence in their test taking ability – these qualified students might take the exam. In our sample, this represents potentially 38 additional test-takers (56.7% of students who are otherwise qualified but do not plan to take the exam).

Perceptions about the exam's difficulty as a deterrent were greater among older students than younger, by those attending public versus private institutions, and by those with more than three-years of work experience compared to those with less work experience. Those with less work experience were also more likely to see the exam as unnecessary compared to their more experienced peers. In general, those with less work experience appeared to be more naïve about the exam: they tended to underestimate the credential's value while at the same time discounting its difficulty.

The factor reported most often that might cause non-test takers to reconsider taking the exam was receiving employee support. While most non-test takers would reconsider if they had employer support, it appears that those who might be nudged most by this factor are females, those with three or fewer years of experience, those 28 or younger, and those who attend public universities.

Overall, our findings indicate that the value proposition of the CPA license needs to be better articulated and communicated. Ideally, communications should target specific communities: younger students, women, and those with less work experience. Our study results imply that younger students need to be better informed about the value of the CPA. Since significantly more women than men are unsure about pursuing the exam, it implies that there are more potential untapped CPA candidates among women than men – suggesting that informational campaigns focusing on women may be appropriate. We also found that those with more work experience seem more certain about their post-educational careers which suggests that recruitment of students from those currently employed – rather than concentrating primarily on undergraduates – might be a way of increasing the CPA pipeline.

Once better informed about the CPA license's value, our results suggest that there are ways to incentivize non-test takers to pursue the exam. Students indicate that the most salient factor for reconsideration of taking the exam is whether they will receive time and support for examination preparation from employers. This is entirely in the hands of employers; bonuses and reimbursements for test preparation are already prevalent, but more can be done. Since graduates with more work experience are more likely to intend to take the exam, accounting firms offering work opportunities with reduced hours while undertaking coursework and or exam preparation may be able to attract more candidates.

It is also imperative to educate current students about the value of CPA licensure. Students not pursuing the exam indicate that they believe licensure is primarily a prestigious accomplishment rather than a necessary requirement for career advancement. This misperception is especially prevalent among younger cohorts, indicating that they need to be better educated about the exam. Colleges and employers should communicate that licensure will be advantageous to one's career beyond prestige. It should be emphasized that licensure is often used as a separating criterion in hiring decisions outside of accounting practice.[3] The gains in salary over a lifetime for CPAs versus non-CPAs need to be reiterated including the premium that CPAs can receive when employed outside of accounting firms.[4] These are messages that both college accounting programs and accounting firms should deliver.

When deciding which of several interventions may be most effective, it is important to remain cognizant of differences that arise when parsing the data based on the factors mentioned earlier: gender, work experience, type of university and age. In our discussion section, we note that more men than women were interested in taking the CPA exam. The gender gap in planning to sit for the CPA exam mirrors that found in the STEM disciplines; perhaps this is indicative of the same gender gap that has been studied in the STEM disciplines (Catalyst, 2022; Kim et al., 2022). University accounting programs might intervene early in the curriculum to increase the number of women interested in taking the CPA exam and seeking employment in the accounting profession. Mentoring and coaching a possible interventions that may prove successful.

In summary, our study reveals significant differences among non-test takers in their reasons for not taking the exam as well as their perceptions of what might induce them to reconsider taking the exam. This indicates that when attempting to persuade non-test takers to reconsider sitting the exam, outreach, and interventions should be focused and target specific groups.

CONCLUSION

The demand for accounting graduates with a CPA credential has increased substantially (National State Boards of Accountancy (NASBA), 2023). However, the number of accounting majors and those seeking a CPA license has declined. Accounting programs may be dedicating insufficient resources to encouraging students to sit for the CPA exam. Additionally, accounting recruiters may be overlooking a candidate pool of older and more experienced workers who might be enticed to consider the accounting field – older workers who enter master's in accounting programs are more likely than their less experienced peers to pursue the CPA. However, the most important focus should be on correcting misperceptions about the CPA exam's value. Of the students surveyed regarding their exam plans, 20% indicated that they were either unsure or not planning to sit for the exam, and we were alarmed to find that 43% of non-test takers felt the exam was unnecessary. If this group's perception of the value of the CPA could be raised, then the pipeline numbers should improve. It also means that 57% of non-test takers believe the exam is important – if time constraints were diminished and confidence in test taking increased, these students might well become exam takers.

An obvious limitation of our study is that we were unable to conduct a complete survey of all accounting students nationally. As is the case in any smaller sized sample, it is possible that the results we found were unique to our sample group. Another potential limitation of our research is that it occurred before the 2024 changes to the exam which introduced a specialized skills testing section to replace the current Business Environment section (i.e., CPA Evolution). As our survey questioned students about their intention to pursue the CPA designation and not about their perceptions about individual sections of the exam, we do not believe that this exam change impacts our results; this is an area of future research that can be conducted. This chapter can also be extended by examining the effects on the pipeline of the NASBA One-Year Extension to successfully complete all exam parts and the 2024 CPA Evolution to the CPA Exam window.

Based on the results in our chapter, we reiterate that without a clear message to potential exam takers of the importance of taking the CPA exam and the value the credential offers, the many initiatives proposed by the AICPA may not fully achieve their goal. We urge the profession to determine how to increase the perception of the CPA's value. Future researchers may also contribute to the quest for solutions by conducting focused behavioral experiments and field research to assess how novel and existing approaches might change the perceived value proposition of the CPA credential, particularly among those who clearly have an interest in accounting but do not plan to pursue the exam.

NOTES

1. Results for test takers are provided for purposes of completeness only. The percentage sum of responses in Table 6.3 Panels A + B equals 100%.
2. Note that four of the 16 comparisons have p-values of 0.088, 0.091, 0.071, and 0.093 for practical (gender), practical (school type), prestigious (gender), and prestigious (school type), respectively.
3. Surveying the resumes of CFOs, Sellers et al. (2016) found that public accounting experience substituted for prestigious educational credentials.
4. The U.S. Bureau of Labor Statistics (2024) gives the average salary of accountants and auditors as $78,000; using the AICPA and CIMA's (2019) salary tool, the latest average salary for members – all CPAs – is $122,000.

ACKNOWLEDGMENTS

The authors thank NASBA for a grant awarded to conduct this research.

REFERENCES

AICPA and CIMA. (2019). *AICPA salary insights 2019*. https://salary.aicpaglobal.com/results?country=US&currency=USD&earning_period=yearly&type=browsing-cpa&us_region=Alabama

AICPA and CIMA. (2023). *Pipeline acceleration plan*. https://www.aicpa-cima.com/resources/article/draft-plan-to-accelerate-talent-pipeline-solutions

Bandla, M. (2023). Expand the accounting pipeline with a mentorship circle. *Journal of Accountancy*. https://www.journalofaccountancy.com/newsletters/academic-update/expand-the-accounting-pipeline-with-a-mentorship-circle.html

Bates, S. B. (2018). *Accounting students' perceptions of the value of pursuing CPA certification and factors that influence their decisions* (Order No. 10812234). ProQuest Dissertations & Theses Global; Social Science Premium Collection. https://www.proquest.com/docview/2038452450?pq-origsite=gscholar&fromopenview=true&sourcetype=Dissertations%20&%20Theses

Bergner, J., Chen, Y., & Simerly, M. (2020). Accounting faculty and professional certifications: Experiences and perceptions. In T. G. Calderon (Ed.), *Advances in accounting education: Teaching and curriculum innovations* (Vol. 24, pp. 143–164). Emerald Publishing Limited.

Bline, D., Perreault, S., & Zheng, X. (2016). Do accounting faculty characteristics impact CPA, exam performance? An investigation of nearly 700,000 examinations. *Issues in Accounting Education*, *31*(3), 291–300.

Bline, D., Perreault, S., & Zheng, X. (2021). Do grades earned in accounting courses predict performance on related sections of the CPA exam? In T. G. Calderon (Ed.), *Advances in accounting education: Teaching and curriculum innovations* (pp. 135–153). Emerald Publishing Limited.

Brink, W., Eaton, T. V., & Heitger, D. (2023). How students view the accounting profession. *Journal of Accountancy*. https://www.journalofaccountancy.com

Burke, J. A., & Polimeni, R. S. (2023). The accounting profession is in crisis: A partial solution to the shortage of accountants. *The CPA Journal*, *93*(9/10), 6–8.

Calderon, T. G., & Nagy, A. L. (2020). A closer look at research on CPA exam success. In T. G. Calderon (Ed.), *Advances in accounting education: Teaching and curriculum innovations* (Vol. 24, pp. 165–178). Emerald Publishing Limited.

Cardona, R. J., Castro-González, K. C., Ríos-Figueroa, C. B., & Vega-Vilca, J. C. (2021). Perceptions of challenges on the CPA exam: Evidence from Puerto Rico. In T. G. Calderon (Ed.), *Advances in accounting education: Teaching and curriculum innovations* (pp. 177–197). Emerald Publishing Limited.

Catalyst. (2022). *Women in science, technology, engineering, and mathematics (STEM) (Quick Take)*. https://www.catalyst.org/research/women-in-science-technology-engineering-and-mathematics-stem/

Castonguay, J. (2023). The AICPA and NASBA's inadequate response to reaching 150 hours. *The CPA Journal*. https://www.cpajournal.com/2023/12/08/the-aicpa-and-nasbas-inadequate-response-to-reaching-150-hours/

Charron, K., & Lowe, D. J. (2009). Becoming a CPA: Evidence from recent graduates. *The Accounting Educators' Journal*, *19*, 11–20.

Coe, M. (2016). Factors that influence a student's intention to sit for the CPA exam. *The CPA Journal*, *86*(8), 21.

Comunale, C. L., Irving, J. H., & Trainor, J. E. (2023). The accounting pipeline. *The CPA Journal*, *93*(9/10), 44–49.

CPA Practice Advisor. (2023). *Opinion: Our obsession with hours is destroying the accounting profession*. https://www.cpapracticeadvisor.com/2023/04/12/our-obsession-with-hours-is-destroying-the-accounting-profession/7864

Crowley, J., & Cadotte, J. R. (2023). CPA engagement boosts student interest in exam, public accounting. *Journal of Accountancy*. https://www.journalofaccountancy.com/issues/2023/sep/cpa-engagement-boosts-student-interest-in-exam-public-accounting.html

Dawkins, M. C., & Dugan, M. T. (2022). An update on the future of accounting education. *The CPA Journal*, *92*(9/10), 20–25.

Dawkins, M. C., Dugan, M. T., Mezzio, S. S., & Trapnell, J. E. (2020). The future of accounting education. *The CPA Journal*, *90*(9), 28–35.

Dickins, D., Hull, R., & Quick, L. (2021). The most effective study methods for passing the CPA exam: A research note. In T. G. Calderon (Ed.), *Advances in accounting education: Teaching and curriculum innovations* (Vol. 25, pp. 155–175). Emerald Publishing Limited.

Gabre, H. G., Flesher, D. L., & Ross, F. (2017). CPA credential perceptions: A case study of Hispanic accountants. *Accounting Education, 26*, 54–77.

Hood, D. (2023). Barriers to entry: Why they're not becoming accountants. *Accounting Today*. https://www.accountingtoday.com

Illinois CPA Society (ICPAS). (2021). *A CPA pipeline report: Decoding the decline.* https://www.icpas.org/information/professional-issues/decoding-the-decline

Kim, J. Y., Brockner, J., & Block, C. J. (2022). Tailoring the intervention to the self: Congruence between self-affirmation and self-construal mitigates the gender gap in quantitative performance. *Organizational Behavior and Human Decision Processes, 169*, 104118.

Morgan, J., Bergin, J. L., & Sallee, L. (2012). Three types of business school accreditation and their relationships to CPA exam scores of graduates. *Advances in Business Research, 3*(1), 25–35.

Mustapha, M., & Hassan, M. H. A. (2012). Accounting students' perception on pursuing professional examination. *International Journal of Education, 4*(4), 1.

National State Boards of Accountancy (NASBA). (2023). *The more things change, the more they stay the same: Addressing the CPA pipeline crisis.* https://nasba.org/blog/2023/03/14/addressing-the-cpa-pipeline-crisis/

New York State Society of Certified Public Accountants (NYSSCPA). (2023). *CPA exam takers in 2022: Fewest in 17 years.* https://www.nysscpa.org/article-content/cpa-exam-takers-in-2022-fewest-in-17-years-053023

Pitstick, H. (2022). What everyone can do to strengthen the next generation of CPAs. *Journal of Accountancy, 234*(3), 28–33.

Sellers, R. D., Fogarty, T. J., & Parker, L. M. (2016). How important is the educational capital of chief financial officers? An examination of educational credentials in the context of other attributes. *Global Perspectives on Accounting Education, 13*, 1–19.

Smith, K. J., & Emerson, D. J. (2017). An analysis of professional competence indicator possession among US accounting faculty. *Issues in Accounting Education, 32*(2), 17–38.

Strickland, B. (2023). AICPA releases expanded plan for addressing CPA pipeline challenges. *Journal of Accountancy*. https://www.journalofaccountancy.com

Taylor, J. (2023). Update on the AICPA pipeline acceleration plan. *Journal of Accountancy*. https://www.journalofaccountancy.com/newsletters/academic-update/update-on-the-aicpa-pipeline-acceleration-plan.html

Trout, B., & Blazer, E. (2017). *Factors influencing accounting students' career aspirations* (pp. 317–325). Northeastern Association of Business, Economics and Technology.

Udeh, I. A. (2022). Factors that influence a private institution student's plan to sit for the CPA exam soon after graduation. In T. G. Calderon (Ed.), *Advances in accounting education: Teaching and curriculum innovations* (pp. 33–54). Emerald Publishing Limited.

U.S. Bureau of Labor Statistics. (2024). *Occupational outlook handbook, accountants and auditors.* https://www.bls.gov/ooh/business-and-financial/accountants-and-auditors.htm

Wen, L., Hao, Q., & Bu, D. (2015). Understanding the intentions of accounting students in China to pursue certified public accountant designation. *Accounting Education, 24*(4), 341–359.

Waggoner, M. (2023). Accounting talent shortage is focus of new advisory group. *Journal of Accountancy*. https://www.journalofaccountancy.com/news/2023/jul/accounting-talent-shortage-is-focus-of-new-advisory-group.html

CHAPTER 7

CPA EXAM PASS RATES AND THE ROLE OF A CPA REVIEW COURSE

Jiayin Li[a], Hussein Issa[b] and Alexander J. Sannella[b]

[a]*University of International Business and Economics, China*
[b]*Rutgers Business School, The State University of New Jersey, USA*

ABSTRACT

Prior literature has studied the factors that impact CPA exam pass rates. Our study extends this research by examining whether a CPA exam review course is associated with exam pass rates and whether the nature of the course matters. We controlled for several factors that prior studies show are associated with student success on the CPA exam. We surveyed 76 US accounting programs and added data from school websites and NASBA publications. After controlling for known collates with CPA exam pass rates, our results provide evidence that offering a CPA review course impacts CPA pass rates for both First-time *and* All Candidates *if it is a credit-bearing elective and there was a reallocation of workload from other accounting courses.*

Keywords: CPA exam; factors affecting pass rates; CPE Exam Review courses; school characteristics; candidate characteristics; review course provider

Employers and prospective students consider several measures of external validation when evaluating the quality of a college or university's accounting program. One of the key elements used to measure the external validation of the quality of college-level accounting programs is the CPA exam pass rate. CPA exam pass rates by school are publicly available in publications issued by the National

Association of State Boards of Accountancy (NASBA). Employers may use them as a factor in recruiting at a particular university, and potential students may use them in selecting among accounting programs. Given the significance of this measure, accounting programs are conscious of the need to improve their CPA exam pass rates. Accordingly, many business schools may be pressured by test-based accountability.

Test-based accountability is often a critical factor in determining accounting curriculum changes, and faculty and administrators may struggle to develop a curriculum that improves CPA exam pass rates. Changes to the curriculum to improve exam pass rates can include course content changes or new course development. Either approach could have a positive impact on pass rates as test content becomes more familiar and test preparation becomes embedded in the curriculum. In this regard, a curriculum change could include adding a mandatory or elective credit-bearing CPA review course to the curriculum. The CPA review course could be delivered by members of the department or purchased from one of the commercial CPA exam review course vendors (e.g., Becker, Roger, and Yeager). While the addition of such a course to the curriculum might enhance students' familiarity with exam content and offer test-taking skills, it is possible that the addition of such a course comes at the expense of dropping or reducing coverage of other valuable skills and abilities.

The total number of credit hours in a college degree is often fixed by the administration or the state and may not be changed unilaterally by the accounting program. Thus, adding a course to the curriculum could mean dropping another, which might impact the range and depth of knowledge, skills, and abilities that the curriculum provides. It is, therefore, possible that even the addition of a mandatory CPA review course to the curriculum might not improve exam pass rates. Several factors impact CPA exam pass rates (Calderon & Nagy, 2020) and merely adding a CPA exam review course may not alter any of those factors.

For various reasons as noted above, it is not entirely clear that the addition of a CPA exam review course to an accounting program will eventually increase pass rates. Additionally, we are not aware of any empirical studies which support the notion that a credit-bearing CPA review course, whether mandatory or elective, increases pass rates. Similarly, there is little current empirical evidence about the role of other nuanced aspects of a CPA review course (e.g., whether the course increased the program length) on exam pass rates. Our study seeks to fill those voids.

Our study examines whether offering a credit-bearing CPA Review course improves exam results for an accounting program.[1] To isolate the impact of offering the course, we identify and control for other critical factors that can impact CPA exam pass rates. Data for the study came from a survey of accounting program administrators, NASBA's published exam pass rates (NASBA, 2006–2019), and a review of accounting program websites. Overall, our results indicate that offering a credit-bearing CPA review course is the most significant factor impacting CPA pass rates after controlling for several known correlates, but only if that course is an elective and there was a reallocation of workload from other accounting courses to make room in the curriculum for the review course. Our results have important implications for curriculum development and CPA exam outcomes.

The remainder of this chapter consists of four sections. The next section reviews the relevant literature and develops our research questions. This is followed by a discussion of our survey data, sample and research method. Next, we present our research results. Our final section provides a summary and discussion of our results and conclusions. This section also includes the limitations of this study, possible policy implications and suggestions for future research.

LITERATURE REVIEW AND RESEARCH QUESTIONS

Previous accounting research has focused on the factors that impact the performance of candidates taking the CPA exam. These factors range from examining the schools' attributes, such as the level of accreditation, to the candidates' own characteristics, including their age and level of education. In addition, researchers have investigated the effect of taking a CPA review course on candidates' performance. However, many of these studies were conducted over 25 years ago (e.g., Ashbaugh & Thompson, 1993), used a sample that became less relevant with changes to the CPA exam (e.g., Howell & Heshizer, 2008) or examined the problem from only one perspective or for a specific school or state (e.g., Bline et al., 2021; Brahmasrene & Whitten, 2001; Cardona et al., 2021). Calderon and Nagy (2020) conducted a comprehensive literature review of the research on CPA exam success but did not re-test any of the factors of interest. None of the prior studies done in the last two decades examines the impact of credit-bearing CPA exam review courses that are embedded in the accounting program.

Zook and Bremser (1982) provide evidence that the characteristics most predictive of successful performance on the CPA exam (auditing, theory, and practice parts) were average study time of at least seven hours per week over the 10-week period prior to sitting for the exam; participation in a CPA review course, SAT above 500 and overall and accounting GPAs above 3.0. Ashbaugh and Thompson (1993) examine the factors associated with passing all four parts of the exam on the first attempt. The most important factors were: CPA review course performance (grade), high-school class rank and high-school class size. Titard and Russell (1989) report that CPA review course had a positive effect on success on all parts of the CPA exam. Grant et al. (2002) find that scholastic aptitude and exam review courses have the highest marginal impact on a candidate's CPA exam success.

In addition, Rudnick and Taylor (2004) discuss the differences between general accounting education and a CPA review course offered by an independent, outside vendor. The authors argue that the outside CPA review course should only be considered a review of the general accounting curriculum, given the short course duration and its focus on what will be on the test rather than general accounting education. Howell and Heshizer (2006, 2008) found a positive relationship between needing fewer attempts to pass the exam and completion of a CPA review course in comparison to self-study preparation.

Shin et al. (2020) found that offering an accounting department-affiliated CPA review course is positively associated with higher CPA exam pass rates if offered as non-credit, but that association is insignificant when the courses are offered for credit (as part of the accounting curriculum). Our chapter differs from Shin et al. (2020) in several respects. First, our sample spans a much longer period (2006–2019), in comparison to 2 years (2013–2014) in Shin et al. (2020). Furthermore, our chapter analyzes both *First-time* and *All* (repeat plus First-time) candidates, whereas Shin et al. focuses on *First-time Candidates*. In addition, our study includes a variable that specifies the provider of the review courses (outside provider such as Becker or internally developed review courses), while Shin et al. do not make this distinction. The control variables in our chapter are also more comprehensive than the cited paper, as we control for recession, transfer students, accreditation, candidates' age, standardized curriculum and departmental exams, and other known correlates (see Table 7.2). Additionally, our chapter employs a unique methodology by combining survey data from 76 US accounting programs with secondary data from NASBA publications and school websites, providing a rich dataset that enables a deeper analysis of the factors influencing CPA pass rates. This approach not only enhances the robustness of the findings but also ensures a more diverse and representative sample, reflecting a wide range of accounting programs across the United States.

Our study re-examines several nuanced aspects of the CPA review course not considered in prior research. For example, we examine whether accounting curriculum content is reallocated to accommodate the CPA review material, the type of the course (for credit/not for credit, elective/required), and the content provider (department/outside vendor). Based on the foregoing discussion, we posit the following research question:

RQ1. Does offering a CPA review course in the accounting program influence CPA pass rates, and are there differences if the review course is credit-bearing as either an elective or a required course?

We further examine the impact of the provider of the CPA exam review course on the exam pass rate. As mentioned earlier, Rudnick and Taylor (2004) posit that a CPA review course that is offered by an outside vendor is best viewed as a condensed refresher of the overall accounting curriculum, rather than a comprehensive accounting education, due to its brief timeframe and emphasis on exam-specific content. Shin et al. (2020) findings suggest that when a CPA review is offered by the accounting department as a not for credit course, it is associated with a higher pass rate on the CPA exam. However, its impact is insignificant if offered for profit. Similarly, if the course is affiliated with a continuing education center rather than the accounting department, the effect of the review course on the pass rate is insignificant. The rationale for further investigating the review course provider's impact is that while review courses developed by outside vendors can be viewed as professionally made with test-taking strategies in mind, review courses offered by accounting departments (in-house) might be more consistent with the academic quality of other courses that make up the university's accounting curriculum. Accordingly, we pose the following question:

RQ2. Does a CPA review course offered by the accounting department affect CPA pass rates?

SAMPLE AND RESEARCH METHODOLOGY

The Survey Instrument

We used a survey (available from the authors) to obtain information regarding school-specific information related to general accounting courses and CPA review classes. The survey consists of eight questions, grouped into three separate categories: the level of the accounting program offered by the school (graduate/undergraduate), the provider and nature of CPA review classes (if any), and other general information related to the school. We also asked whether the core accounting courses (which are part of the general accounting curriculum and not CPA exam-oriented) are provided for undergraduates only or both undergraduate and graduate. In addition, the survey includes questions to determine if the accounting program uses departmental exams, course leaders (coordinators) and whether standardized curricula are used across all sections of a course. Regarding the CPA review classes, we asked if the school provided a CPA review class and if the review classes are credit-bearing. The survey also includes questions designed to determine who provided the review courses: the department or an outside vendor. Finally, we inquired as to the percentage of transfer students enrolled at the school.

Data and Sample

Surveys were sent to 937 schools (445 AACSB schools and 492 non-AACSB schools). We obtained 76 usable responses, 59 of which are from AACSB schools and 17 from non-AACSB schools.

All usable responses were matched to the CPA exam pass rate data from the year 2006 to 2019.[2] The CPA exam pass rates were obtained from the CPA exam performance data published by NASBA's *Candidate Performance on the Uniform CPA Examination*. The data include CPA pass rate information for both *First-time Candidates* and *All Candidates*. It also includes pass rates for the overall exam and four separate sections, FAR, BEC, REG, and AUD. Therefore, we were able to examine the performance of both *First-time Candidates* and *All Candidates* in our statistical tests. We also test performance on the total exam and each individual part for both groups.

Matching the 76 usable responses to the CPA pass rate data led to 946 school-year observations. We excluded six responses (94 school-year observations) with missing values in any of our independent variables. Our final sample consisted of 852 school-year observations for *All Candidates* and *First-time Candidates*. These two candidate groups have the same number of observations because although the number of *First-time Candidates* should be less than or equal to the number of overall candidates, our sample is aggregated at the school level. Every school that responded to our survey had both *first-time and repeat candidates*. Table 7.1 presents our initial sample and final number of observations.

Regression Models

Based on the review of existing literature on CPA exam performance, we used the following regression model to examine our research questions:

$$Pass\%_{i,j} = \alpha_0 + \alpha_1 * REV\_CLSS_i + \alpha_2 * REV\_CLSS\_PROV_i + Controls_i + \varepsilon_i \quad (1)$$

The variables used in the model and the data sources are defined in Table 7.2. The dependent variable is a set of pass rates[3] for school i in year j. Our main variables of interest are the type of review courses and the provider of review courses for school i, which are indicated by variables REV_CLSS_i and $REV\_CLSS\_PROV_i$, respectively. We also include a comprehensive set of control variables in the model (see Table 7.2). The first group of control variables comes from the survey, including the level of review courses $PRGM\_LVL_j$), the percentage of transfer students in school i ($TSFR_j$), whether the accounting program administers departmental exams in school i (DPT_EXM_j), whether courses in school i used standardized syllabi across sections (STD_CUR_j), whether accounting classes have a course leader in school i ($CRSE\_LDR_j$).

To adequately account for other factors that can affect CPA exam performance, we included several additional control variables in our model. First, we included school characteristics, such as AACSB accreditation, if the school is public or private, the average SAT score, and the average age of candidates in school i (acquired from NASBA's performance reports). Our study also includes a control (RCSS) for the financial crisis in 2008 and 2009. To control for the unobserved changes across each year and to avoid multicollinearity between year fixed effects and the recession dummy, we include a time trend (Year – 2005) to control for year fixed effects in the model. In addition, to control for the potential correlations among several observations for each school, we cluster standard errors at the school level.[4]

Table 7.1. Sample and Number of Observations.

	Number of Unique Schools	Number of School-Year Observations
Surveys sent	937	–[a]
Surveys received	76	–[a]
Complete responses merged with CPA exam data from year 2006 to 2019	70	946
Observations with missing variables	(6)	(94)
Merged responses without missing variables	64	852

[a]The first and second lines will not have the number of school-year observations because the data were not merged with the CPA exam data at that point. That is, the data in the first and second lines are at the school level, while the remaining portion of the table is at the school-year level.

Table 7.2. Variable Definitions and Data Sources.

Variable	Name	Definitions	Data Sources
Dependent Variables			
	Pass rate FT	Pass rates of *First-time Candidates* in all sections	NASBA Reports
	AUD PR FT	Pass rates of *First-time Candidates* in AUD section	NASBA Reports
	BEC PR FT	Pass rates of *First-time Candidates* in BEC section	NASBA Reports
	FAR PR FT	Pass rates of *First-time Candidates* in FAR section	NASBA Reports
	REG PR FT	Pass rates of *First-time Candidates* in REG section	NASBA Reports
	Pass rate All	Pass rates of *All Candidates* in all sections	NASBA Reports
	AUD PR All	Pass rates of *All Candidates* in AUD section	NASBA Reports
	BEC PR All	Pass rates of *All Candidates* in BEC section	NASBA Reports
	FAR PR All	Pass rates of *All Candidates* in FAR section	NASBA Reports
	REG PR All	Pass rates of *All Candidates* in REG section	NASBA Reports
Independent Variables			
Type of CPA review class	REV_CLSSnoncredit	"The course is offered as a non-credit bearing course": 1; Others: 0	Survey
	REV_CLSS_elective	"The course is offered as an elective": 1; Others: 0	Survey
	REV_CLSS_reallocate	"The course was included by reallocating credits from other courses": 1; Others: 0	Survey
	REV_CLSS_major	"The course increased the number of credits required for the major": 1; Others: 0	
	REV_CLSS_nocourse	"The review course is not provided": 1; Others: 0	
Who provides review courses	REV_CLSS_PROV	"Provided by an outside vendor (e.g., Becker)" or "Both provided by the department and an outside vendor": 1 "Provided by the department": 0	Survey
Control Variables			
Accounting program offer level	PRGM_LVL	Undergraduate and graduate: 1 Undergraduate: 0	Survey
Percentage of transfer students	TSFR	Less than 10%: 1; 10%–30%: 2; 30%–50%: 3; >=50%: 4	Survey
Does your department administer departmental exams?	DPT_EXM	Equals to 1 if the answer for this question in the survey is Yes; otherwise 0.	Survey
Standardized curriculum?	STD_CUR	Equals to 1 if the answer for this question in the survey is Yes; otherwise 0.	Survey
Course leader	CRSE_LDR	Equals to 1 if the answer for this question in the survey is Yes; otherwise 0.	Survey

(*Continued*)

Table 7.2. (Continued)

Variable	Name	Definitions	Data Sources
Average age of candidates	AGE (FT/All)	The logged number of average age of the *First-time/All Candidates*	NASBA Reports
School is accredited or not	AACSB	Equals to 1 if the school is AACSB credited school; otherwise 0.	AACSB
Public or private	PBLC	Equals to 1 if the school is a public school; otherwise 0.	Wiki[a]
Average Sat	SAT	The logged number of schools' average accepted SAT	PrepScholar[b]
Recession	RCSS	Equals to 1 if the year is 2008 or 2009, otherwise 0.	NBER[c]
Time trend		Equals to year minus 2005 to avoid the collinearity with recession dummy	

Note: Variables in this list were selected based on such studies as Calderon and Nagy (2020), Bline et al. (2021), Cardona et al. (2021), and Shin et al. (2020).

[a]The type of school comes from high school list provided by Wiki. See https://en.wikipedia.org/wiki/Lists_of_schools_in_the_United_States.
[b]The average SAT score is searched on the website of PrepSchool. See https://www.prepscholar.com/.
[c]See https://www.nber.org/research/business-cycle-dating.

RESULTS

Table 7.3 presents descriptive statistics for each variable used in our model. The percent pass rate of the *"All Candidates"* group is 49.4%, which is slightly lower than the *First-time Candidates* group's average of 52.5%. On the other hand, the average score of the two groups was approximately the same. As for the age of the candidates, the average age for the *All Candidates* group was 28.08 years, compared to 27.39 years for the *First-time Candidates*. Examining each part of the CPA exam separately yields some interesting results. While the Auditing part's pass rates for the two groups are similar, it was interesting to find that the other parts' pass rates for the *First-time* candidate's group were slightly higher than those of the all-candidates group.

A summary of the results for the main variables of interest appears in Table 7.4. This table highlights our primary findings and compares them with the results of prior studies. A more detailed discussion of our results appears below.

The results for the OLS regressions using the CPA exam pass rates of *First-time Candidates* are presented in Table 7.5-Panel A. The first column includes the results where the dependent variable is defined as the overall CPA exam pass rates of *First-time Candidates* in all four sections, while Columns (2)–(5) present the results where the dependent variable is specified as the pass rates of *First-time Candidates* in each CPA exam section. All regressions include year-fixed effects, and the standard errors are clustered at the school level. The numbers in parentheses are *t*-statistics.

Based on the results reported in Table 7.5-Panel A, for *First-time Candidates*, we determined that factors that positively affected the CPA pass rates include the offering of a review course where some material was taken out of other courses to accommodate the CPA review topics. Using available class time and not adding extra hours to cover the CPA review topics seems to be received positively by the *First-time Candidates*. Consistent with that logic, we find that review courses offered by an outside entity (as opposed to in-house offerings) had a negative impact on pass rates.

Table 7.5-Panel B reports the OLS regressions using the CPA exam pass rates of *All Candidates* as the dependent variable. The table structure and column numbers in this table are as defined for Table 7.5-Panel A. The results reported in Table 7.5-Panel B for *All Candidates* are not significantly different from those reported in Table 7.5-Panel A for *First-time Candidates*, with three notable exceptions for certain control variables. First, age was not a significant factor for *All Candidates*. The second difference between *First-time* and *All Candidates* is that offering a non-credit CPA review course is negatively associated with exam pass rates. We would expect that the non-credit course would not be effective given the fact that this course would be added to an already intensive accounting curriculum. We also found that offering an elective CPA review course did not have a significant impact on the CPA exam pass rates. We posit that many candidates from the *"All Candidates"* group are out of school, limiting the possibility for elective courses.

Table 7.3. Summary of Statistics.

Statistic	N	Mean	p25	Median	p75	St.Dev	min	max
Dependent Variables								
PercentPass All	852	0.494	0.418	0.491	0.564	0.112	0.063	0.929
AverageScore All	852	71.797	69.6	71.95	74.3	3.762	48.8	85
AverageAge All	852	28.08	25.9	28	29.8	2.851	0.255	39.2
AUD All	852	80.831	25	57.5	107	77.209	2	486
AUD PR All	852	0.491	0.412	0.491	0.57	0.124	0	1
BEC All	852	74.54	24	54	100	69.348	1	444
BEC PR All	852	0.541	0.429	0.54	0.655	0.164	0	1
FAR All	852	78.765	24	55.5	106	74.402	1	459
FAR PR All	852	0.473	0.38	0.469	0.56	0.135	0	1
REG All	852	78.015	25	54.5	106	75.365	1	451
REG PR All	852	0.492	0.41	0.497	0.567	0.125	0	1
PercentPass FT	852	0.525	0.429	0.53	0.615	0.137	0.071	0.92
AverageScore FT	852	72.007	69.05	72.4	75.3	4.908	48.8	85.3
AverageAge FT	852	27.39	25.2	27.1	29.1	2.658	22	38.2
AUD FT	852	48.464	14	33	62	49.59	1	314
AUD PR FT	852	0.501	0.4	0.5	0.61	0.158	0	1
BEC FT	852	47.958	14	32	62	49.826	1	338
BEC PR FT	852	0.601	0.483	0.61	0.74	0.184	0	1
FAR FT	852	48.704	15	33	64	50.165	0	323
FAR PR FT	852	0.496	0.38	0.5	0.61	0.171	1	1
REG FT	852	46.748	14	31.5	60	48.751	1	315
REG PR FT	852	0.513	0.406	0.514	0.609	0.161	0	1
Independent Variables								
REV_CLSS_noncredit	852	0.061	0	0	0	0.24	0	1
REV_CLSS_elective	852	0.211	0	0	0	0.408	0	1
REV_CLSS_reallocate	852	0.016	0	0	0	0.127	0	1
REV_CLSS_major	852	0.031	0	0	0	0.172	0	1
REV_CLSS_nocourse	852	0.131	0	0	0	0.338	0	1
REV_CLSS_PROV	852	0.178	0	0	0	0.383	0	1

CPA Exam Pass Rates

Control Variables								
PRGM_LVL	852	1.8	2	1			0.4	2
TSFR	852	1.934	2	1			0.881	4
DEP_EXM	852	0.232	0	0			0.423	1
STD_CUR	852	0.563	1	0			0.496	1
CRSE_LDR	852	0.624	0	0			0.485	1
AGE (FT)	852	3.306	3.3	3.227	3.371	3.091	0.095	3.643
AGE (All)	852	3.326	3.332	3.254	3.395	−1.366	0.186	3.669
AACSB	852	0.838	1	1	1	0	0.369	1
PBLC	852	0.561	1	0	1	0	0.497	1
SAT (log of SAT Score)	852	7.048	7.048	7.003	7.123	6.234	0.131	7.244

Table 7.4. Summary of Results for Research Questions Testing.

Research Questions	First-time Candidates	All Candidates	Prior Literature
RQ1. Review course-non-credit (review course is offered as a non-credit bearing course)	Not significant	Significant (−)	Significant (+) (Shin et al., 2020)
RQ1. Review course-elective (review course is offered as an elective course)	Significant (+)	Not significant	None
RQ1. Review course-reallocate (review course requires replacing content from major courses)	Significant (+)	Significant (+)	None
RQ1. Review course-major (review course increases credits required for the major)	Significant (−)	Significant (−)	Not significant (Shin et al., 2020)
RQ1. Review course-no course (no review course is offered)	Not significant	Not significant	Significant (−) (Howell & Heshizer, 2006, 2008)
RQ2. Review course Provider (accounting department=0 and outside provider = 1)	Significant (−)	Significant (−)	Posit (+) (Rudnick & Taylor, 2004)

Note: This table represents the summary of our results, together with relative results from prior literature. "+" and "−" correspond to positively and negatively associated, respectively.

Table 7.5: Panel A. Factors Affecting the CPA Pass Rates of First-time Candidates.

VARIABLES	(1) PercentPass_FT	(2) AUD PR FT	(3) BEC PR FT	(4) FAR PR FT	(5) REG PR FT
REV_CLSS_noncredit	−0.036	−0.035	−0.030	−0.025	−0.063
	(−0.970)	(−1.106)	(−0.669)	(−0.655)	(−1.530)
REV_CLSS_elective	0.006	0.009	0.011	−0.002	−0.002
	(0.236)	(0.356)	(0.383)	(−0.059)	(−0.047)
REV_CLSS reallocate	0.415*	0.325**	0.683*	0.395**	0.283***
	(2.695)	(2.157)	(4.194)	(2.136)	(1.972)
REV_CLSS_major	−0.090**	−0.072**	−0.050	−0.157*	−0.111*
	(−2.399)	(−2.077)	(−1.006)	(−4.149)	(−2.883)
REV_CLSS_nocourse	0.024	−0.019	0.068	0.018	0.030
	(0.408)	(−0.348)	(0.923)	(0.283)	(0.484)
REV_CLSS_PROV	−0.008	0.005	−0.049	−0.007	0.031
	(−0.266)	(0.178)	(−1.427)	(−0.207)	(0.865)
PRGM_LVL	0.014	−0.002	0.003	0.040	0.021
	(0.298)	(−0.039)	(0.052)	(0.870)	(0.450)
TSFR	−0.026***	−0.023***	−0.034**	−0.027***	−0.019
	(−1.847)	(−1.673)	(−2.116)	(−1.878)	(−1.246)
DEP_EXM	−0.003	−0.009	0.010	−0.010	−0.011
	(−0.128)	(−0.336)	(0.334)	(−0.326)	(−0.406)
STD_CUR	−0.039	−0.034	−0.040	−0.050	−0.020
	(−1.361)	(−1.298)	(−1.253)	(−1.517)	(−0.737)
CRSE_LDR	−0.013	−0.015	−0.020	−0.009	−0.010
	(−0.595)	(−0.738)	(−0.716)	(−0.348)	(−0.431)
AGE (FT)	−0.299**	−0.281**	−0.286**	−0.388**	−0.189
	(−2.461)	(−2.608)	(−2.004)	(−2.616)	(−1.451)
AACSB	0.003	−0.016	0.035	−0.054**	0.024
	(0.097)	(−0.651)	(0.880)	(−2.127)	(0.759)
PBLC	0.075*	0.058**	0.093*	0.082*	0.067**
	(2.901)	(2.298)	(3.278)	(2.751)	(2.571)
SAT	0.528*	0.512*	0.768*	0.459**	0.401**
	(2.896)	(2.870)	(3.997)	(2.081)	(2.341)
Recession	0.023*	0.045*	−0.010	0.024**	0.032**
	(2.696)	(3.568)	(−0.935)	(2.246)	(2.515)
Constant	−2.226	−2.147	−3.956**	−1.404	−1.753
	(−1.579)	(−1.550)	(−2.609)	(−0.816)	(−1.304)
Observations	852	852	852	852	852
R-squared	0.354	0.220	0.361	0.260	0.174
Time trend	Yes	Yes	Yes	Yes	Yes
Robust SD	Yes	Yes	Yes	Yes	Yes

Notes: This table represents the results of OLS regressions using the CPA exam pass rates of *First-time Candidates* are presented. Column (1) includes the results where the dependent variable is defined as the overall CPA exam pass rates of *First-time Candidates* in all four sections, while Columns (2)–(5) present the results where the dependent variable is specified as the pass rates of *First-time Candidates* in each CPA exam section. All regressions include time trend, and the standard errors are clustered at the school level. The numbers in parentheses are *t*-statistics. Numbers in parentheses are *t*-statistics based on standard errors clustered at the school level. All variables are defined in Table 7.2.
*, **, and *** correspond to 1%, 5%, and 10% significance levels, respectively.

Table 7.5: Panel B. Factors Affecting the CPA Pass Rates of *All Candidates*.

VARIABLES	(1) PercentPass_All	(2) AUD_PR_All	(3) BEC_PR_All	(4) FAR_PR_All	(5) REG_PR_All
REV_CLSS_noncredit	−0.034	−0.035	−0.040	−0.019	−0.043
	(−1.043)	(−1.201)	(−0.949)	(−0.589)	(−1.234)
REV_CLSS_elective	0.005	−0.001	0.002	0.012	0.007
	(0.211)	(−0.034)	(0.077)	(0.473)	(0.256)
REV_CLSS_reallocate	0.361**	0.271**	0.623*	0.292***	0.235***
	(2.512)	(2.016)	(3.790)	(1.725)	(1.855)
REV_CLSS_major	−0.078**	−0.079*	−0.074***	−0.067***	−0.096*
	(−2.534)	(−2.870)	(−1.851)	(−1.892)	(−3.380)
REV_CLSS_nocourse	0.022	0.030	0.029	0.023	0.018
	(0.434)	(0.661)	(0.469)	(0.396)	(0.393)
REV_CLSS_PROV	−0.012	−0.001	−0.033	−0.026	0.009
	(−0.471)	(−0.030)	(−1.024)	(−0.961)	(0.305)
PRGM_LVL	0.007	0.008	−0.008	0.015	0.015
	(0.168)	(0.206)	(−0.154)	(0.357)	(0.424)
TSFR	−0.023**	−0.025**	−0.029**	−0.024***	−0.017
	(−2.023)	(−2.329)	(−2.043)	(−1.998)	(−1.485)
DEP_EXM	−0.003	−0.017	0.012	0.001	−0.010
	(−0.144)	(−0.787)	(0.404)	(0.028)	(−0.445)
STD_CUR	−0.035	−0.031	−0.041	−0.039	−0.019
	(−1.358)	(−1.394)	(−1.309)	(−1.335)	(−0.766)
CRSE_LDR	−0.009	0.009	−0.019	−0.016	−0.008
	(−0.454)	(0.498)	(−0.706)	(−0.772)	(−0.422)
AGE (All)	−0.235**	−0.167***	−0.361*	−0.342*	−0.117
	(−2.472)	(−1.893)	(−3.023)	(−3.026)	(−1.227)
AACSB	−0.003	0.029	−0.010	−0.027	−0.009
	(−0.134)	(1.314)	(−0.318)	(−0.858)	(−0.395)
PBLC	0.064**	0.040***	0.086*	0.067**	0.058**
	(2.644)	(1.838)	(3.056)	(2.391)	(2.546)
SAT	0.459*	0.407**	0.685*	0.373***	0.318**
	(2.701)	(2.554)	(3.512)	(1.860)	(2.129)
Recession	0.025*	0.045*	0.004	0.019**	0.032*
	(3.679)	(4.344)	(0.473)	(2.151)	(3.235)
Constant	−1.962	−1.836	−3.135**	−0.964	−1.384
	(−1.532)	(−1.467)	(−2.104)	(−0.637)	(−1.223)
Observations	852	852	852	852	852
R-squared	0.363	0.236	0.416	0.269	0.161
Time trend	Yes	Yes	Yes	Yes	Yes
Robust SD	Yes	Yes	Yes	Yes	Yes

Notes: This table represents the results of OLS regressions using the CPA exam pass rates of all-time candidates are presented. Column (1) includes the results where the dependent variable is defined as the overall CPA exam pass rates of all-time candidates in all four sections, while Columns (2)–(5) present the results where the dependent variable is specified as the pass rates of all-time candidates in each CPA exam section. All regressions include time trend, and the standard errors are clustered at the school level. The numbers in parentheses are *t*-statistics. Numbers in parentheses are *t*-statistics based on standard errors clustered at the school level. All variables are defined in Table 7.2.
*, **, and *** correspond to 1%, 5%, and 10% significance levels, respectively.

We note that including the recession in our model did not change any of the conclusions about our variables of interest for either *First-time Candidates* or the *All Candidates* group. The recession itself had a positive impact on CPA pass rates. In this case, it is logical to assume that with job loss, candidates may have been able to spend more time studying. In addition, passing the CPA exam would be added to a candidate's resume, and this fact could increase the incentive to pass the exam. The chances of employment would increase if the parts passed or if the entire exam was passed were included on the candidate's resume.

Table 7.6-Panel A presents the results for the OLS regressions where the CPA exam pass rate is the dependent variable, but we exclude the public/private school indicator variable and the recession variable. Overall, the results are consistent with our prior findings, except that after removing the effect of the type of institution (public or private), AACSB accreditation became a significant factor in increasing CPA pass rates for both *First-time* and *All Candidates*. Our sample of public schools consists mainly of AACSB-accredited schools. As a result, it is likely that the significance of the Public/Private variable was impacted by the fact that they were AACSB accredited. In other words, the public/private variable is probably impounding the AACSB effect, which can explain why AACSB accreditation was mostly non-significant in Table 7.5 but became significant when we excluded the public/private indicator, as shown in Table 7.6 (Panels A and B).

Table 7.6: Panel A. Results for Pass Rates of First-time Without the Public/Private School and Recession Variable.

	Pass Rates of *First-time Candidates*				
	(1)	(2)	(3)	(4)	(5)
VARIABLES	PercentPass_FT	AUD PR FT	BEC PR FT	FAR PR FT	REG PR FT
REV_CLSS_noncredit	−0.043	−0.041	−0.040	−0.033	−0.070***
	(−1.248)	(−1.451)	(−0.974)	(−0.857)	(−1.715)
REV_CLSS_elective	0.001	0.003	0.005	−0.008	−0.007
	(0.025)	(0.115)	(0.146)	(−0.212)	(−0.225)
REV_CLSS_reallocate	0.296***	0.238	0.533*	0.262	0.180
	(1.806)	(1.538)	(3.028)	(1.364)	(1.163)
REV_CLSS_major	−0.065	−0.055	−0.017	−0.127*	−0.090**
	(−1.504)	(−1.440)	(−0.289)	(−3.282)	(−2.138)
REV_CLSS_nocourse	−0.000	−0.038	0.038	−0.008	0.009
	(−0.002)	(−0.632)	(0.440)	(−0.120)	(0.123)
REV_CLSS_PROV	−0.011	0.002	−0.053	−0.010	0.028
	(−0.333)	(0.071)	(−1.298)	(−0.278)	(0.733)
PRGM_LVL	0.015	−0.002	0.003	0.041	0.021
	(0.267)	(−0.030)	(0.051)	(0.763)	(0.402)
TSFR	−0.022	−0.021	−0.029	−0.023	−0.016
	(−1.370)	(−1.404)	(−1.530)	(−1.370)	(−0.940)
DPT_EXAM	−0.003	−0.009	0.011	−0.009	−0.010
	(−0.078)	(−0.273)	(0.296)	(−0.234)	(−0.313)
STD_CUR	−0.067**	−0.057**	−0.075**	−0.081**	−0.046***
	(−2.528)	(−2.516)	(−2.395)	(−2.630)	(−1.672)

Table 7.6: Panel A. (*Continued*)

	Pass Rates of *First-time Candidates*				
	(1)	(2)	(3)	(4)	(5)
VARIABLES	PercentPass_FT	AUD PR FT	BEC PR FT	FAR PR FT	REG PR FT
CRSE_LDR	0.001	−0.004	−0.003	0.006	0.002
	(0.027)	(−0.205)	(−0.111)	(0.232)	(0.090)
AGE (FT)	−0.253***	−0.225***	−0.245	−0.351**	−0.136
	(−1.836)	(−1.890)	(−1.506)	(−2.177)	(−0.922)
AACSB	0.026	0.002	0.065	−0.029	0.045
	(0.770)	(0.058)	(1.291)	(−1.034)	(1.276)
SAT	0.372***	0.400**	0.571*	0.285	0.267
	(1.939)	(2.210)	(2.754)	(1.262)	(1.461)
Constant	−1.212	−1.493	−2.576	−0.266	−0.917
	(−0.776)	(−1.015)	(−1.503)	(−0.144)	(−0.610)
Observations	852	852	852	852	852
R-squared	0.325	0.221	0.342	0.242	0.176
Cluster school	Yes	Yes	Yes	Yes	Yes
Year FE	Yes	Yes	Yes	Yes	Yes

Notes: This table represents the results of OLS regressions using the same model as in Table 7.5, Panel A, except for the excluding of the public/private school indicator variable and the recession indicator variable. Column (1) includes the results where the dependent variable is defined as the overall CPA exam pass rates of *First-time Candidates* in all four sections, while Columns (2)–(5) present the results where the dependent variable is specified as the pass rates of *First-time Candidates* in each CPA exam section. All regressions include year-fixed effects, and the standard errors are clustered at the school level. The numbers in parentheses are *t*-statistics. Numbers in parentheses are *t*-statistics based on standard errors clustered at the school level. All variables are defined in Table 7.2.
*, **, and *** correspond to 1%, 5%, and 10% significance levels, respectively.

Table 7.6: Panel B. Results for Pass Rates of All-time Without the Public/Private School Variable and Recession Variable.

	Pass Rates of *All Candidates*				
	(1)	(2)	(3)	(4)	(5)
VARIABLES	PercentPass_All	AUD_PR_All	BEC_PR_All	FAR_PR_All	REG_PR_All
REV_CLSS_noncredit	−0.040	−0.040	−0.048	−0.026	−0.049
	(−1.321)	(−1.469)	(−1.214)	(−0.879)	(−1.424)
REV_CLSS_elective	−0.000	−0.004	−0.004	0.007	0.002
	(−0.001)	(−0.252)	(−0.139)	(0.297)	(0.096)
REV_CLSS_reallocate	0.260***	0.210	0.484*	0.185	0.146
	(1.754)	(1.579)	(2.776)	(1.104)	(1.092)
REV_CLSS_major	−0.057	−0.067**	−0.043	−0.044	−0.078*
	(−1.618)	(−2.272)	(−0.923)	(−1.083)	(−2.688)
REV_CLSS_nocourse	0.001	0.016	0.001	0.002	−0.001
	(0.018)	(0.319)	(0.011)	(0.031)	(−0.015)
REV_CLSS_PROV	−0.015	−0.003	−0.037	−0.029	0.006
	(−0.522)	(−0.107)	(−0.965)	(−0.952)	(0.204)

(*Continued*)

Table 7.6: Panel B. (*Continued*)

	Pass Rates of *All Candidates*				
	(1)	(2)	(3)	(4)	(5)
VARIABLES	PercentPass_All	AUD_PR_All	BEC_PR_All	FAR_PR_All	REG_PR_All
PRGM_LVL	0.007	0.008	−0.007	0.015	0.015
	(0.151)	(0.186)	(−0.130)	(0.309)	(0.379)
TSFR	−0.020	−0.024**	−0.024	−0.021	−0.014
	(−1.521)	(−2.049)	(−1.428)	(−1.534)	(−1.116)
DPT_EXAM	−0.003	−0.017	0.012	0.001	−0.009
	(−0.095)	(−0.668)	(0.342)	(0.041)	(−0.333)
STD_CUR	−0.059**	−0.047**	−0.073**	−0.064**	−0.041***
	(−2.562)	(−2.488)	(−2.484)	(−2.550)	(−1.784)
CRSE_LDR	0.003	0.016	−0.003	−0.004	0.002
	(0.139)	(1.018)	(−0.112)	(−0.179)	(0.096)
AGE (FT)	−0.196***	−0.129	−0.318**	−0.305**	−0.072
	(−1.789)	(−1.332)	(−2.306)	(−2.396)	(−0.662)
AACSB	0.017	0.042***	0.017	−0.006	0.009
	(0.561)	(1.710)	(0.442)	(−0.151)	(0.393)
SAT	0.326***	0.329**	0.503**	0.233	0.202
	(1.898)	(2.114)	(2.461)	(1.200)	(1.303)
Constant	−1.106	−1.376	−1.869	−0.086	−0.665
	(−0.807)	(−1.078)	(−1.137)	(−0.055)	(−0.535)
Observations	852	852	852	852	852
R-squared	0.326	0.232	0.392	0.244	0.155
Cluster school	Yes	Yes	Yes	Yes	Yes
Year FE	Yes	Yes	Yes	Yes	Yes

Notes: This table represents the results of OLS regressions using the same model as in Table 7.5, Panel B, except for the excluding of the public/private school indicator variable and the recession indicator variable. Column (1) includes the results where the dependent variable is defined as the overall CPA exam pass rates of all-time candidates in all four sections, while Columns (2)–(5) present the results where the dependent variable is specified as the pass rates of all-time candidates in each CPA exam section. All regressions include year-fixed effects, and the standard errors are clustered at the school level. The numbers in parentheses are *t*-statistics. Numbers in parentheses are *t*-statistics based on standard errors clustered at the school level. All variables are defined in Table 7.2.
*, **, and *** correspond to 1%, 5%, and 10% significance levels, respectively.

CONCLUSION

Our results partially support the thesis that offering a non-credit CPA review course may have a significant negative effect on pass rates. Our evidence showed this to be true for the *All Candidates* group, but it was not significant for the *First-time* group. As for offering the course as a credit-bearing elective, we found that pass rates were significant and positive for *First-time Candidates* but not for the *All Candidates* group. On the other hand, including the CPA review course but reducing the overall program workload was significant and positively associated with higher CPA pass rates for both groups. The results support the notion that students will devote more time and effort to a credit-bearing CPA course that is embedded into the minimum number of credits required for an accounting degree. In addition, reallocating and reducing the workload within a very intensive accounting curriculum would provide additional time to focus on the CPA exam material. Interestingly, a CPA Review Course provided by outside providers was associated with a lower CPA exam pass rate compared to a CPA Review Course provided by the department.

This chapter has several practical implications for passing the uniform CPA exam for *First Time Candidates* as well as *All Candidates*. For instance, the results strongly suggest that offering a review course for credit significantly improves the chances of CPA exam success. Specifically, our results suggest that offering a review course for credit as an elective and with a workload reduction in the curriculum significantly improves the chances of successfully passing the exam.

This study has various limitations, which may trigger opportunities for future research. For example, despite the relatively large sample surveyed in this study, there was a lack of balance between AACSB and non-AACSB accredited respondents. Perhaps future studies might explore whether the experience of smaller, non-AACSB accredited programs mirrors our finding of a significant impact of embedded CPA review courses in the accounting program. Similarly, our sample did not include any non-US institutions and it is unclear whether students in accounting programs at those institutions might benefit from embedded professional examination review courses in their respective curricula. Thus, a comparative analysis between US and non-US universities might be useful for shedding light on this issue. Furthermore, our study was conducted pre-CPA Evolution and it would be useful to shed more definitive light on the efficacy of embedded CPA review courses in accounting programs post-CPA evolution. Finally, candidate schools are self-reported in the NASBA database. These data are not always accurate, particularly in cases where the candidate transfers from one university to another, completes graduate and undergraduate degrees at different universities, or earns a degree at one university and then completes pre-CPA exam qualifying course work at a different institution. Future researchers might consider addressing these concerns through a longitudinal study of known students from a small sample of universities who take the CPA exams with and without an embedded CPA review course in their respective curricula.

NOTES

1. It is important to note that our study was conducted prior to the announcement and implementation of the 2024 CPA Evolution. As accounting programs review and modify their curricula to accommodate the new exam content and structure, it is possible that the new structure of the exam might add a new dimension to the issues studied in this chapter. An extension of this chapter for future research would include a replication after the CPA evolution is place for several years, which would potentially enable the comparison of candidates' performance pre- and post-CPA evolution.

2. Based on a review of the CPA exam blueprint over our sample period, we conclude that there were no substantial changes in the form and content of the exam.

3. As stated previously, the set of pass rates includes pass rates for two candidate groups: *First-time Candidates* and *All Candidates*, and for each group, we include the pass rates for the overall examination and the individual exam sections.

4. In untabulated analysis, we also repeat our regressions with robust standard errors, and the results are consistent.

ACKNOWLEDGMENT

We would like to thank Rutgers University Research Council for their partial funding of this research study.

REFERENCES

Ashbaugh, D. L., & Thompson, A. F. (1993). Factors distinguishing exceptional performance on the uniform CPA exam. *Journal of Education for Business, 68*(6), 334–337.

Bline, D., Perreault, S., & Zheng, X. (2021). Do grades earned in accounting courses predict performance on related sections of the CPA exam? *Advances in Accounting Education: Teaching and Curriculum Innovations, 25*, 135–153.

Brahmasrene, T., & Whitten, D. (2001). Assessing success on the uniform CPA exam: A logit approach. *Journal of Education for Business, 77*(1), 45–50.

Calderon, T. G., & Nagy, A. L. (2020). A closer look at research on CPA exam success. *Advances in Accounting Education: Teaching and Curriculum Innovations, 24*, 165–178.

Cardona, R. J., Castro-González, K. C., Ríos-Figueroa, C. B., & Vega-Vilca, J. C. (2021). Perceptions of challenges on the CPA exam: Evidence from Puerto Rico. *Advances in Accounting Education: Teaching and Curriculum Innovations, 25*, 177–197.

Grant, C. T., Ciccotello, C. S., Dickie, M. (2002). Barriers to professional entry: How effective is the 150-hour rule? *Journal of Accounting and Public Policy, 21*(1), 71–93.

Howell, C., & Heshizer, B. (2006). AACSB accreditation and success on the uniform CPA exam. *Journal of Applied Business and Economics, 6*(3), 9–17.

Howell, C., & Heshizer, B. (2008). Characteristics that assist future public accountants pass the CPA exam on fewer attempts. *The Journal of Applied Business and Economics, 8*(3), 57.

National Association of State Boards of Accountancy (NASBA). (2006–2019). *Candidate performance on the uniform CPA examination.*

Rudnick, M., & Taylor, V. A. (2004). Do college accounting curriculums teach to the CPA exam? Should they? *Journal of College Teaching & Learning (TLC), 1*(9), 45–48.

Shin, H., Lacina, M., Lee, B. B., & Pan, S. (2020). Schools' CPA review course affiliations and success on the uniform CPA examination. *Journal of Accounting Education, 50*, 100642.

Titard, P. L., Russell, K. A. (1989). Factors affecting CPA examination success. *Accounting Horizons, 3*(3), 53.

Zook, D. R., & Bremser, W. G. (1982). A correlation between the characteristics of candidates and performance on the uniform CPA examination. *Delta Pi Epsilon Journal, 24*(2), 45–52.

CHAPTER 8

DEVELOPING AND ASSESSING WELLBEING IN THE ACCOUNTING CURRICULUM

Matt Bjornsen, Sarah Borchers and Steven Hall

University of Nebraska at Kearney, USA

ABSTRACT

Although the mental and physical health of students on college campuses has been under scrutiny, little has been done at the program level to assess and improve an accounting student's overall wellbeing. This chapter describes a wellbeing program integrated into the curriculum of a small accounting program in the American Midwest. It documents the implementation steps, what was learned from the program, and how it can be used to improve both individual student wellbeing, as well as the accounting program as a whole. Integrating a concern for student wellbeing into our accounting curriculum and creating awareness around the areas of wellbeing has been beneficial for both students and faculty. Students are able to learn about the wellbeing principles and apply them to their lives. Faculty gain insight into the lives of students and are able to understand them better. With that understanding, faculty can alter programs and approaches, which may then help with student retention, and enable students to be better ambassadors for our program and for the accounting profession.

Keywords: Wellbeing; wellness; accounting; curriculum; students; burnout; stress

Although the mental and physical health of students on college campuses has been under scrutiny (Baik et al., 2019; Lipson & Eisenberg, 2018; Long et al., 2021; Stallman, 2011), little has been done at the program level to assess and improve a student's overall wellbeing. College students are at high risk of psychological distress and mental disorders (Baik et al., 2019), and prolonged mental health difficulties are associated with lower motivation, and overall academic dissatisfaction (Lipson & Eisenberg, 2018). Although many universities have taken steps to address students' wellbeing through programs for stress management and improving mental health, the evidence of their success is limited (Long et al., 2021; Stallman, 2011).

Not only are burnout and stress motivating factors for students leaving the accounting profession after graduation, but they also play a role in student decisions to drop the accounting major. In fact, according to Smith et al. (2020),

> Accounting educators worldwide should take note that failing to cultivate coping strategies to reduce stress and burnout among accounting students may lead to voluntary departure from the major and a conspicuous lack of effective workplace coping skills among those who successfully complete their accounting studies and enter the profession. (pp. 77–78)

In addition, job stress and burnout significantly contribute to turnover in the accounting profession (Chong & Monroe, 2015). As the pipeline of Certified Public Accountants (CPAs) shrinks due to baby boomers retiring, declining college enrollments, a lower number of accounting graduates, and CPA exam changes, it is critical that educators play a role early on to increase and retain accounting students (Reisig, 2023). We, faculty of a small accounting program at a state university in the American Midwest, seek to foster an environment that lends itself to improved student wellbeing by focusing on wellbeing at the program level throughout accounting students' courses and experiences. We maintain that our study enables this improvement through increased awareness as well as various tools and programs that students can take with them to be successful long into their careers as accounting professionals.

The remainder of this chapter describes our experience with exposing students to concepts of wellbeing. The next section details how we focused on wellbeing. It is followed by what we learned, and then a conclusion.

HOW WE FOCUSED ON WELLBEING

How Wellbeing Was Integrated into the Curriculum

Our wellbeing initiative grew from our accounting department's AACSB-Accounting initial accreditation process. Through this process, our small faculty came to a consensus that a focus on student mental health was important. Therefore, we decided to make a conscious effort to incorporate a wellbeing component into our accounting curriculum. After researching various options, we opted to use *Wellbeing: The Five Essential Elements* (Rath & Harter, 2010) as the wellbeing-related resource for our classes. We found this book provided the most comprehensive list of wellbeing factors that were the most applicable to our students, in order to give students a more holistic view of wellbeing that can be incorporated into each aspect of their lives. The book is published by Gallup Press, and the information and recommendations it contains are based on surveys and studies that the Gallup organization has conducted over the years. The reputable nature of the Gallup organization was also a factor in the selection of this particular book.[1]

The text covers a wide array of wellbeing concepts and incorporates five distinct areas of wellbeing including career wellbeing, social wellbeing, financial wellbeing, physical wellbeing, and community wellbeing. To cover the material, each of those five areas was assigned to one particular required accounting class. An initial assessment was conducted at the very beginning of Intermediate Accounting I (when students "begin" the accounting major), and a final assessment was provided in Auditing after students had progressed through the accounting program. Each of the wellbeing pillars was then assigned throughout the accounting curriculum in the individual required courses. Physical wellbeing was assigned to Cost Accounting; financial wellbeing was assigned to Accounting Information Systems; community wellbeing was assigned to Tax Accounting; and career wellbeing and social wellbeing were assigned to Intermediate Accounting I. Each instructor had discretion over how the assigned wellbeing area(s) would be integrated into the course.

How Wellbeing Was Assessed

We developed an assessment instrument similar to several that are available in the public domain. After receiving IRB approval as an exempt protocol for secondary data analysis of deidentified data, we asked students to rate themselves relative to ten statements for each of the five areas of wellbeing, for a total of fifty statements.[2] Statements reflect ideas emphasized in the Gallup text. Students were given the following instructions. "Rank each statement on a five-point scale from 1 – This is not at all true for me, to 5 – This is very true for me." If the statement is a positive statement, for example, "I manage my money well," then a 1 is scored as zero points, 2 as 0.25 points, 3 as 0.5 points, 4 as 0.75 points, and 5 as 1 point. If the statement is a negative statement, for example, "I often feel sad and lonely," then the scores are reversed and a response of 1 is scored 1 point and a response of 5 is scored 0. Scores in each area of wellbeing are then summed to get an overall score. Those scores may range from 0 to 10.

An initial assessment of student wellbeing was given early in the student's first Intermediate Accounting class. A final assessment of wellbeing was given in the student's Auditing course which is most often taken in the last semester of the students' undergraduate education. Our hope was that students were able to take what they were learning about wellbeing throughout their college years and improve from their baseline assessment from Intermediate Accounting. One caveat worth mentioning is that in order to encourage honest assessment feedback, we opted to keep it anonymous (students receive credit just for completing it). A resulting limitation is that we are unable to track and compare wellbeing scores on a micro, student-based level.

WHAT WE FOUND

Focusing on the wellbeing of students produces benefits for both our students and our program. Such a wellbeing focus not only improves the individual wellbeing of the students and equips students with valuable life skills as they enter their careers in accounting, but also improves the instructors' understanding of the students as well.

Benefits to the Students

By reviewing students' responses to the wellbeing assignments, we were able to see benefits to students. For example, in Cost Accounting, students were given the following assignment in the online learning management system discussion board:

Read the chapter in your Wellbeing book that examines physical wellbeing.

By the end of February, post on the discussion board something valuable that you learned. If you already knew everything you read, then post about what you thought was most important.

By the end of March, comment something meaningful on the posts of at least two other students.

A sample of the threads students created in response appears below. Student names have been removed, but student writing is unaltered. *Italics* are added for emphasis.

Student 1:

Over the course of the chapter, I found quite a few facts that were *valuable to me in my daily life* as well as important to my mental wellbeing in addition to my physical wellbeing. The most valuable idea that I took from the chapter *and will use in my life in the future* is the fact that exercising is much more effective at getting rid of fatigue than any prescription drug could. I find myself experiencing frequent fatigue after working, so *this knowledge will be very helpful to me in the near future*.

Student 2:

Student 1, I took my capstone class on the Science of Play, which talks a lot about how exercise or playing some type of game that you enjoy can benefit your mental and physical health. I liked how you said "exercising is much more effective at getting rid of fatigue than any prescription drug could" because that is something that I learned in the capstone course when it came to depression, anxiety, and stress. Today, many do take prescriptions thinking they'll be the cure-all, however, adding more time for exercise may just be the thing that works. Good post!

Student 3:

Student 1, I agree that being active is a great way to get rid of fatigue. On days that I am active I find myself less likely to feel tired or drowsy during the day. I try to get in some activity every day when I can so I can feel better throughout the day.

Student 4:

The physical wellbeing chapter taught me that getting enough exercise, sleeping enough, and eating healthy is crucial for a good lifestyle. Unfortunately, I was unaware of how important these three things were for my wellbeing. Another valuable piece of information that I learned was that our choices could genetically influence our children. For example, I didn't know that being malnourished as an adolescent puts my future children at a higher risk of having heart disease. *The reading also left me motivated to start the process of embracing a more active lifestyle*. It is nice to see that only 20 minutes of exercise are more than enough to boost my mood. I also didn't know that exercise is an excellent supplement to help combat fatigue. *I also plan to get 8 hours of sleep every night* because it helps a lot with processing information and waking up with lots of energy.

Student 1:

Hello Student 4! The knowledge and the eye-opening realization that the choices we make about our physical wellbeing today have profound impacts upon our future generations was honestly a little bit frightening to me, personally. But when one takes these facts into account in the form of their daily nutrition and exercise habits, healthy lifestyles can be achieved by all those impacted by such decisions. The biggest relief that can be acknowledged is the fact that one can always work to improve their physical wellbeing with a bit of time and effort. Sleep and dietary nutrition are key to my own physical wellbeing, and I hope you can make strides in the account of your own by increasing the hours of sleep you are getting and the time you spend exercising as well.

Student 2:

Student 4, before college, I never really cared how much sleep I got, thinking that as long as I'm in bed at a somewhat reasonable time, I'll be fine. I'll be honest, college provided me with a wake-up call in realizing how getting enough sleep can benefit me every day. Like you said in your post, sleeping helps to process and retain information which is crucial to getting good grades, and it helps with overall energy levels because you never know what the day might throw at you. Good points!

Student 5:

Student 4, I was also shocked by the fact that early health issues could translate to generations down the line. I was also interested in the fact that 20 minutes of exercise a day can have such a lasting impact on health, energy, and mood. *I took these facts to heart and will accustom my lifestyle to the facts I learned.* I do recommend 8 hours of sleep, though. I can't function without it.

Student 6:

Student 4, I also was surprised to learn that even 20 minutes of exercise can boost my mood and help me combat fatigue. I thought exercise would make me feel more tired and unmotivated. *I've decided to incorporate more exercise into my life as well. I also plan on getting at least seven or eight hours of sleep.* When I sleep less than seven hours, I feel tired and struggle to get anything done. I believe making these changes to our routines will help us develop a better lifestyle overall.

Student 5:

After reading the physical wellbeing portion of the book, I found many interesting things. The most interesting, to me, was the fact that leading a healthy lifestyle isn't just a health-conscious decision, but a financial one. For example, the book outlines that healthcare alone equates to 16% of the total economy and that number is only climbing. On top of that, 62% of all bankruptcies were related to health issues in 2007. While the physical wellbeing of a person is more inclined toward health, it was interesting how it held a financial impact as well.

Student 3:

Student 5, I would agree that a healthy lifestyle can also affect your financial health. I feel that a healthy lifestyle can affect your decision making throughout the day. Being healthy can lead to better financial and future decisions. I would not have thought about that if you had not brought it up. Thank you!

Student 7:

Hello, Student 6. It is shocking how much of the total economy is related to health concerns. People sometimes justify eating unhealthy foods because "healthy foods are too expensive." However, it is better to pay a little more now for healthy foods than to pay a lot later due to unhealthy food decisions.

Student 6:

Student 5, the correlation between the economy and overall physical health is both shocking and not shocking at the same time. Usually with poor financial health comes more stress, and more stress leads to poor physical health. The numbers are shocking though. Luckily, I think our culture is becoming more and more health conscious about what we put into our bodies and how we regulate stress.

Several things can be learned from these student responses. First, students are learning things about physical wellbeing. Second, they are making the connection to their own personal lives. Third, they are applying or making plans to apply the things they have learned. They are doing this while never being asked to make the connections to their personal lives nor to apply what they learned. Based on the findings presented in Table 8.1, it appears that the most significant improvements during the accounting program were seen in the areas of financial and community wellbeing. In no cases did wellbeing significantly decline over the time period, which, in itself, could be considered a student victory, as student responsibilities and stressors tend to increase as they progress further into the accounting major. As this initiative is in its early stages, we will continue to evaluate and look for emerging trends and make adjustments as necessary. Overall, from these replies, we can conclude that the exercise has done some good and has had a positive impact on the students.

Benefits to the Program

Through our focus on student wellbeing, we learned some significant things about our students. Some of the things we learned can help us alter our program in new ways to address student needs. Others would be better addressed at the college level, and there are others that will simply help us better understand and connect with our students.

Assessment results improve our understanding of our students. Due to the categorically repetitive nature of the survey questions within each pillar of wellbeing, for brevity purposes, selected assessment results are presented in Table 8.1. Average scores on the assessment instrument reveal some interesting things about our students.

For example, when it comes to career wellbeing, the students that are in their last semester enjoy what they do every day and feel they are treated with respect. On the other hand, they have a lot of stress in their lives. Although faculty have heard this anecdotally, seeing this consistently expressed by students indicates that it is an area to be addressed going forward, not only to help students in their college careers, but to also give them tools to help them in their professional careers after college.

In the area of social wellbeing, the most positive results indicate that students in their last semester feel they have someone they can count on and have a lot of love in their lives. On the flip side, the lowest score was relative to religion being an important part of their daily lives. We also find the scores to be somewhat low for having a group where they belong and for feeling sad and lonely.

Table 8.1. Self-assessment of Wellbeing.

	Intermediate #	Intermediate Score	Auditing #	Auditing Score	t-stat	p-Value
Career Wellbeing	27	6.60	26	6.86	0.652	0.259
I like what I do each day	27	0.67	26	0.71	0.784	0.218
I am treated with respect every day	27	0.68	26	0.73	1.259	0.107
I have a lot of stress in my life	27	0.38	26	0.30	−0.929	0.179
Social Wellbeing	26	7.07	26	6.89	−0.697	0.269
If I were in trouble, I have someone I can count on	27	0.92	26	0.87	−1.232	0.112
Religion is an important part of my daily life	26	0.52	26	0.48	−0.102	0.460
I have a lot of love in my life	27	0.82	26	0.78	−0.517	0.304
I have a group where I belong, where I am accepted	27	0.74	26	0.65	−0.935	0.177
I often feel sad or lonely	27	0.63	26	0.64	0.063	0.475
Financial Wellbeing	27	5.38	26	6.64	5.026	**0.000**
I am satisfied with my standard of living and all the things I can buy and do	27	0.70	26	0.76	1.006	0.160
There have been times in the last year when I did not have enough money to buy food that I or my family needed	27	0.75	26	0.92	1.808	**0.039**
I will have enough money in the future	27	0.61	26	0.70	1.158	0.126
I manage my money well	27	0.73	26	0.77	0.712	0.240
I have worried about money in the last few days	27	0.61	26	0.66	0.652	0.259
Physical Wellbeing	27	6.26	26	6.14	−0.296	0.384
During the last month, poor health did not keep me from doing my usual activities on any day	27	0.69	26	0.73	0.200	0.421
I feel good about my physical appearance	27	0.57	26	0.49	−0.739	0.232
I exercise regularly because I am health conscious	27	0.60	26	0.62	0.543	0.295
I have a very healthy diet	27	0.40	26	0.42	0.295	0.197
I have had a lot of energy every day this last week	27	0.43	26	0.47	0.766	0.224
Community Wellbeing	27	6.06	26	6.48	0.930	0.178
I feel safe walking alone at night in the community where I live	27	0.54	26	0.73	1.569	**0.061**
If a neighbor found my wallet or purse that contained items of great value to me, I think it would be returned with its contents	27	0.56	26	0.68	1.283	0.103
The place where I live is perfect for me	27	0.55	26	0.55	0.483	0.315
I always feel safe and secure	27	0.66	26	0.71	0.916	0.182

Notes: This table presents wellbeing scores from each category of wellbeing, as well as scores for select questions within each area. The number of respondents is indicated as well. An initial assessment was conducted at the very beginning of Intermediate Accounting I (when students "begin" the accounting major), and a final assessment was provided in Auditing after students had progressed through the accounting program. The *t*-statistics and *p*-values provided represent the significance in the change in scores from between the beginning of the accounting major and the end of the accounting major. Bold values represent significance at the 0.10 level or better.

Students in their final semester have greater financial wellbeing than students who are starting out in accounting. By their last semester, most of these students have had accounting internships where they have been compensated better than they have ever been before. Many of them will also have full-time positions lined up for after graduation. Their financial futures will likely be much more secure and tangible than they were when they originally took the wellbeing assessment.

Relative to physical wellbeing, the majority of the students do not have health problems that keep them from doing daily activities; however, they are not all living healthy lifestyles. The majority do not eat a healthy diet, are lacking energy, and do not feel good about their physical appearance. Results indicate there may be room for improvement in the areas of physical wellbeing.

Finally, students at the end of their college careers seem to have greater community wellbeing than those starting out. One could speculate that this could be the result of living off campus, being more plugged into the community as they get older and more involved, or it could even be the result of having greater financial means to enhance their living conditions.

When educators better understand students, they are better able to help them succeed (Aljohani, 2016). In reviewing the results, it becomes evident that there are several areas where faculty could help students to be more successful. For example, it is concerning that thirty percent of our students (see Table 8.1) did not give a positive score to the statement "I have a group where I belong and feel accepted" (i.e., a four or a five rating). In addition, for those students that do have a group where they belong, it is unclear whether that group is associated with the university. While we have an innate desire that our students feel like they belong, we are also aware that integration into the academic and social systems of the institution is one of the greatest predictors of student retention (Aljohani, 2016). Remedies might include more social time in accounting club meetings, meaningful service activities, more group discussions in class, and/or more interaction with faculty. Creating a community among students through peer learning or participation in faculty mentorships may prove to be beneficial to students. For example, Kern and Kingsbury (2019) find that the likelihood of returning the following semester doubles for students in learning communities, as compared to those not living in learning communities. Accordingly, a best practice may be for faculty to proactively encourage students to consider living in a learning community if offered at the institution.

It is not surprising that student responses indicate high levels of stress. Some may speculate that college students' stress levels are at an all-time high. Further, students in the field of accounting may experience greater stress than others throughout their college years as well as into their careers. Accounting students face various impactful life choices very early in their college experience such as whether to complete an internship, pursue a master's degree as a path toward the 150 credit hour requirement for licensure (Barrios, 2022), explore private or public accounting, or sit for the CPA exam. In our experience at our institution, accounting courses are often some of the most challenging in the business college and attract some of the most dedicated and brightest students who are used to doing very well academically, creating an environment rich in stress.

According to the 2023 AICPA trends report, the supply of accounting graduates has been trending downward for both bachelor's and master's levels, while the demand for accounting graduates has steadily been trending upward (American Institute of Certified Public Accountants, 2023). Given the burnout and turnover rates found in the accounting profession, the increase in those reaching retirement age, and the decreasing supply of accounting graduates, it is arguably more important than ever that accounting students develop a skillset to deal with the ever-increasing challenges of the profession.

At our institution, we provide training and activities to help students get their first job and transition into the professional accounting world. We help them with resume writing, networking opportunities, social and communication skills, interviewing, and other related skills. Perhaps it would also be beneficial to add stress management skills to the list. For example, one option would be to bring in a qualified, licensed expert in this area (potentially from the counseling/psychology department) to speak with accounting students about stress management skills.

CONCLUSION

Integrating a concern for student wellbeing into our accounting curriculum has produced benefits for our students and for our program. Creating awareness around the areas of wellbeing has been extremely beneficial for both students and faculty. Students are able to learn and apply the principles of wellbeing to their lives. Faculty gain insight into the lives of students and are able to understand them better. With that understanding, faculty can alter programs and approaches in order to help students where they struggle. Doing so should also help with retention in the accounting program and at the university. If we are able to help them be healthier in these five areas of wellbeing and if they have a more positive experience overall, we think that they will also be better ambassadors for our program and for the accounting profession.

We recognize our chapter is not without limitations. As it is beyond the scope of our study, the benefits we suggest are not assessed empirically, nor have we linked stress management with student performance in accounting. Also, while we were able to develop consensus at our institution for helping students to be more stress-aware, this could be more challenging at other larger institutions as there may not be agreement in faculty roles and responsibilities. These limitations offer opportunities for future research in this area.

NOTES

1. For example, Gallup. (2023) has over 80 years of data collection experience, spanning 160 countries, and is trusted by over 90% of Fortune 500 companies.
2. We adapted our statement and rating system from Gallup's Wellbeing Finder.

REFERENCES

Aljohani, O. (2016). A comprehensive review of the major studies and theoretical models of student retention in higher education. *Higher Education Studies, 6*(2), 1–18.

American Institute of Certified Public Accountants (AICPA). (2023). *2023 trends*. Retrieved October 18, 2023, from https://www.aicpa-cima.com/professional-insights/download/2023-trends-report

Baik, C., Larcombe, W., & Brooker, A. (2019). How Universities can enhance student mental wellbeing: The student perspective. *Higher Education Research and Development, 38*(4), 674–687.

Barrios, J. M. (2022). Occupational licensing and accountant quality: Evidence from the 150-hour rule. *Journal of Accounting Research, 60*(1), 3–43.

Chong, V., & Monroe, G. (2015). The impact of the antecedents and consequences of job burnout on junior accountants' turnover intentions: A structural equation modelling approach. *Accounting & Finance, 55*(1), 105–132.

Gallup. (2023). *Gallup*. Retrieved April 18, 2023, from https://www.gallup.com/corporate/212381/pressing-problems-solved.aspx

Kern, B., & Kingsbury, T. (2019). Curricular learning communities and retention. *Journal of the Scholarship of Teaching and Learning, 19*(1), 41–52. https://doi.org/10.14434/josotl.v19i1.26779

Lipson, S., & Eisenberg, D. (2018). Mental health and academic attitudes and expectations in University populations: Results from the healthy minds study. *Journal of Mental Health, 27*(3), 205–213.

Long, R., Halvorson, M., & Lengua, L. J. (2021). A mindfulness-based promotive coping program improves wellbeing in college undergraduates. *Anxiety, Stress, & Coping, 34*(6), 690–703.

Rath, T., & Harter, J. (2010). *Wellbeing: The five essential elements*. Gallup Press.

Reisig, R. (2023). *The more things change, the more they stay the same: Addressing the CPA pipeline crisis*. National Association of State Boards of Accountancy. Retrieved April 18, 2023, from https://nasba.org/blog/2023/03/14/addressing-the-cpa-pipeline-crisis/

Smith, K., Haight, T., Emerson, D., Mauldin, S., & Wood, B. (2020). Resilience as a coping strategy for reducing departure intentions of accounting students. *Accounting Education, 29*(1), 77–108.

Stallman, H. M. (2011). Embedding resilience within the tertiary curriculum: A feasibility study. *Higher Education Research & Development, 30*(2), 121–133.

THEME 4

PERSPECTIVES ON ACCOUNTING THEORY AND INTEGRATED THINKING AND LEARNING

CHAPTER 9

A MODEL TO DEVELOP INTEGRATED THINKING SKILLS OF PROSPECTIVE PROFESSIONAL ACCOUNTANTS

Erica du Toit, Ben Marx and Rozanne Smith

University of Johannesburg, South Africa

ABSTRACT

The International Integrated Reporting Council introduced the concept of integrated thinking skills to the accounting world overall. This study uses a constructivist approach to address the development of integrated thinking skills for future professional accountants during higher education. This issue is relevant as many professional accounting bodies expect that integrated thinking skills are developed during the higher education of prospective professional accountants. Despite this expectation, there is limited guidance available to academics in the accounting education field to do so. By means of a literature review as well as an empirical study, this chapter develops a constructivist model that can be used by academics to develop integrated thinking skills during the higher education of prospective professional accountants. The model addresses the foundation, appropriate pedagogies, disciplinarity type, and point of introduction of integrated thinking principles in accounting education.

Keywords: Constructivist approach; higher education; integrated thinking and learning; inter-disciplinary; professional accountant skills and abilities; South African accounting academics; trans-disciplinary

The research question that this study strives to address is: "How can integrated thinking skills be developed in higher education for future professional accountants?" This research question is relevant as many professional accounting bodies expect that integrated thinking skills are developed during the higher education of prospective professional accountants. Despite this expectation, there is limited guidance available to academics in the accounting education field to do just this. By means of a literature review as well as an empirical study, this study develops a model that can be used by academics to develop integrated thinking skills during the higher education of prospective professional accountants.

From a professional accounting perspective, the concept of integrated thinking gained significant popularity when the International Integrated Reporting Council (IIRC) published the International Integrated Reporting <IR> Framework toward the end of 2013, which introduced a novel approach to corporate disclosure. The IIRC states that integrated thinking contributes to integrated decision-making and activities that address value generation, preservation, and erosion in the short-, medium-, and long-term (IIRC, 2021). This definition demarcates integrated thinking purely from an organizational perspective.

The reform of higher education to embody integrated thinking starts with an intentional teacher who is continuously questioning, observing, and aware of their teaching methods (Chaves, 2006; Duke, 2013; Ginsburg-Block et al., 2006; VanLehn, 2011). If teachers do not master the art of integrated thinking themselves, they can never hope to embed this quality in their students (Blackshields et al., 2015). Traditional teaching methods (Qureshi & Stormyhr, 2012; VanLehn, 2011) in higher education have led to narrow specialism (Holley, 2017), delving deep to try and answer the questions of an insatiable audience. This specialist knowledge has a narrow endpoint with several side effects, such as compartmentalization, fragmentation, and detachment (Klein, 2005). In a post-normal world with massive complexity and an ever-faster rate of change, these side effects have become even more pronounced and worrying (Blackshields et al., 2015). Contemporary society requires students to cooperate, apply higher order thinking abilities to real-world problems, manage cultural complexity, and make meaningful connections across disciplines, which calls for a fundamental shift in current characterized teaching and learning (Boix Mansilla, 2008). The teaching and learning of integrated thinking skills play a significant role in overcoming the previous century's knowledge fragmentation in order to provide a grounded education that is relevant and appropriate for contemporary life (Boix Mansilla, 2008). Consequently, integrated teaching and learning is a diverse and all-encompassing method focused on the learner that aims to correlate different viewpoints, foster an inter-/trans-disciplinary mindset, construct integrated systems of knowledge, and apply them in real-world settings. The 21st century skills are also related to integrated learning (Ignjatović, 2020).

The concept of integrated thinking is still evasive and only gained popularity as a research topic in recent years (Adams, 2017; Maroun et al., 2022; McGuigan et al., 2020). There are numerous practitioner publications relating to integrated thinking published by professional accounting bodies, such as the International Federation of Accountants (IFAC, 2015), the Chartered Institute of Management

Accountants (CIMA, 2014), the IIRC (2020), and the South African Institute of Chartered Accountants (SAICA, 2015, 2021), but despite their significant value, these sources cannot replace the thorough, independent study carried out by scholars (Maroun et al., 2022). Most of the academic research relating to integrated thinking deals with the concept at the organizational level (Busco et al., 2021; Dumay & Dai, 2017; Guthrie & Parker, 2016), and there remains a significant void in the research on the development of integrated thinking on an individual level (Lorson & Paschke, 2015; McGuigan et al., 2020).

Despite the above void in the literature, many professional accounting bodies are now turning toward higher education institutions to develop integrated thinking skills in students who are prospective professional accountants. There is a need for guidance on exactly how higher education institutions should go about developing integrated thinking skills in their students. The purpose of this study is to develop a model that lecturers[1] can use to develop integrated thinking skills in students studying toward a professional accounting designation. The contribution that this study makes is to provide structured guidance to academics regarding the most effective manner to develop integrated thinking skills in students. This study addresses a gap in the literature in that it specifically relates to the development of integrated thinking skills in the accounting education field and not just education in general.

The study is structured as follows: a literature review section that discusses the underpinning components of the developed model; a method and findings section that describes how the empirical portion of the study was conducted and presents the empirical findings, followed by the proposed constructivist model; and a final section that presents conclusions, recommendations, and opportunities for further research.

LITERATURE REVIEW

The Current State of Accounting Education

The role of a professional accountant has changed significantly due to Industry 4.0, Industry 5.0, and the COVID-19 pandemic (Du Toit et al., 2023). The professional accountant of today and the future requires a different skill set than before (Tavares et al., 2022). Incorporating the principles of the International <IR> Framework into the accounting education curriculum is not a case of copy and paste, but intentional learning strategies that model integrated ways of thinking (McGuigan et al., 2020). There are significant criticisms of modern accounting education in that the higher education curriculum is too technically orientated and that students do not obtain the vocational nor personal skills they need for an ambiguous and fast-changing business world where the role of the professional accountant has changed significantly (Gittings et al., 2020; Hassall & Joyce, 2014). The focus of accounting education needs to shift to preparing students for complexity, ambiguity, and uncertainty (McGuigan, 2021). By broadening the accounting education curriculum, that is, an increased focus on professional skills, values, and ethics; there is less of a technical focus and a greater emphasis is placed on conceptual understanding (McGuigan, 2021). The manner in which accounting degrees are currently structured divides a comprehensive subject into manageable units that are taught separately (McGuigan & Kern, 2016). With this cookie-cutter method (McGuigan & Kern, 2015), students fail to recognize the links and relationships in accounting education and instead perceive it as a technical and impartial discipline (McGuigan & Kern, 2016). Hence to move forward in accounting education, a great deal of unlearning by both lecturers and students is required (McGuigan, 2021). The development of critical thinking skills has received a lot of attention in the accounting education field for many years. However, it is important to understand that integrated thinking and learning are not the same as critical thinking although integrated thinking requires students to think critically (see Du Toit et al., 2024, for a contrast of these two related concepts).

Globally, accounting education is heavily influenced by and connected with several professional bodies, such as IFAC, the Association of Chartered Certified Accountants (ACCA), the International Accounting Education Standards Board (IAESB), and country specific professional bodies (Rodgers et al., 2017). In South Africa, the SAICA accredited undergraduate and postgraduate curriculums at universities are prescribed by the SAICA Competency Framework. The designation Chartered Accountant – South Africa (CA(SA)), cannot be obtained unless an individual meets all prescribed competencies as determined by the SAICA Competency Framework. The vast amount of knowledge required by professional bodies, namely SAICA in South Africa, leads to teaching at higher educational level having an extremely technical focus (De Villiers & Venter, 2010). Many view the list of skills that accounting professional bodies require of entry level accountants as excessive and state that the majority of senior executives do not even possess all of these skills (Rebele & Pierre, 2019). Educators frequently forget, or simply do not have time, to connect and integrate (for instance) the tax elements of a transaction to its accounting, financial, or economic ramifications in their attempt to cover every computational rule that could affect a calculation (Bayerlein, 2014). Although lecturers have limited control over the technical content of the curriculum due to accreditation requirements, the delivery mode of the content is within the control of lecturers (Van Oordt & Mulder, 2016). It is thus crucial that lecturers make use of a creative combination of student-centered pedagogies to facilitate integrated learning and thinking.

The empirical part of this study took place in South Africa where the Heads of Department of all SAICA accredited universities participated in a questionnaire to provide their views on the development of integrated thinking skills. The higher education of prospective Chartered Accountants in South Africa is structured as follows:

- A three-year undergraduate qualification at a SAICA accredited university, followed by;
- A one-year postgraduate qualification at a SAICA accredited university. The postgraduate qualification is referred to as the Postgraduate Diploma in Accounting (PGDA).

In this study, reference will be made to both professional accountants and CAs(SA). All CAs(SA) are professional accountants, as IFAC defines a professional accountant as a person who is a member of an IFAC member body (Rutherford, 2011). Thus although the study is based on the South African model of developing professional accountants, the study is also applicable to professional accountants at large.

The model developed in this study is built on the following foundations: constructivism, the development of creativity, and a blended teaching and learning approach. The literature relating to these three concepts is discussed below.

Foundation of Model

Constructivism
Constructivist teaching and learning methods are associated with integrated thinking abilities and many academic researchers firmly believe that a constructivist approach is a prerequisite for the successful development of integrated thinking skills (Higgs et al., 2010; Klein, 2006; Lima et al., 2004; Quattrone, 2000). Students should be taught how to be curious and receptive to innovative ideas, as well as how to think creatively and process other metacognitive skills (Scheer et al., 2012). According to constructivism, learning should be self-directed, innovative, creative, and focused on the individual learner, and learning should be a process of ongoing adaptation to circumstances that involve shifting relationships between subject, object, and context (Lattemann & Fritz, 2014). There is no denying that universities today lack a multi-epistemic process and that the focus of education today is on individual subjects and specialized disciplines (Eagen et al., 2010; Lattemann & Fritz, 2014). The traditional teacher-centered approach, which discourages the use of higher order thinking skills, nevertheless predominates in classrooms and assessment procedures despite the emphasis on the constructivist approach in higher education institutions (Lombard & Grosser, 2008). The constructivist theory is predicated on the notion that individuals build their own knowledge based on their own experiences (Duffy & Cunningham, 1996; Stentoft, 2017) as opposed to being fed information passively by a lecturer. Constructivism is successful because it equips students to solve complex problems in a complex world (Crawford & Jenkins, 2018). Integrated and inter-disciplinary teaching challenges the traditional roles of lecturers and students as the conventional functions of teachers (i.e., directing and telling) are replaced by the functions of mentor, facilitator, and mediator (Klein, 2005).

The pedagogies alluded to in this study are all constructivist in nature. Interdisciplinary learning is influenced and shaped by the readiness of the students as well as their prior academic and professional experiences (Ashby & Exter, 2019). Students enter learning with prior theories or experiences relating to the topic being studied and although invisible, these prior theories frame and shape the added information received (Bransford et al., 2000). If students' original understanding is not engaged, they may not understand the innovative ideas and material being taught, or they may learn them for assessment purposes only, returning to their initial understanding outside of the classroom (National Research

Council, 2000). The implication of the above is of course that lecturers need to draw out these pre-existing and original understandings and build on them during the lecture (National Research Council, 2000).

Development of Creativity
The absence of creative abilities in higher education, according to contemporary educationalists, is personally, professionally, and socially restrictive (Dewey, 2009). Without creativity, problem-solving and integrated thinking becomes an impossible task (Blackshields et al., 2015). Literature claims that teaching should be more artistic than procedural, more reactive than proactive (Dewey, 2016; Herr, 2015) and that the purpose of education is to help students respond not only critically, but also creatively to the problems they are presented with (Herr, 2015; Reed, 1997). Students are expected to take a creative approach to their education by putting a significant emphasis on constructivist-based pedagogical design and reflective practice in accounting education (McGuigan & Kern, 2016). They are asked to actively create their own learning, unlearning, and relearning of accounting (McGuigan & Kern, 2016). Students are prepared for an uncertain future in which creativity, resilience, agility, flexibility, and integrated cognition will be crucial and highly valuable qualities (Davies et al., 2011). From a dispositional perspective, creativity includes a variety of attitudes that include the willingness to take risks, learn from mistakes, and search for solutions outside of a specific discipline (Amabile et al., 1996). This is exactly what is required of students if a problem is to be solved in an integrated manner. Although it is helpful if a student has a natural aptitude for this type of creative thinking, it is vital that creative practice is modeled by lecturers to further develop and promote integrative thinking (Blackshields et al., 2015).

From a professional accountant perspective, there is a firm expectation that accounting graduates are innovative, creative, and integrated problem solvers (Lawson et al., 2014). However, despite these firm expectations, creativity is not traditionally associated with professional accountants (Rossetto & Chapple, 2019). Accounting is often stereotyped as a black and white world where there is only one correct answer using stringent rules. However, professional accountants are expected to exercise their judgment when solving ill-structured and complex problems among many shades of gray (Pathways Commission, 2015).

Blended Teaching and Learning Approach
In an era where academic programs in higher education are expanding their reliance on technology, an important question that needs to be addressed is whether a blended teaching and learning environment supports the development of integrated thinking skills. A blended teaching and learning approach should put students at the center of curriculum planning and promote their ability to learn independently (Chigeza & Halbert, 2014). If this is done, blended learning becomes constructivist in nature and students are able to build and construct their own knowledge through their personal experience in this manner active learning takes place; thus, this is considered to be truly student-centered in nature

(Abraham & Jones, 2016; Crawford & Jenkins, 2018; Russo et al., 2022). To accomplish this strategic objective and meet the expectations of a diverse student body, higher education institutions cannot ignore technology, especially because technology-rich classrooms have been proven to improve students' academic performance (Donnelly, 2010). In addition to the above, a blended teaching and learning approach provides the necessary pedagogical innovation to address the multiple learning preferences of an increasingly diverse student body globally (Mihret et al., 2017). A blended teaching and learning approach assists in optimizing face-to-face contact time as theoretical components can be dealt with by using Information and Communication Tools (ICT), such as podcasts, vodcasts, and voice-over PowerPoints (Van Oordt & Mulder, 2016).

According to the literature, many of the pedagogies used to enhance integrated thinking in higher education, as described in this study, can successfully be used in a blended teaching and learning setting, such as problem-based learning (Donnelly, 2010), e-portfolios (Blackshields et al., 2015), flipped classroom (Danker, 2015), and capstone courses (Muhammad et al., 2021). Several researchers indicated that a blended learning approach can assist in the development of integrated thinking skills (Blessinger & Wankel, 2013; McDonald et al., 2021; Swan, 2009).

The model developed in this study indicates the appropriateness of the various levels of inter-disciplinarity in each academic year. Further discussion of inter-disciplinarity appears below.

Inter-disciplinarity

In today's complex and globally connected society, problems "rarely arise within orderly disciplinary categories, and neither do their solutions" (Palmer, 2001, p. vii). However, many graduates lack the necessary skills to effectively synthesize multiple disciplinary fields. An inter-disciplinary learning environment can provide the necessary tools for students to solve ill-structured problems that stretch across more than one discipline (Ashby & Exter, 2019). Inter-disciplinary education refers to the integration of knowledge from various disciplines to address complex problems that are unsolvable from a single disciplinary perspective (Boix Mansilla, 2016; Holley, 2017).

A particularly important ability that an intentional integrated teaching and learning approach will assist with, is the concept of transfer. That is, the ability to apply knowledge acquired in one discipline to solve a new dissimilar problem in another (McLoughlin & Finlayson, 2015). Studies to date show a disconcerting but consistent finding that transfer is, in fact, even more difficult than might have been considered (Galoyan & Betts, 2021; McLoughlin & Finlayson, 2015). An inter-disciplinary approach in higher education is also viewed as an effective way of developing creativity, teamwork, and innovation (Ashby & Exter, 2019; Haynes, 2017).

The Differences Between Integrated Learning and Inter-disciplinarity

Inter-disciplinarity is closely linked to the concept of integrated learning and can be seen as a subset of integrated learning (Ashby & Exter, 2019; Klein, 2005). Integrated learning is a broader concept than inter-disciplinarity and is an overarching concept that includes frameworks, strategies, and exercises that span a variety of divides, including introductory and advanced levels, general education and the majors, classroom experiences, experiences out of the classroom, theory and practice, and disciplines (Klein, 2005; Leonard, 2012). Contrastingly, inter-disciplinarity refers exclusively to the subset of integrated learning where the focus is solely on the fusion of disciplines (Ashby & Exter, 2019). One of the stated objectives of inter-disciplinary learning is the development of integrated thinking skills (Mino, 2013) and inter-disciplinary courses undergo a fundamental shift when both instructors and students participate in the process of synthesizing new knowledge (Armstrong, 1980).

Typology of Disciplinarity

It is important to distinguish between the most common forms of disciplinarity, that is, intra-disciplinarity, multi-disciplinarity, cross-disciplinarity, inter-disciplinarity, and trans-disciplinarity. It is vital to make this distinction because transitioning from the most common approach to teaching and learning (intra-disciplinary) to one that offers the most potential for integrated thinking and learning (trans-disciplinary) necessitates a scaffolded and structured approach that requires an understanding of the underpinning differences. Table 9.1 highlights differences that could be expected as one transitions from intra-disciplinary to trans-disciplinary approaches to teaching and learning.

The difference between inter- and trans-disciplinarity is opaque and sometimes these two terms are used interchangeably (Stentoft, 2017). Although integrated thinking and inter-disciplinarity are often used interchangeably in the literature (McLoughlin & Finlayson, 2015; Sill, 1996; Woodside et al., 2020), from the respective definitions of inter-disciplinarity and trans-disciplinarity, it is clear that integrated thinking skills will be developed more successfully in a trans-disciplinary approach seeing that this approach moves beyond the field of disciplinarity and also integrates the domain beyond mere disciplines (Hampson, 2013; McGuigan, 2021; Sill, 1996). Typically, from a professional accountant's perspective, this would imply the incorporation of business, relational, and digital acumen into the curriculum.

From Table 9.1, which shows a typology of disciplinarity, it can be concluded that teaching and learning in an integrated manner is achieved by using a range of different "disciplinarities" (Ignjatović, 2020). Ultimately, a combination of inter-disciplinarity and trans-disciplinarity will be the most effective approach of developing integrated thinking skills (Klein, 2005; Leicht et al., 2018; Newell, 1999). Literature suggests that an integrated teaching and learning model should be implemented in stages (Bloom, 2014; McComas, 2009). From the above, it can be reasoned that undergraduate students start with an intra-disciplinarity approach and then progress to multi-disciplinarity, cross-disciplinarity, inter-disciplinarity, and finally, trans-disciplinarity.

The model developed in this study will refer to the point of introduction of integrated thinking skills during higher education. The relevant literature pertaining to this issue will be discussed hereunder.

Table 9.1. A Typology of Disciplinarity.

Disciplinarity Type	Brief Description	Distinguishing Aspects
Intra-disciplinarity	Teaching and learning within a singular discipline which usually includes several subdisciplines (Miller, 2010)	• Focus is on a single discipline. • Discipline-based curriculum with foundational and specialized courses (UNESCO-IBE, 2013)
Multi-disciplinarity	Disciplines are seen as parallel units with no integration (Klein, 2005). Team-teaching lacks integration (Holley, 2017)	• Encyclopaedic approach (Holley, 2017) • With team teaching each lecturer offers a separate perspective and connects their own discipline to the theme (Drake, 1991)
Cross-disciplinarity	Borrowing of theories, ideas, and tools from another discipline to help delineate a specific problem (Klein, 2010; Lattuca et al., 2004)	• Contributing discipline is passive and lecturers from different disciplines maintain their own epistemology (Holley, 2017) • Easy to embed in course as it does not require significant design or change (Ashby & Exter, 2019)
Inter-disciplinarity	Truly integrated pedagogy as knowledge from disparate disciplines is integrated to arrive at an outcome that is not doable if a solitary discipline is used (Holley, 2017)	• Team teaching is truly collaborative and focuses on the synthesis of disciplines (Klein, 2005) • Discussions are question-, theme- or problem-based (Klein, 2005)
Trans-disciplinarity	Synthesis of disciplines to the point where knowledge can no longer be attributed to a single discipline (Ashby & Exter, 2019; Holley, 2017)	• Knowledge is co-constructed and entails collaboration with the community and other stakeholders (Lattuca et al., 2004) • Moves beyond the field of disciplinarity and integrates the domain beyond mere disciplines (Hampson, 2013)

Introduction of Integrated Thinking Skills During Higher Education

Undergraduate and Postgraduate Integration and Inter-disciplinarity

It makes sense that the development of integrated thinking skills is easier in a postgraduate environment as postgraduate students have an undergraduate foundation with an abundance of prior learning experience and a depth of knowledge (Holley, 2017). On the other hand, undergraduate students lack a depth of knowledge and experience integration and inter-disciplinarity at a much lower cognitive level (Holley, 2017; Rodgers et al., 2017). Despite the above, William H. Newell, an influential expert in the field of inter-disciplinarity and integration, strongly suggests that students should be introduced to inter-disciplinary coursework in their first year of higher education as this will encourage an openness to different thinking styles from the onset (Newell, 2001). Inter-disciplinary integration can and should take place at the undergraduate level (Abbott & Nantz, 2012; Newell, 2006). In fact, inter-disciplinarity is becoming particularly popular at the undergraduate level (Holley, 2017). The depth of integration and inter-disciplinarity will of course differ from undergraduate to postgraduate and at undergraduate level it is more about identifying and understanding a problem rather than solving it (Castellana, 2005). In the accounting discipline, there is often a tendency to seek solutions and accordingly, students are presented with relatively structured scenarios and problems that are solved within the context of an intra-disciplinary pedagogy. This, of course, limits the preparation of students to solve more complex problems that requires an inter-disciplinary orientation and integrated thinking.

Stand-alone Versus Integrated Courses

Researchers seem to disagree about the processes that take place when students engage in higher order thinking and whether lecturers should teach these abilities as a stand-alone subject or in conjunction with other discipline specific courses (Cobb, 2017). A study performed in 2006 reached the conclusion that critical thinking should be developed across different disciplines rather than in a stand-alone course (Hatcher, 2006). It makes sense that the same can be said of the development of integrated thinking skills. If the students are to learn how to think in an integrated manner, it should be infused throughout their academic programs in both undergraduate as well as postgraduate programs (Holley, 2017; Newell, 2001, 2006). Many researchers are in favor of infusing and scaffolding integrated thinking throughout the curriculum as opposed to teaching the concepts in a stand-alone course (Huber, 2006; Mino, 2013; Mino & Sandoval, 2014) as this will assist students to not compartmentalize the ability to think in an integrated manner to a six-month stand-alone course hidden somewhere in their academic programs. There are however also proponents of using a stand-alone course to introduce students to the concept of integrated thinking (Durrant & Hartman, 2015).

Pedagogical Considerations of Inter-disciplinary and Integrated Education

Teaching inter-disciplinary courses necessitates cultivating inter-disciplinary habits of mind through active learning and reflective thinking techniques (Newell & Luckie, 2019). Pedagogical approaches for inter-disciplinary learning usually align with those of integrated learning (Holley, 2017). To make integrated and interdisciplinary education effective, teachers must reassess their own ideologies and instructional techniques (Barisonzi & Thorn, 2003). Pedagogy relates to the type of interaction between lecturers, students, the learning environment, learning outcomes, and the task (Gittings et al., 2020). While each of the pedagogies used in this study is distinct, it is also particularly important to notice that they can and should be integrated as part of an overall integrated thinking strategy (Newell, 1999). Research has shown that an intentional pedagogical approach is required to enable students to think in an integrated manner (Dean et al., 2020). All the pedagogies included in this study are well recognized and researched examples of intentional approaches to developing integrated thinking skills. There is no particular nor exclusive pedagogy for teaching in an integrative inter-disciplinary manner (Klein, 2005). It is about the combination of strategies (Newell, 2001). This combination of strategies amplifies their power to develop integrated thinking skills during higher education (Haynes, 2002). The successful development of integrated thinking skills relies as much on the integrated curriculum as the pedagogies adopted (Hovland et al., 2015).

The following strategies are recognized as enablers of the development of integrated and inter-disciplinary skills during higher education: team teaching, capstone courses,[2] e-portfolios, and problem-based learning (Klein, 2005). In addition to these mentioned pedagogies, this study also includes the following pedagogies which have been proven in the literature to assist with the development of integrated thinking skills: modeling and the think-out-loud method (Foster et al., 2020; Herr, 2015; Mino, 2013), flipped classroom (Williams et al., 2019), peer learning and group work (Mahoney & Schamber, 2011), experiential learning skills (Gale, 2006; Newell, 1999), and tutorials (Duke, 2013).

METHOD AND EMPIRICAL FINDINGS

Method

This study applies a positivist paradigm and uses a descriptive research design. Researchers using the positivist paradigm favor quantitative data over qualitative data and according to this paradigm, the observation of numbers leads to the creation of facts (Smith, 2021). In this study, we emphasize the empirical findings for the development of the proposed model. An online questionnaire (available from the authors) with close-ended questions was designed after the completion of the literature review. The contents of the questionnaire as well as the distribution of the questionnaire to respondents were ethically cleared by our university. SAICA approved and supported the study and provided the link to the questionnaire via email to the Heads of Department of Accounting Departments of all 23 SAICA accredited universities. The Heads of the Department were specifically selected as they are regarded as accounting education experts due to their position, qualifications, experience, and close collaboration with SAICA. All Heads of Department in the sample were involved in teaching and curriculum design within their respective accounting departments. SAICA very much involves these Heads of Department in all accounting education matters. Largely due to SAICA's involvement, we obtained a response rate of 82.6%. We used SPSS to analyze the survey data.

Views on Effectiveness of Alternative Pedagogies

We used a 5-point Likert scale ranging from extremely effective (1) to not at all effective (5) to ask department heads which pedagogies academics perceive to be most beneficial in the development of integrated thinking skills in students. The pedagogies listed in this question are based on those identified in the preceding literature review. Results appear in Table 9.2.

The following eight pedagogies (listed from the most to the least effective) are perceived as most beneficial in the development of integrated thinking skills in students:

Table 9.2. Effectiveness of Integrated Pedagogies.

	1	2	3	4	5	n	M	Md	SD
Problem-based learning	6	11	2	0	0	19	1.79	2.00	0.631
Capstone courses	4	13	1	1	0	19	1.95	2.00	0.705
Modeling of integrated thinking by lecturer	3	12	4	0	0	19	2.05	2.00	0.621
Compulsory experiential learning during higher education	6	7	4	2	0	19	2.11	2.00	0.994
Inter-disciplinary tutorials	4	9	6	0	0	19	2.11	2.00	0.737
Inter-disciplinary case studies (working in groups)	3	11	5	0	0	19	2.11	2.00	0.658
Inter-disciplinary case studies (working as an individual)	4	7	7	1	0	19	2.26	2.00	0.872
Student-centered learning	1	12	5	1	0	19	2.32	2.00	0.671
Inter-disciplinary formal lectures with team-teaching	2	7	9	1	0	19	2.47	3.00	0.772
Flipped classroom	1	7	9	2	0	19	2.63	3.00	0.761
E-portfolios	0	9	7	3	0	19	2.68	3.00	0.749
Peer mentorship programs	1	5	11	2	0	19	2.74	3.00	0.733

Key: n = number of respondents who answered the question; M = Mean; Md = Median; and SD = Standard deviation.

Model to Develop Integrated Thinking Skills

- problem-based learning (1.79M);
- capstone courses (1.95M);
- modeling of integrated thinking by the lecturer (2.05M);
- compulsory experiential learning during higher education (2.11M);
- inter-disciplinary tutorials (2.11M);
- inter-disciplinary case studies (working in groups) (2.11M);
- inter-disciplinary case studies (working as an individual) (2.26M); and
- student-centered learning (2.32M).

Appropriateness for Each Academic Level of Study

The purpose of this question is to determine which recognized integrated learning pedagogies are most appropriate for each academic level of study for aspirant professional accountants. Questionnaire respondents could choose as many pedagogies as they feel are appropriate for each academic year. The frequency indicates how many respondents (of the total of 19 respondents) selected a particular pedagogy. This is an exploratory question as, according to the author's knowledge, no such mapping of pedagogies to academic levels has been performed before in literature. To a limited extent, a study performed in 2021 indicated that PBL, exposure to ICT, and tutoring are effective methods to apply throughout the entire undergraduate curriculum, with experiential learning being appropriate for second- and third-year students (García & De los Ríos, 2021).

The remainder of this section will discuss the results gathered for this question per academic year. The top six pedagogies per academic year of study will be identified for each academic year.

First Academic Year

Table 9.3 shows, that for the first academic year during the higher education of aspirant professional accountants, respondents indicated (in order of most selected to least selected) that the top six pedagogies to use for the development of integrated thinking skills in students are:

Table 9.3. Integrated Pedagogies Appropriate for the First Academic Year.

	Frequency	Percentage (%)	N
Inter-disciplinary tutorials	16	84	19
Student-centered learning	15	79	19
Problem-based learning	12	63	19
Peer mentorship programs	11	58	19
Modeling of integrated thinking by lecturer	10	53	19
E-portfolios	9	47	19
Flipped classroom	8	42	19
Inter-disciplinary case studies (working in groups)	4	21	19
Inter-disciplinary case studies (working as an individual)	2	11	19
Inter-disciplinary formal lectures with team-teaching	2	11	19
Compulsory experiential learning during higher education	2	11	19
Capstone courses	1	5	19

- inter-disciplinary tutorials (84%);
- student-centered learning (79%);
- problem-based learning (63%);
- peer mentorship programs (58%);
- modeling of integrated thinking by the lecturer (53%); and
- e-portfolios (47%).

Second Academic Year
Table 9.4 shows that for the second academic year during the higher education of aspirant professional accountants, respondents indicated (in order of most selected to least selected) that the top six pedagogies to use for the development of integrated thinking skills in students are:

- inter-disciplinary tutorials (89%);
- student-centered learning (89%);
- flipped classroom (89%);
- modeling of integrated thinking by lecturer (84%);
- problem-based learning (79%); and
- peer mentorship programs (74%).

Third Academic Year
Table 9.5 shows, that for the third academic year during the higher education of aspirant professional accountants, respondents indicated (in order of most selected to least selected) that the top seven pedagogies to use for the development of integrated thinking skills in students are:

- inter-disciplinary tutorials (100%);
- student-centered learning (100%);
- flipped classroom (100%);
- peer mentorship programs (100%);

Table 9.4. Integrated Pedagogies Appropriate for the Second Academic Year.

	Frequency	Percentage (%)	N
Inter-disciplinary tutorials	17	89	19
Student-centered learning	17	89	19
Flipped classroom	17	89	19
Modeling of integrated thinking by lecturer	16	84	19
Problem-based learning	15	79	19
Peer mentorship programs	14	74	19
E-portfolios	12	63	19
Inter-disciplinary case studies (working in groups)	10	53	19
Compulsory experiential learning during higher education	8	42	19
Inter-disciplinary case studies (working as an individual)	7	37	19
Inter-disciplinary formal lectures with team-teaching	6	32	19
Capstone courses	3	16	19

Model to Develop Integrated Thinking Skills

Table 9.5. Integrated Pedagogies Appropriate for the Third Academic Year.

	Frequency	Percentage (%)	N
Inter-disciplinary tutorials	19	100	19
Student-centered learning	19	100	19
Flipped classroom	19	100	19
Peer mentorship programs	19	100	19
Problem-based learning	18	95	19
Inter-disciplinary case studies (working in groups)	18	95	19
Inter-disciplinary case studies (working as an individual)	18	95	19
Modeling of integrated thinking by lecturer	17	89	19
Inter-disciplinary formal lectures with team-teaching	17	89	19
Capstone courses	16	84	19
Compulsory experiential learning during higher education	15	79	19
E-portfolios	13	68	19

- problem-based learning (95%); and
- inter-disciplinary case studies (both working in groups and individually) (95%).

Seven instead of six pedagogies were selected seeing that problem-based learning and inter-disciplinary case studies achieved the same frequency, that is, 95%.

Post Graduate Diploma in Accounting

Table 9.6 shows, that for the PGDA year during the higher education of aspirant professional accountants, respondents indicated (in order of most selected to least selected) that the top six pedagogies to use for the development of integrated thinking skills in students are:

- inter-disciplinary case studies (working as an individual) (100%);
- inter-disciplinary tutorials (95%);
- student-centered learning (95%);
- inter-disciplinary formal lectures with team-teaching (95%);
- capstone courses (95%); and
- problem-based learning (89%).

Table 9.6. Integrated Pedagogies Appropriate for the PGDA.

	Frequency	Percentage (%)	n
Inter-disciplinary case studies (working as an individual)	19	100	19
Inter-disciplinary tutorials	18	95	19
Student-centered learning	18	95	19
Inter-disciplinary formal lectures with team-teaching	18	95	19
Capstone courses	18	95	19
Problem-based learning	17	89	19
Modeling of integrated thinking by lecturer	16	84	19
Inter-disciplinary case studies (working in groups)	15	79	19
E-portfolios	15	79	19
Flipped classroom	14	74	19
Peer mentorship programs	12	63	19
Compulsory experiential learning during higher education	8	42	19

A Stand-alone Course Versus Integration Across The Curriculum

The purpose of this question is to determine respondents' views on how integrated thinking skills should be developed. The question asks whether integrated thinking skills should be developed in a stand-alone course, integrated throughout the curriculum or a combination of both. The results of this question are set out in Table 9.7.

The results of the study show that the majority of respondents (68.4%) believe that integrated thinking skills should be developed in a combination of a stand-alone course and integrated throughout the curriculum. A smaller number of respondents (31.6%) think that integrated thinking skills should be developed throughout the curriculum. None of the respondents indicated that integrated thinking skills should be developed exclusively in a stand-alone course.

Ideal Approach to Develop Integrated Thinking Skills

We asked department heads whether respondents believe face-to-face instruction or a blended teaching and learning approach is the most effective manner of developing integrated thinking skills. The frequency indicates the number of respondents (out of a total of 19 respondents) who chose each option. The results of this question are set out in Table 9.8.

The majority (78.9%) of respondents are of the opinion that a blended teaching and learning approach is more suitable than face-to-face instruction (21.1%) to develop integrated thinking skills.

Views on a Constructivist Approach

The aim of this question is to determine whether respondents believe that a constructivist approach will assist in the development of integrated thinking skills. The results of this question are set out in Table 9.9.

All the respondents (100%) believe that a constructivist approach will assist in the development of integrated thinking skills.

Developing Creativity Skills During Higher Education

This question asks respondents whether they believe that creative skills can be developed during higher education. The results of this question are set out in Table 9.10.

Table 9.7. Stand-alone Versus Integration Throughout Curriculum.

	Frequency	Percentage (%)
In a stand-alone course	0	0.0
Integrated throughout the curriculum	6	31.6
In a combination of a stand-alone course and integrated throughout the curriculum	13	68.4
Total (*n*)	**19**	**100.0**

Table 9.8. Ideal Method to Develop Integrated Thinking Skills.

	Frequency	Percentage (%)
A blended teaching and learning approach	15	78.9
Face-to-face instruction	4	21.1
Total (*n*)	**19**	**100.0**

Table 9.9. Constructivist Pedagogical Approach.

	Frequency	Percentage (%)
A constructivist approach will assist in developing integrated thinking skills	19	100.0
A constructivist approach will not assist in developing integrated thinking skills	0	0.0
Total (*n*)	**19**	

Table 9.10. Development of Creativity.

	Frequency	Percentage (%)
Creativity should not be developed in higher education	2	10.5
Creativity should be developed in higher education	17	89.5
Total (*n*)	**19**	**100.0**

Of the total number of respondents, 89.5% feel that creativity can be developed in students. The respondents' views are completely in line with what the literature tells us about creative skills being developed during higher education.

BUILDING A CONSTRUCTIVIST MODEL

Model and Appropriate Pedagogies

From the empirical findings, the researchers built a model to indicate the six most effective pedagogies per year of academic study for the CA(SA) as a professional accountant. This model is visually represented in Fig. 9.1. As discussed above, respondents to the questionnaire ranked 12 integrated pedagogies from the most appropriate to the least appropriate per academic level of study. From this ranking, the six most appropriate pedagogies are identified. Student-centered learning ranked highly across all academic years and thus was selected as a foundation of the model.

Disciplinarity and Scaffolding of Integration and Inter-disciplinarity

The disciplinarity of each academic year is scaffolded in the model from the simplest form of disciplinarity in the first year (i.e., multi-disciplinarity) through to the most complex form of disciplinarity in the PGDA year (i.e., trans-disciplinarity). The levels of disciplinarity are not covered in the empirical

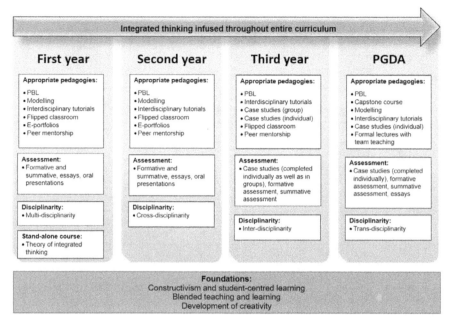

Fig. 9.1. Model to Develop Integrated Thinking Skills During Higher Education.

study but are based on the recommendations of the available literature. The recommended use of disciplinarity is thus, as follows:

- first year: multi-disciplinarity;
- second year: cross-disciplinarity;
- third year: inter-disciplinarity; and
- PGDA year: trans-disciplinarity.

In addition, it is recommended that the level of integration is also scaffolded. Integration should take place within a discipline before it is expanded to integration between different disciplines. For example, in the first academic year, the main focus should be on developing the ability of students to integrate all topics within a specific module with limited integration with other modules. As the student progresses through the academic levels, integration within a discipline should still take place, but with a growing emphasis on integration between disciplines/modules and non-technical factors as well. In developing the integrated curriculum, care should be taken to include all non-core modules.

Stand-alone Course in First Year And Integration Throughout The Curriculum

Most questionnaire respondents (68.4%) indicated that integrated thinking principles should be presented in a stand-alone course as well as integrated throughout the curriculum. The developed model for integrated thinking thus indicates that the theoretical principles of integrated thinking are presented in a stand-alone course in the first year and subsequent to the stand-alone course, integrated thinking is infused in the entire undergraduate and postgraduate curriculums.

Foundations of an Integrated Thinking Model

The following are considered the foundations of an integrated thinking model as presented in Fig. 9.1:

- *Constructivism and student-centered learning*: As discussed in both the literature review and the empirical findings, a constructivist and student-centered approach is prescribed in the development of integrated thinking skills.
- *Blended teaching and learning*: As discussed in both the literature review and the empirical findings, a blended teaching and learning approach is the optimal way in which to develop integrated thinking skills during higher education.
- *Development of creativity*: As discussed in both the literature review and the empirical findings, the development of creativity during higher education is crucial for the development of integrated thinking skills.

CONCLUSION

It takes intentional learning strategies that represent integrated ways of thinking to incorporate the International <IR> framework's tenets into the accounting education curriculum (McGuigan et al., 2020). The development of integrated thinking skills should be an intentional and structured approach (Dean et al., 2020). There is a misconception that students are intuitively able to make meaningful connections across disciplines and contexts. However, research has shown that an intentional pedagogical approach is required to enable students to think in an integrated manner (Dean et al., 2020; Huber & Hutchings, 2004).

Many professional accounting bodies expect higher education institutions to develop integrated thinking skills in students studying toward a professional accounting designation. To date, the literature does not provide a model addressing how different pedagogies can be used in conjunction with each other in the different academic years to develop integrated thinking skills. In addressing this gap in the literature, the contribution of this study is to develop a structured model that deals with all aspects of an integrated teaching and learning approach, namely the foundations thereof, appropriate pedagogies, disciplinarity type, and point of introduction of integrated thinking principles. This model provides our answer to the research question, which is "How can integrated thinking skills be developed in higher education for future professional accountants?"

The empirical findings of this study are based on the views of South African SAICA accredited universities, and the model addresses the undergraduate and postgraduate structure as required by SAICA. This poses a limitation to the study. Further research should be performed internationally that will assist with the development of integrated thinking skills during higher education of all prospective professional accountants. It would be useful to understand the extent to which the views of educators and administrators in different jurisdictions converge and the resulting impact on comparative constructivist approaches to integrative thinking and learning across those jurisdictions. Another limitation of this study is that only Heads of Departments were surveyed; thus, a follow-up study is recommended where non-administrators are also surveyed.

NOTES

1. This study was conducted in South Africa where teachers at the university level are broadly referred to as lecturers. This is similar to the use of the term instructor in the USA to refer to teachers at the university level.
2. Even though capstone courses are traditionally used at the end of an academic program, a capstone course to promote integrated thinking and learning can also be used during any academic year to bring together the knowledge obtained in that specific academic year (Collins & Dunne, 1996).

REFERENCES

Abbott, W., & Nantz, K. A. (2012). Building students' integrative thinking capacities: A case study in economics and history. *Issues in Integrative Studies, 30,* 19–47.

Abraham, A., & Jones, H. (2016). Facilitating student learning in accounting through scaffolded assessment. *Issues in Accounting Education, 31*(1), 29–49.

Adams, C. A. (2017). *Understanding integrated reporting: The concise guide to integrated thinking and the future of corporate reporting.* Routledge.

Amabile, T. M., Collins, M. A., Conti, R., Phillips, E., Picariello, M., Ruscio, J., & Whitney, D. (1996). *Creativity in context.* Westview Press.

Armstrong, F. (1980). Faculty development through interdisciplinarity. *Journal of General Education, 32*(1), 52–63.

Ashby, I., & Exter, M. (2019). Designing for interdisciplinarity in higher education: Considerations for instructional designers. *TechTrends, 63*(2), 202–208.

Barisonzi, J., & Thorn, M. (2003). Teaching revolution: Issues in interdisciplinary education. *College Teaching, 51*(1), 5–8.

Bayerlein, L. (2014). Curriculum innovation in undergraduate accounting degree programmes through "virtual internships." *Education and Training, 39*(8), 916–931.

Blackshields, D., Cronin, J., Higgs, B., Kilcommins, S., McCarthy, M., & Ryan, A. (Eds.). (2015). *Integrative learning: International research and practice.* Routledge.

Blessinger, P., & Wankel, C. (2013). Novel approaches in higher education: An introduction to web 2.0 and blended learning technologies. *Cutting-Edge Technologies in Higher Education, 6*(G), 3–16.

Bloom, R. (2014). Integrating the accounting curriculum. In R. M. S Wilson (Ed.), *Routledge companion to accounting education* (pp. 332–351). Routledge.

Boix Mansilla, V. (2008). Integrative learning: Setting the stage for a pedagogy of the contemporary. *Peer Review, 10*(4), 31–32.

Boix Mansilla, V. (2016). Interdisciplinary learning: A cognitive-epistemological foundation. In R. Frodeman, J. T. Klein, & R. C. S Pacheco (Eds.), *Oxford handbook of interdisciplinarity* (pp. 261–275). Oxford University Press.

Bransford, J. D., Brown, A., & Cocking, R. (2000). *How people learn: Brain, mind, experience and school.* National Academy Press.

Busco, C., Granà, F., & Achilli, G. (2021). Understanding integrated thinking: Evidence from the field, the development of a framework and avenues for future research. *Meditari Accountancy Research, 29*(4), 673–690. https://doi.org/10.1108/MEDAR-04-2021-1263

Castellana, R. (2005). Becoming interdisciplinary: Pioneer text on IDS has political significance. *Association for Integrative Studies Newsletter, 27*(2), 1–4.

Chaves, J. A. (2006). Self, peer, and tutor assessments of MSN competencies using the PBL-evaluator. *Journal of Nursing Education, 45*(1), 25.

Chigeza, P., & Halbert, K. (2014). Navigating e-learning and blended learning for pre-service teachers: Redesigning for engagement, access and efficiency. *Australian Journal of Teacher Education, 39*(11), 133–146.

CIMA. (2014). *Integrated thinking*. AICPA-CIMA. Retrieved September 23, 2023, from https://www.aicpa-cima.com/resources/download/integrated-thinking-in-integrated-reporting

Cobb, J. L. (2017). *Critical and reflective thinking in an intermediate financial accounting course: An action research study* [Doctoral thesis, Texas Christian University]. https://www.proquest.com/openview/5a67a7f12a235ba412aa6189983d5366/1?pq-origsite=gscholarandcbl=18750

Collins, R., & Dunne, A. (1996). Utilizing multilevel capstone course in an integrated agribusiness curriculum. *Agribusiness, 12*(1), 105–112.

Crawford, R., & Jenkins, L. E. (2018). Making pedagogy tangible: Developing skills and knowledge using a team teaching and blended learning approach. *Australian Journal of Teacher Education, 43*(1), 127–142. https://doi.org/10.14221/ajte.2018v43n1.8

Danker, B. (2015). Using flipped classroom approach to explore deep learning in large classrooms. *The IAFOR Journal of Education, 3*(1), 171–186.

Davies, A., Fidler, D., & Gorbis, M. (2011). *Future work skills 2020*. Retrieved September 19, 2023, from https://uqpn.uq.edu.au/files/203/LIBBY%20MARSHALL%20future_work_skills_2020_full_research_report_final_1.pdf

De Villiers, C., & Venter, E. (2010). The influence of the accounting profession on the academy: A cautionary case study. *Meditari Accountancy Research, 46*(3), 1246–1278.

Dean, B. A., Perkiss, S., Simic Misic, M., & Luzia, K. (2020). Transforming accounting curricula to enhance integrative learning. *Accounting and Finance, 60*(3), 2301–2338. https://doi.org/10.1111/acfi.12363

Dewey, J. (2009). *Democracy and education: An introduction to the philosophy of education*. WLC Books.

Dewey, J. (2016). *Democracy and education*. University of Chicago Press.

Donnelly, R. (2010). Harmonizing technology with interaction in blended problem-based learning. *Computers and Education, 54*(2), 350–359. https://doi.org/10.1016/j.compedu.2009.08.012

Drake, S. (1991). How our team dissolved the boundaries. *Educational Leadership, 49*(2), 20–22.

Duffy, T. M., & Cunningham, D. J. (1996). Constructivism: Implications of the design and delivery of instruction. In D. H. Jonassen (Ed.), *Handbook of research for educational communications and technology* (pp. 170–198). Simon and Schuster Macmillan.

Duke, C. J. (2013). *Integrative learning within tutoring in higher education: Contexts for connections* [Doctoral thesis, Appalachian State University]. https://libres.uncg.edu/ir/asu/f/Duke,%20Cama_2013_Dissertation.pdf

Dumay, J., & Dai, T. (2017). Integrated thinking as a cultural control? *Meditari Accountancy Research, 25*(4), 574–604. https://doi.org/10.1108/MEDAR-07-2016-0067

Durrant, K. L., & Hartman, T. P. (2015). The integrative learning value of field courses. *Journal of Biological Education, 49*(4), 385–400.

Du Toit, E., Marx, B., & Smith, R. J. (2023). The Impact of Industries 4.0 and 5.0 on the professional accountant and auditor's integrated thinking skills skillset and other pervasive skills. *International Journal of Business Innovation, 2*(4). e32786. https://doi.org/10.34624/ijbi.v2i4.32786

Du Toit, E., Marx, B., & Smith, R. J. (2024). Delineating the parameters of integrated thinking: A synthetic literature review. *Journal of Economic and Financial Sciences, 17*(1), 891.

Eagen, W., Cukier, W., Bauer, W., & Ngwenyama, O. (2010). *Design thinking: Can creativity be taught?* [Conference presentation]. In Proceedings from the international conference: The future of education, Florence, Italy.

Foster, W., Sweet, L., & McNeill, L. (2020). Linking out loud (LOL): Developing critical thinking. *MedEdPublish, 9*(42), 11–14.

Gale, R. (2006). *Fostering integrative learning through pedagogy*. Retrieved August 7, 2023, from http://gallery.carnegiefoundation.org/ilp/uploads/pedagogy_copy.pdf

Galoyan, T., & Betts, K. (2021). Integrative transfer of learning model and implications for higher education. *Journal of Continuing Higher Education, 69*(3), 169–191. https://doi.org/10.1080/07377363.2020.1847970

García, J. L., & De los Ríos, I. (2021). Model to develop skills in accounting students for a 4.0 industry and 2030 agenda: From an international perspective. *Sustainability, 13*(17), 1–31. https://doi.org/10.3390/su13179699

Ginsburg-Block, M. D., Rohrbeck, C. A., & Fantuzzo, J. W. (2006). A meta-analytic review of social, self-concept, and behavioral outcomes of peer assisted learning. *Journal of Educational Psychology, 98*(4), 723.

Gittings, L., Taplin, R., & Kerr, R. (2020). Experiential learning activities in university accounting education: A systematic literature review. *Journal of Accounting Education, 52*, 1–13. https://doi.org/10.1016/j.jaccedu.2020.100680

Guthrie, J., & Parker, L. D. (2016). Whither the accounting profession, accountants and accounting researchers? Commentary and projections. *Accounting, Auditing and Accountability Journal, 29*(1), 2–10. https://doi.org/10.1108/AAAJ-10-2015-2263

Hampson, G. P. (2013). Toward a genealogy and topology of Western integrative thinking. *Research and Praxis, 9*(2), 46–75.

Hassall, T., & Joyce, J. (2014). The use of experiential learning in accounting education. In R. M. S. Wilson (Ed.), *The Routledge companion to accounting education* (pp. 376–398). Routledge.

Hatcher, D. L. (2006). Stand-alone versus integrated critical thinking courses. The *Journal of General Education, 55*(3), 247–272.

Haynes, C. (Ed.). (2002). *Innovations in interdisciplinary teaching*. Oryx Press.

Haynes, A. (2017). In support of disciplinarity in teaching sociology: Reflections from Ireland. *Teaching Sociology, 45*(1), 54–64.

Herr, J. (2015). *Thinking out loud: Exploring the dynamics of student engagement within facilitated whole-class dialogues* [Doctoral thesis, Texas Wesleyan University]. https://www.proquest.com/openview/84d3bf6e4027ea0dbd94b8ba3999ca2b/1?pq-origsite=gscholarandcbl=18750

Higgs, B., Kilcommins, S., & Ryan, T. (2010). *Making connections: Intentional teaching for integrative learning*. Retrieved July 27, 2023, from http://login.ezproxy.library.ualberta.ca/login?url=https://eprints.teachingandlearning.ie/id/eprint/2518/1/NAIRTL%20Making%20Connections%20Intentional%20Teaching%20for%20Integrative%20Learning.pdf

Holley, K. (2017). Interdisciplinary curriculum and learning in higher education. In G. W. Noblit (Ed.), *Oxford research encyclopaedia of education*. https://doi.org/10.1093/acrefore/9780190264093.013.138

Hovland, K., Anderson, C., & Ferren, A. (2015). Interrogating integrative learning. *AACU Peer Review, 17*(4/1), 2014–2015.

Huber, M. T. (2006). *Fostering integrative learning through the curriculum*. Retrieved October 21, 2023, from http://gallery.carnegiefoundation.org/ilp/uploads/curriculum_copy.pdf

Huber, M. T., & Hutchings, P. (2004). *Integrative learning: Mapping the terrain*. Retrieved June 14, 2023, from https://www.researchgate.net/publication/254325229_Integrative_Learning_Mapping_the_Terrain

IFAC. (2015). *Creating value with integrated thinking. The role of professional accountants*. Retrieved November 22, 2023, from https://www.ifac.org/_flysystem/azure-private/publications/files/Creating-value-with-iIntegrated-thinking-role-of-accountants.pdf

Ignjatović, G. (2020). Integrative learning approach in ESP/ELP: Theoretical framework of intra-disciplinary, multi-disciplinary, interdisciplinary, and trans-disciplinary integration. *Zbornik Radova Pravnog Fakulteta u Niso, 59*(88), 179–198. https://doi.org/10.5937/zrpfn0-27891

IIRC. (2020). *Integrated thinking and strategy: State of play report*. Retrieved October 29, 2023, from https://integratedreporting.org/wp-content/uploads/2020/01/Integrated-Thinking-and-Strategy-State-of-Play-Report_2020.pdf

IIRC. (2021). *International integrated reporting framework*. Retrieved October 29, 2023, from https://integratedreporting.org/wp-content/uploads/2021/01/InternationalIntegratedReportingFramework.pdf

Klein, J. T. (2005). Integrative learning and interdisciplinary studies. *Peer Review, 7*(4), 8–10.

Klein, J. T. (2006). A platform for a shared discourse of interdisciplinary education. *Journal of Social Science Education, 5*(2), 10–18.

Klein, J. T. (2010). A taxonomy of interdisciplinarity. In R. Frodeman (Ed.), *The Oxford handbook of interdisciplinarity* (pp. 15–30). Oxford University Press.

Lattemann, C., & Fritz, K. (2014). Learning integrative thinking. In M. Searson & M. N. Ochoa (Eds.), *Society for Information Technology and Teacher Education international conference* (pp. 1857–1864). Association for the Advancement of Computing in Education.

Lattuca, L., Voigt, L., & Fath, K. (2004). Does interdisciplinarity promote learning? Theoretical support and researchable questions. *The Review of Higher Education, 28*(1), 23–48.

Lawson, R. A., Blocher, E. J., Brewer, P. C., Cokins, G., Sorensen, J. E., Stout, D. E., Sundem, G. L., Wolcott, S., & Wouters, M. J. F. (2014). Focusing accounting curricula on students' long-run careers: Recommendations for an integrated competency-based framework for accounting education. *Issues in Accounting Education, 29*(2), 295–317. https://doi.org/10.2308/iace-50673

Leicht, A., Heiss, J., & Buyn, W. J. (2018). *Issues and trends in education for sustainable development.* UNESCO Publishing.

Leonard, J. J. B. (2012). Integrative learning: A grounded theory. *Issues in Integrative Studies, 30*(30), 48–74.

Lima, M., Koehler, M. J., & Spiro, R. J. (2004). Collaborative interactivity and integrated thinking in Brazilian business schools using cognitive flexibility hypertexts: The Panteon project. *Journal of Educational Computing Research, 31*(4), 371–406. https://doi.org/10.2190/TTK2-TDRP-D0DX-M8XN

Lombard, B. J. J., & Grosser, M. (2008). Critical thinking: Are the ideals of OBE failing us or are we failing the ideals of OBE? *South African Journal of Education, 28*, 561–579.

Lorson, P., & Paschke, R. (2015). Worum geht es beim integrated thinking: Ansatze zur begriffsbestimmung und umsetzung. *WPg - Die Wirtschaftsprufung, 68*(17), 939–948.

Mahoney, S., & Schamber, J. (2011). Integrative and deep learning through a learning community: A process view of self. *Journal of General Education, 60*(4), 234–247.

Maroun, W., Ecim, D., & Cerbone, D. (2022). Refining integrated thinking. *Sustainability Accounting, Management and Policy Journal, 14*(7) 1–25. https://doi.org/10.1108/sampj-07-2021-0268

McComas, W. F. (2009). Thinking, teaching and learning: Science outside the boxes. *Science Teacher, 76*(2), 24–28.

McDonald, P. L., Schlumpf, K. S., Weaver, G. C., & Corcoran, M. (2021). *Integrative blended learning.* Routledge.

McGuigan, N. (2021). Future-proofing accounting education: Educating for complexity, ambiguity and uncertainty. *Revista Contabilidade e Financas, 32*(87), 383–389. https://doi.org/10.1590/1808-057X202190370

McGuigan, N., Haustein, E., Kern, T., & Lorson, P. (2020). Thinking through the integration of corporate reporting: Exploring the interplay between integrative and integrated thinking. *Meditari Accountancy Research, 29*(4), 775–804. https://doi.org/10.1108/MEDAR-04-2020-0872

McGuigan, N., & Kern, T. (2015). Developing a creative environment for learning: Nurturing reflective thought amongst accountants. In K. S. Coleman, & A. Flood (Eds.), *Capturing creativity: The link between creativity and teaching creatively* (pp. 145–167). Common Ground Publishing LLC.

McGuigan, N., & Kern, T. (2016). CreActive accounting education: Visioning future-oriented accounting programs through a reflective unlearning of current practice. *Journal of University Teaching and Learning Practice, 13*(2), 1–23.

McLoughlin, E., & Finlayson, O. E. (2015). Interdisciplinary science – Integrative learning in first-year undergraduate science. In D. Blackshields, G. R. Cronin, B. Higgs, S. Kilcommins, M. McCarthy, & A. Ryan (Eds.), *Integrative learning: International research and practice* (pp. 195–206). Routledge.

Mihret, D. G., Abayadeera, N., Watty, K., & McKay, J. (2017). Teaching auditing using cases in an online learning environment: The role of ePortfolio assessment. *Accounting Education, 26*(4), 335–357. https://doi.org/10.1080/09639284.2017.1292466

Miller, R. C. (2010). Interdisciplinarity: Its meaning and consequences. In N. Sandal (Ed.), *Oxford research encyclopedia of international studies.* https://doi.org/10.1093/acrefore/9780190846626.013.92

Mino, J. (2013). Link aloud: Making interdisciplinary learning visible and audible. *Learning Communities Research and Practice, 1*(1), 4.

Mino, J., & Sandoval, P. (2014). Learning beyond cognition: Embodying integration from seminar to the stage. In D. Blackshields, J. G. Cronin, B. Higgs, S. Kilcommins, M. McCarthy, & A. Ryan (Eds.), *Integrative learning* (pp. 229–243). Routledge.

Muhammad, A. J., Arrington-Slocum, A., & Hughes, L. (2021). Capstone courses and major projects for enhancing generation Z career readiness through general higher education classroom curriculum. *Journal of Higher Education Theory and Practice, 21*(7), 63–75.

National Research Council. (2000). *How people learn: Brain, mind and experience, and school*. National Academies Press.

Newell, W. H. (1999). The promise of integrative learning. *About Campus, 4*(2), 17–23.

Newell, W. H. (2001). Powerful pedagogies. In B. L. Smith & J. McCann (Eds.), *Reinventing ourselves: Interdisciplinary education, collaborative learning, and experimentation in higher education* (pp. 196–211). Anker Publishing Company.

Newell, W. H. (2006). Interdisciplinary integration by undergraduates. *Issues in Integrative Studies, 24*, 89–111.

Newell, W. H., & Luckie, D. B. (2019). Pedagogy for interdisciplinary habits of mind. *Journal of Interdisciplinary Studies in Education, 8*(1), 6–20.

Palmer, C. L. (2001). *Work at the boundaries of science: Information and the interdisciplinary research process*. Springer Science and Business Media.

Pathways Commission. (2015). *The Pathways Commission: In pursuit of accounting's curricula of the future*. Retrieved May 13, 2023, from https://aaahq.org/portals/0/images/education/pathways/15-9-61866.pdf?ver=2021-02-23-175219-123

Quattrone, P. (2000). Constructivism and accounting research: Towards a trans-disciplinary perspective. *Accounting, Auditing and Accountability Journal, 13*(2), 130–155. https://doi.org/10.1108/09513570010323047

Qureshi, M. A., & Stormyhr, E. (2012). Group dynamics and peer-tutoring a pedagogical tool for learning in higher education. *International Education Studies, 5*(2), 118–124. https://doi.org/10.5539/ies.v5n2p118

Rebele, J. E., & Pierre, E. K. S. (2019). A commentary on learning objectives for accounting education programs: The importance of soft skills and technical knowledge. *Journal of Accounting Education, 48*, 71–79. https://doi.org/10.1016/j.jaccedu.2019.07.002

Reed, R. (1997). Lost times/recovered times. *The Journal of Philosophy for Children, 13*(1), 34–36.

Rodgers, W., Simon, J., & Gabrielsson, J. (2017). Combining experiential and conceptual learning in accounting education: A review with implications. *Management Learning, 48*(2), 187–205. https://doi.org/10.1177/1350507616669479

Rossetto, C., & Chapple, S. (2019). Creative accounting? The critical and creative voice of students. *Assessment and Evaluation in Higher Education, 44*(2), 216–232.

Russo, A., Warren, L., Neri, L., Herdan, A., & Brickman, K. (2022). Enhancing accounting and finance students' awareness of transferable skills in an integrated blended learning environment. *Accounting Education, 31*(1), 67–91. https://doi.org/10.1080/09639284.2021.1961087

Rutherford, B. (2011). *Definition of professional accountant*. Retrieved May 16, 2023, from https://www.ifac.org/system/files/meetings/files/Definition%20of%20Professional%20Accountant%20Presentation.pptx

SAICA. (2015). *SAICA: Integrated thinking, an exploratory survey*. Retrieved November 23, 2023, from https://www.integratedreporting.org/resource/saica-integrated-thinking-an-exploratory-survey/

SAICA. (2021). *The exploration and development of the concept of integrated thinking*. Retrieved November 28, 2023, from https://saicawebprstorage.blob.core.windows.net/uploads/resources/THE-CONCEPT-OF-INTEGRATED-THINKING.pdf

Scheer, A., Noweski, C., & Meinel, C. (2012). Transforming constructivist learning into action – Design thinking in education. *Design and Technology Education: An International Journal, 17*(3), 8–19.

Sill, D. (1996). Integrative thinking, synthesis and creativity in interdisciplinary studies. *Journal of General Education, 45*(2), 129–151.

Smith, R. J. (2021). *The application of corporate governance in large and medium-sized South African auditing firms*. [Doctoral thesis, University of Johannesburg]. https://www.proquest.com/openview/2774989571f0730ede64ec3e0077edac/1?pq-origsite=gscholar&cbl=2026366&diss=y

Stentoft, D. (2017). From saying to doing interdisciplinary learning: Is problem-based learning the answer? *Active Learning in Higher Education, 18*(1), 51–61. https://doi.org/10.1177/1469787417693510

Swan, K. (2009). Blended learning at class level. *Journal of the Research Center for Educational Technology*, *5*(1), 1.

Tavares, M. C., Zimba, L. N., & Azevedo, G. (2022). The implications of industry 4.0 for the auditing profession. *International Journal of Business Innovation*, *1*(1), 1–21.

UNESCO-IBE. (2013). *International Bureau of Education: Glossary of curriculum terminology*. Retrieved April 10, 2023, from https://www.ibe.unesco.org/en/document/glossary-curriculum-terminology

Van Oordt, T., & Mulder, I. (2016). Implementing basic e-learning tools into an undergraduate taxation curriculum. *Meditari Accountancy Research*, *24*(3), 341–367. https://doi.org/10.1108/MEDAR-08-2015-0054

VanLehn, K. (2011). The relative effectiveness of human tutoring, intelligent tutoring systems and other tutoring systems. *Educational Psychologist*, *46*(4), 197–221.

Williams, B., Horner, C., & Allen, S. (2019). Flipped v's traditional teaching perspectives in a first-year accounting unit: An action research study. *Accounting Education*, *28*(4), 333–352. https://doi.org/10.1080/09639284.2019.1609436

Woodside, J. M., Augustine, F. K., Chambers, V., & Mendoza, M. (2020). Integrative learning and interdisciplinary information systems curriculum development in accounting analytics. *Journal of Information Systems Education*, *31*(2), 147–156.

CHAPTER 10

THEORY AND ITS ABSENCE IN ACCOUNTING EDUCATION RESEARCH

Timothy J. Fogarty

Case Western Reserve University, USA

ABSTRACT

This chapter argues that the accounting literature in general and the accounting education literature in particular has under-invested in theory. The few theories that we officially believe are in use but are used quite poorly. Many theories that could be used are not used at all despite the promise that they appear to hold. Accounting education would be better understood if more of an effort was made to bring theory to the table in a variety of ways.

Keywords: Accounting literature; use of theory; accounting teaching; education using theory; practical application of accounting theory

Of all the elements of academic work, theory is the least well appreciated. This lacuna is more extreme in highly applied areas such as accounting. And within these very instrumental fields, the theory is even more obscured when it is brought to bear on the pedagogy of those disciplines. The purpose of this chapter is to develop some systematic thought around accounting theory as it exists today and is used in the ongoing evolution of accounting education research.

Following a brief introduction to the idea of theory in the first section, a second section describes the premise of a singular accounting theory. The third and longest section illustrates the possibilities of emergent accounting theory that can be found through inductive approaches. The chapter concludes with two sections that offer implications for what has been found and not found, and a conclusion that aims to summarize the theory agenda.

BACKGROUND TO THEORY IN ACADEMIC WORK

We have been taught to believe that theory is important to have and to use. That would be true even if we could not agree about what theory was and about the specific ways that we should deploy it. This provides a starting point comprising how to define theory. Without pretense, we can assert that theory is knowledge that is systematically organized and wide in its applicability. With such scope and breadth, theory still needs to articulate some fundamental assumptions about the state of nature that potentially rule out other viable and reasonable ways of seeing. Thus, it highlights some dimensions of a phenomenon at the purposeful expense of others. Theoretical statements usually include some rules of analysis and agreements about causality. Theory almost invariably promises some degree of prediction about future states, although this is often quite implicit. Preferred solutions usually follow axiomatically rather than being part of the formal theory. The theoretical process can be deductive in which existing conditions can be tested against expectations, or inductive in which selection criteria help identify otherwise unobserved patterns.

The abstract definitions of theory might sound desirable but certainly factor in convincing us to seek it out and to use it correctly. "Why use theory" can be approached as a question for individual researchers and for the discipline as a whole. In fact, theory asserts the variegated decision-making that must be done in first selecting projects. These include insuring that the data gathered is acceptable and that it is appropriately testable. Theory adds perspective such that results are portable to other contexts, thereby enhancing reader interest. Without theory, data tend to be a morass (Wheeler, 1970) and its implications are not much more than a compendium of best practices (Hopwood, 1987). For the discipline, theory modulates standards of acceptability for research contributors to follow. That which is judged sufficiently interesting to publish exists in an often unrecognized theoretical filter of data and its proper testing. Furthermore, the theory is a critical contributor to external parties' view of a discipline's legitimacy (Díaz Andrade et al., 2023).

ACCOUNTING AND THE PURSUIT OF AN OVER-ARCHING THEORY

Many of us have been schooled at the feet of Thomas Kuhn. In *The Structure of Scientific Revolutions*, Kuhn (1970) argued that disciplines historically shift from one paradigm to another in rare moments of change. In the interregnums, academics practice "normal science" which illustrates the acceptance of the worldview of the times they work within. However, efforts to position accounting within this model have produced confusing results (e.g., Cushing, 1989; Wells, 1976). A large part of the problem is the schism between the double entry of practice and the diverse work done by academe that connects only parenthetically with that.

We must accept the distinct possibility that accounting does not have the overarching theory that, in a perfect world, it should. Among the several writers of prominence that have come to such a conclusion include those who found it fragmented (e.g., Mattessich, 1993) or impossible (Beaver, 1998). Most would not go as far as Gaffikin (2016) who asserts that accounting has no theory of its own. But perhaps what these scholars have in mind might be too ambitious or in fact altogether different in nature since theory can mean many different things.

The accounting field compounds the theory problem. Accounting as a practice has murky origins (see Sangster, 2016) but nobody would question that it stretches back over more than the last 500 years and has grown up and flourished with capitalism. Accounting education as something more than an informal apprenticeship claims a legacy somewhat co-equal to the modern business school, extending over a period of perhaps 125 years. An accounting academy that aspired to much more than instruction, can lay claim to only about half of that shorter period in which much attempt was made to systematically add to the knowledge of the emergent discipline. This unique history makes it necessary to first search for theory in practice and education.

If theory was truly important in accounting practice, it would serve as a criterion for professional admission. This would be predicated on the idea that practice cannot be reduced to rules and practices but instead is imbued with essential values and normative preferences. Such a premise was illustrated in the late 20th century by a stand-alone theory section of the CPA examination which has subsequently disappeared, apparently a victim of exam evolution. Although the theory section may never have achieved its potential and may have been little more than a set of non-mathematical abstractions about or rationalizations for the central calculations, it served as a placeholder for the role of theory in the minimally acceptable preparation of new practitioners. It also served to distinguish accountants from others vaguely interested in business by reiterating professional claims. The extant theory of practice is particularly germane for accounting education which rejects the necessity of a bifurcation of research into a separate discovery endeavor.

The pressure put on adequate theory magnifies if one expects it to be coextensive with the scope of services spanned by modern accountants. The major lines of business are difficult to coherently rationalize. Whereby financial accounting and tax are rule-based, the latter's exclusive governmental control and its essential bureaucratic logic remove it from the theoretic template of the former. Managerial accounting and work focused on information systems, as practiced within businesses, are too driven by what works at any given time, or what delivers the most insight efficiently, to bother with theory. Therefore, a more constrained definition of accounting must be accepted to meaningfully denominate the nature of accounting theory.

The vacuum is at least partially filled by financial accounting which has experienced what Gaffikin (1988) characterizes as "great effort" in the attempt to gradually build out theoretical rationales for external reporting. This can be illustrated by the fact that textbooks that dare to use the word "theory" in their titles tend to be almost exclusively financial in their orientation (e.g., Schroeder et al., 2001; Wolk et al., 2016). Also marked as theory, works in accounting history identify broad eras in the nature of operating company external disclosures as the criteria of theory (Previts & Merino, 1998).

If accounting is little other than an extension or alter ego of a nation's economic control over its private sector, the prospects for accounting theory are diminished by the specificity that such a reductionistic view necessitates. Accounting rules are necessarily sensitive to the politics of a country which in turn reflect a specific culture and history. This is tantamount to accepting the impossibility of a transnational accounting theory. Such deep cultural penetration cuts into the research design that are selected and therefore cannot be controlled with binary variables in regressive equations.

The light commitment of accounting research to theory suggests that its function is something other than officially described. The relative absence of theory in what is published should be contrasted with its high importance in unpublished dissertations. This suggests that theory is a mostly unattainable aspiration that is purposefully used to do the soft gatekeeping that makes the academic accounting discipline somewhat exclusive. Theory is not only a cudgel used to beat doctoral students but also something journal referees use to admonish putative authors about the deficiency of their manuscripts. Theory is what theory does.

If one never forgets that accounting originally existed as an interesting area of economics, the continued dependence of accounting research on economic theory is no surprise. As elaborated by the modern finance discipline (a field with a similar historical connection to economics), ample theoretical materials exist in economies to make a unique or singular accounting theory unnecessary for the purpose of sustaining literature. Although such a massive adoption might have been predicted by the watershed turn toward an empirical archival methodology usually attributed to Ball and Brown (1968), a longer gravitation in that direction has been documented (Al-Adeem & Fogarty, 2010). However, its adoption is highly selective and insufficiently rigorous.

Some might say that sufficient financial accounting theory exists within its basic postulates that identify the basic unit of analysis (entity, time, context (markets and measurement unit) and aspiration (objectivity, consistency and quantification). Whereas the ground rules for how accounting should be best done are essential, they collectively fall well short of a theory. The sanctioning of completely opposite techniques suggests that the postulates wherever they have been expressed are a better historical compilation than a theoretical statement. Alternatively expressed, the theory we think we have needs to be more theoretical.

SEARCHING FOR THEORY IN PUBLISHED ACCOUNTING RESEARCH

An inductive approach to the search of accounting theory would be based on the idea that a systemic knowledge base of a discipline could not exist without theory. This suggests that which is published must contain the *defacto* theory to which we subscribe. Why else would the most prestigious journals of the discipline be willing to display such work? Doing so, one is first struck by the failure of various conceptual framework projects undertaken over the years to compose a theoretical structure. The non-appearance of these efforts to guide or even remotely influence the trajectory of research of the field is noteworthy.

Then again, accounting research merely uses economic theory rather than acts to contribute to it in a way that would materially elaborate it. Its concerns are with economic quantities, consequences and sectors, but not its assumptions and limitations. As illustrated by calls for special editions and collections, substantive applications tend to be the building blocks of accounting research. As a mere user of these foundational ideas mostly as they relate to accounting choices by corporate entities and new regulatory pronouncements that support extant professional practice, accounting work is not cited in the economic literature with any regularity. Nonetheless, the centrality of the markets to the accounting literature cannot be gainsaid. If their operation is primarily economic in nature, accounting research cannot afford to deviate too widely.

Among economic theories, agency theory (Watts & Zimmerman, 1978) looms large for mainstream accounting work. This theory fits well if one imagines that the central act of concern is the selection of accounting technique that separately creates bottom-line consequences for the entity. Agency theory engenders speculation regarding the motives of the people in command of this, and how controls might be placed on this discretion for the benefit of others. While a debate about the limitations of this perspective exceeds the scope of this chapter, a more obvious observation is that the accounting literature tends not to do much with agency theory beyond its basic invocation as a motivation vehicle. In that sense, reciting a grounding in agency theory has devolved into a "check the box" *modus operandi*.

The relative absence of a specifically identified theory in the accounting literature seems rather ironic, given the ongoing advance of that literature's methodological and data analysis sophistication. Although more nuanced and better articulated theory could certainly exist in an environment that also required better quantifications and more rigorous displays of disproof for alternative explanations, the two upward trajectories have not simultaneously occurred. This suggests that the latter has displaced the former as the *sine qua non* of high-quality academic accounting work. Work that delivers large data sets, comprehensive regressions and careful modeling of effects may get scant scrutiny of its underpinning theoretical assumptions and origins. Although both fronts represent a version of progress, their failure to move apace also threatens stagnation. The more method becomes independent from rational, the more isolated academe becomes from practice and the classroom.

Theory in Accounting Education Research

Accounting education research is similarly available for the quest to identify underpinning theoretical assumptions and origins. Although it cannot be said that this subset of the discipline forms its vanguard, or even that the majority of academic accountants participate in its articulation, accounting education possesses unique importance. Accounting education lies at the center of the reason that the discipline has emerged from practice and therefore serves as a common denominator of all its academics. Theory would seem as appropriate here as anywhere.

On the whole, the accounting education literature is primarily practical. Instructors, often starting with a serendipitous observation made in their classes, systematically deploy innovative pedagogies that can be reasonably associated with better learning outcomes. There is much to be interrogated about the validity and reliability of such a vision and its design. Reviewers should be concerned with whether or not the project would be interesting to accounting educators, and whether it is sufficiently practical for others to use. Accounting education research work is unique in that it can never interfere with the educational process that it studies and is in the process of unfolding as research is conducted. This creates limits on permissible experimental manipulation, especially prohibiting the delivery of an inferior experience to any group of students. Thus, we often must accept less than definitive proof regarding outcomes and the permanency of effects.

With work devoted to these aspirations, the absence of much meaningful theory is scarcely noticed by readers and rarely mentioned or acknowledged in print by authors. Normally all that is required is that a palatable stimulus can be associated with a plausible response. With outcomes that are limited to self-reported change, some hand waving is often done about the so-called theory of planned behavior (Fishbein & Ajzen, 1975). This allows reported attitudes to be taken as the convenient equivalent of actual behavior in action. The real theory at work is often simple exposure, in that students given a chance to do X will respond differently than other students, or to how they responded before the application of X. For these purposes, X could be new course content (e.g., ESG), a new delivery method (e.g., flipped classroom) or even new curricular scheduling (e.g., journal entry bootcamp). These attempts, nonetheless, possess meaning for the readership because everyone appreciates the general baseline from which they depart. Thus, educational work has a strong template for its authors, even in the absence of actual theory.

Many have studied how people learn and why. However, it is surprising how little penetration exists for the easiest and best theoretical representative, John Dewey, into the accounting literature. Dewey's works from nearly a century ago remain fresh and rich (see Sikandar, 2015). More generally, few cites also are found in the more modern educational scholarship. The existence of several accounting educational journals allows the body of research to be a constrained self-referential island. As such, major tenets of educational thought find little expression in the accounting discipline. One might also suggest that the hard questions about learning addressed in theoretical formulations outside accounting have merely been passed over.

Theory can more readily be found in the small corner of the accounting education field that removes itself from the actual education process by looking at those who are professionally involved in it (e.g., faculty and administrators) or those that seek to regulate it (e.g., accreditors and governments). This component concerns itself with how higher education is best organized and delivered, and therefore studies focuses attention on faculty in accounting departments and their positioning in business schools. In that this scope includes the role of higher education in society, it allows the permeation of the many theories of formal organizations and sociology. These theories bear upon how a not-for-profit sector with a unique mission can contribute to an economy and the well-spent lives of people in it. However, the few authors who work above the individual level of analysis usually find it necessary to soft pedal the theory to which they adhere. One notable exception can be found in Tuttle and Dillard (2007) who use institutional theory to identify the diminishment of diversity in the published work of the discipline.

As a mental characteristic, learning exists within the ambit of psychological phenomena. As such, one would expect the accounting education literature to depart substantially from the rest of the academic accounting literature by eschewing the traditions of economic theory for the equally rich theories of psychology. However, what tends to happen is quite short of the use of theories from psychology. What tends to be used is the rationalizations behind isolated variables in a somewhat belated realization that people (usually students) might differ in their reactions to any particular stimuli. Rarely does psychological variation form the main thrust of accounting education research efforts. Too often, accounting education also treats demographic differences such as gender as a destiny that need not be further explored.

An increasingly large part of the accounting education literature constitutes a compendium of cases that are offered as instructional material for college courses in the discipline. The collective volume of this material, often larger in page counts than regular research pieces, argues that it cannot be ignored in discussions of accounting education. Cases also bridge the schism that exists for authors between the production of new knowledge and the desire to best influence the thinking of students.

Cases tend to be driven by current events gleaned from the mass market reporting of issues usually faced by corporations. Especially in an era where students are less likely to be conversant with the events of the day, a formal education that brings the student into such participation and awareness has incremental value. Developed in such a way, accounting cases are decidedly atheoretical (Fogarty, 2022). Writers believe that the currency of facts speaks for itself. The facts assume great importance as writers create those that are needed to disguise true identities and to make them fit the intended lessons better. The case writers' task is to juxtapose these superannuated facts with proper accounting procedures as such is revealed by regulations and professional standards. Such a template does not allow much room for theory except perhaps the way in which recommended corporate governance protocols are consistent with the general outline of agency theory. The dramaturgy of moral hazard made possible by the embedded information asymmetry of corporate governance, if not always hinted at by case authors, can be highlighted by instructors.

IMPLICATIONS

The assessment that theory has not made a sufficiently vibrant contribution to academic accounting necessitates some thought about a path forward. That theory has not achieved its potential and cannot be easily reversed even if some incremental steps are apparent. A good part of this process is fuller realizations about theory, where it can be found, and where it can be used.

History and theory are intimately intertwined. The denial of theory is essentially an assertion that the past is not very relevant. Accounting seems to have a "here and now" bias that tends to erase the past as educators attempt to stay up with new regulations and the ever-changing trajectory of the capital and labor markets. Theory needs to meet the test of time as our acceptance of it builds with the accumulation of insights and applications. Looking at theory as a bridge with our intellectual traditions and forebearers prevents its marginalization. Imagining our history to be broader than just what has been explicitly labeled "accounting" reduces the impact of the silos that segregate us from rich intellectual traditions.

That said, we cannot afford to be slaves to the past. Our job is to make judgments about what has changed and what continues to be true. I suspect that most of that which should matter to our work does not change with any regularity. Alternatively put, we tend to more predictably err by believing that fundamental change has occurred when in fact it is ephemeral. There may be new things under the sun, but upon closer inspection, they closely resemble the familiar objects that we have always had.

I have periodically suggested that the schism between accounting practice and academic accounting always underlies many of the serious problems in the discipline (e.g., Fogarty & Black, 2014; Zimmerman et al., 2017). Uncharacteristically, I see the schism as insufficiently wide in this application. Colleagues who see themselves as accountants who just happen to be academics have little use for theory since they imagine their function to be securing the labor pipeline for the profession and explaining practice difficulties to those accountants actively servicing a clientele. If colleagues saw themselves as academics who just happen to specialize in accounting, incorporating and deploying theory would be more salient. This occupational perspective would put them into the service of ideas, with the hope that such would benefit present and future practitioners in a longer time frame. Theory would be given breathing space to deepen meaning and extend the timeliness of such contributions. To engineer the production of the proper perspective requires that we review what we are doing in doctoral education. Getting serious about inter-disciplinary perspectives would be a first obvious step.

Room in our minds needs to be made for theory. The specific case of academic accounting is that, to a large extent, such space is currently occupied by governmental regulation and the standards pronounced by professional bodies. Whereas it is true that a good part of our value to our educational institutions and our students exist in our mastery of such, it tends to displace our appreciation for theory. The rules governing practice generally are responses to the exigencies of the day and as such have little permanence. Many will be effectively countermanded during our work lives, as alternative forces emerge. Although theories also ebb and flow, they provide firmer foundation upon which to build reputations and sustainable contributions.

Academic accounting continues to be challenged by the progress of information technology. Some have fashioned this as an existential crisis by posing the question of whether accounting as we know it is still worthwhile as a subject. A lesser version of the question would be the debate over the proper scope of accounting. One has to believe that theory could be useful here. Accounting should be broader than public company corporate disclosures but needs to be narrower than all information useful to businesses. The current placement of ESG begs the question that might be answered if theory provided accounting with useful self-definitions. Various analytical frontiers (aka big data and artificial intelligence) also pose similar problems for the range of our activities relative to other groups.

CONCLUSION

In deference to the often-forgotten notion that academic accountants have the liberty to serve as the conscience of the profession, theory serves as a useful reminder that what we do is not primarily dictated by its profitability. Ethical conceptions and the primacy of the public interest provide good examples of theory-driven dimensions of our trade. Abstract notions of who benefits and what sacrifices must be made abound in this area. Deeper indulgences in theory might be an open invitation to push the boundaries of academic freedom and to voluntarily be more controversial.

If you are convinced that we need more theory, where should we get it? Alternative directions exist. One could double down on economics and finance where a receptive home can be found without difficulty. Even within agency theory, much more than the conventional "drive-by shooting" or fleeting glance could be done. Journal reviewers and editors could insist that every paper make a substantive contribution to the theory that is invoked. Mainstream economics is rich with theory awaiting application. Beyond that mothership, sociology awaits. The fact that academic accountants outside the USA have already performed review papers on the accounting applications of writers like Foucault (e.g., Armstrong, 1994) and Bourdieu (e.g., Malsch et al., 2011) could advance sociology as an underpinning theory of accounting. Institutional theory remains a powerful source of explanation for higher level accounting phenomenon (e.g., Joseph, 2024; Wukich et al., 2023) as in the related legitimacy theory (Martens & Bui, 2023). The explanation of the associated language in the tradition of various rhetorical theories has yet to begin. The idea that theory is for European academics and America is too practical to bother with that needs to end.

Theory, like anything else, has an opportunity cost. Investments in it prevent us from doing other things, some of which have desirable payoffs for research and education. Currently, the incentive systems at many universities may very well drive accounting academics away from theory. The drumbeat that is never silenced, demanding that accounting research needs to better demonstrate its relevance to practice, threatens to take us further away from theory. In accounting education, the emphasis on designing accounting curricula that prioritize what is tested on the CPA exams presents a similar challenge. Theory will never be emphasized beyond lip service when we focus on short run issues such as the current "pipeline" crisis. Theory is the epitome of a long-term bet for the accounting discipline in general and accounting education in particular. Notwithstanding its current challenges, everything we do in the name of accounting would be better understood if more of an effort was made to bring theory to the table in a variety of ways.

REFERENCES

Al-Adeem, K., & Fogarty, T. (2010). *Accounting theory: A neglected topic for academic accounting researchers*. Lambert Academic Publishing.

Armstrong, P. (1994). The influence of Michel Foucault on accounting research. *Critical Perspectives on Accounting, 5*(1), 25–55.

Ball, R., & Brown, P. (1968). An empirical evaluation of accounting income numbers. *Journal of Accounting Research, 6*, 159–178.

Beaver, W. (1998). *Financial reporting: An accounting revolution*. Prentice Hall.

Cushing, B. E. (1989). A Kuhnian interpretation of the historical evolution of accounting. *Accounting Historians Journal, 16*(2), 1–41.

Díaz Andrade, A., Tarafdar, M., Davison, R. M., Hardin, A., Techatassanasoontorn, A. A., Lowry, P. B., Chatterjee, S., & Schwabe, G. (2023). The importance of theory at the *Information Systems Journal*. *Information Systems Journal, 33*(4), 693–702.

Fishbein, M., & Ajzen, I. (1975). *Belief, attitude, intention, and behavior: An introduction to theory and research*. Addison-Wesley.

Fogarty, T. (2022). A review of published tax cases: Contents, value-added and constraints. *Advances in Accounting Education, 26*, 175–190.

Fogarty, T., & Black, W. (2014). Further tales of the Schism: US accounting faculty and professional certification. *Journal of Accounting Education, 32*, 223–237.

Gaffikin, M. J. (1988). Legacy of the golden age: Recent developments in the methodology of accounting. *Abacus, 24*(1), 16–36.

Gaffikin, M. J. (2016). A brief historical appreciation of accounting theory? But who cares? In J. Haslam & P. Sikka (Eds.), *Pioneers of critical accounting: A celebration of the life of Tony Lowe* (pp. 109–142). Springer.

Hopwood, A. (1987). The archeology of accounting systems. *Accounting, Organizations and Society, 12*, 207–234.

Joseph, G. (2024). *Institutional entrepreneurship and integrating sustainability in a developing country context*. Unpublished working paper.

Kuhn, T. S. (1970). *The structure of scientific revolutions* (2nd ed.). University of Chicago Press.

Malsch, B., Gendron, Y., & Grazzini, F. (2011). Investigating interdisciplinary translations: The influence of Pierre Bourdieu on accounting literature. *Accounting, Auditing & Accountability Journal, 24*(2), 194–228.

Martens, W., & Bui, C. N. M. (2023). An exploration of legitimacy theory in accounting literature. *Open Access Library Journal, 10*(1), 1–20.

Mattessich, R. (1993). Paradigms, research traditions and theory nets of accounting. In M. J. Mumford & K. V. Peasnell (Eds.), *Philosophical perspectives on accounting* (pp. 62–122). Routledge.

Previts, G. J., & Merino, B. (1998). *A history of accountancy in the United States: The cultural significance of accounting*. Ohio State Press.

Sangster, A. (2016). The genesis of double entry bookkeeping. *The Accounting Review, 91*(1), 299–315.

Schroeder, R. G., Clark, M. W., & Cathey, J. M. (2001). *Accounting: Theory and analysis*. John Wiley & Sons.

Sikandar, A. (2015). John Dewey and his philosophy of education. *Journal of Education and Educational Development, 2*(2), 191.

Tuttle, B., & Dillard, J. (2007). Beyond competition: Institutional isomorphism in US accounting research. *Accounting Horizons, 21*(4), 387–409.

Watts, R. L., & Zimmerman, J. L. (1978). Towards a positive theory of the determination of accounting standards. *The Accounting Review, 53*(1), 112–134.

Wells, M. C. (1976). A revolution in accounting thought? *The Accounting Review, 51*(3), 471–482.
Wheeler, J. T. (1970). Accounting theory and research in perspective. *The Accounting Review, 45*(1), 1–10.
Wolk, H. I., Dodd, J. L., & Rozycki, J. J. (2016). *Accounting theory: Conceptual issues in a political and economic environment.* Sage Publications.
Wukich, J. J., Neuman, E. L., & Fogarty, T. J. (2023). Show me? Inspire me? Make me? An institutional theory exploration of social and environmental reporting practices. *Journal of Accounting & Organizational Change, 19*(5), 673–701.
Zimmerman, A., Fogarty, T., & Jonas, G. (2017). Is accounting an applied discipline? An institutional theory assessment of the value of practice work experience in academic labor markets. *Journal of Accounting Education, 41*, 33–47.

CHAPTER 11

A COMMENTARY ON TEACHING A FINANCIAL ACCOUNTING THEORY COURSE

Jerry E. Trapnell[a] and Michael T. Dugan[b]

[a]Clemson University, USA
[b]University of Alabama, USA

ABSTRACT

An advanced graduate-level financial accounting theory course should provide integral content for all accounting programs. However, we are aware that such courses are not always required at either the undergraduate or graduate level. We taught the accounting theory class at three institutions for many years, and as a result, we provide our views about the opportunities and challenges of placing the class at the undergraduate level while supporting our belief that the best placement is at the graduate level. As well, we strongly support a theoretical approach over a more short-term functional approach that stresses preparation for the Certified Public Accountant (CPA) examination. We offer our views supporting these perspectives along with a general framework for a theory class.

Keywords: Teaching; financial accounting theory; CPA exam preparation; general framework; hybrid approach

An advanced financial accounting theory course is often offered in many accounting programs at the undergraduate and/or graduate level. However, we are aware that such courses are not always required at either level because of the need and/

or desire to address new or other areas such as data analytics, forensic accounting, cybersecurity, advanced auditing, and similar contemporary topics. Based on our experience with teaching the class at three institutions, we offer our reasoning about why the course should be taught at the graduate level. Also, we strongly support a theoretical approach including a review of relevant research over a more short-term functional approach that stresses preparation for the CPA examination. In this chapter, we offer our views supporting these perspectives and provide a broad general framework for the theory class.

GRADUATE VERSUS UNDERGRADUATE

As an overall argument, placing the theory class at the graduate level after completing an undergraduate accounting curriculum is appropriate in order to build on a level of "financial accounting maturity" and relevant knowledge in finance, economics, and other business fields. However, we are aware that some accounting programs do not offer a graduate degree resulting in placing any advanced classes at the undergraduate level. Like most technical/scientific disciplines, basic, foundational concepts and theories are presented early and expanded and applied as advanced issues and problems are encountered in upper division undergraduate and/or graduate courses. Accounting follows a similar process.

If placement in an undergraduate accounting program is chosen or essential because of the lack of a graduate accounting program, we strongly support establishing the course as a capstone accounting course for all undergraduate accounting students with at least a solid set of prerequisites through advanced accounting, managerial areas, and auditing. We note, in our view, an undergraduate class probably needs to focus on professional pronouncements and related case literature and likely has some limitations in terms of the level of rigor that can be incorporated (e.g., a strong focus on accounting research). Another factor affecting an undergraduate theory class is limitations on available credit hours to add a required course at the undergraduate level. Most undergraduate accounting programs have required general education components and a substantive business core (finance, management, marketing, business law, etc.). The space for an additional required accounting class along with the traditional accounting classes may be difficult and may have to be an elective class only. Faculty resources may be an issue as well.

If a masters'-level graduate accounting degree is offered, the graduate-only approach is more strongly recommended. Drawing on the full array of undergraduate accounting classes as well as content from finance and economics, a more rigorous graduate accounting theory class can explore advanced analysis and application of recognized accounting theories and concepts, incorporate a strong focus on case analyses, and incorporate seminal accounting research publications. Adding a focus on accounting research provides an opportunity to explore the relevant academic and professional literature. With such an approach, the course may be more appropriately titled "Accounting Theory and Research."

ACCOUNTING THEORY AS A CPA REVIEW CLASS

As noted, one approach for an "accounting theory" class could be a sole focus on a review for the "Financial Accounting and Reporting" (FAR) section of the CPA examination. If the CPA exam is the prime focus, student performance on the exam may be enhanced in the short run, but in our view, long-term frameworks for addressing complex accounting issues are not sufficiently developed. More in-depth analysis of accounting in the context of concepts, theories, and standards is preferred for preparing accounting graduates for a lifetime of learning to support a successful professional career. As such, we do not recommend a CPA exam approach as the sole focus of the theory course at either level, and our consistent student feedback supports this conclusion. We have observed some graduate accounting programs offering a non-credit CPA exam review program as a co-curricular part of the masters' program, and such an approach takes the exam focus out of the graduate credit-based class sections retaining the focus on theory and application based on a sound understanding of accounting concepts, principles, and standards.

A GRADUATE FOCUS

The ultimate outcome of a graduate-level class should be based on advanced exploration of the theoretical framework, supporting concepts, and standards. This focus should be structured with a strong focus on student development of higher order analytical, understanding, and problem-solving skills and knowledge needed to address complex accounting issues/problems that often do not fit neatly into simple binary solutions for such issues.

Again, a graduate accounting theory course can be structured in a purely theoretical context somewhat similar to a doctoral seminar; however, we recommend a blended coverage of theories and concepts with limited coverage of content related to the FAR section of the CPA examination. Each faculty member must decide what areas to incorporate from the CPA exam, but we recommend the dominant coverage of issues requiring more analysis, research, and deep emersion into concepts and principles.

From a pedagogical perspective, we recommend the course be structured with a strong focus on active learning experiences that can include case analyses and presentations, discussion, review, and analysis of actual financial statements across various industries that lead to oral and written presentations individually and/or in a team format. Requiring students to review actual financial statements and related disclosures across such areas as manufacturing, financial and other service firms, hospitality, transportation, technology, and construction enhances students' understanding of various financial reporting challenges unique to these different industry sectors.

Given our recommendations above, we offer a set of possible learning objectives for a graduate accounting theory/research class in Table 11.1. We recognize these learning objectives may vary depending on a faculty member's preference for emphasis.

Table 11.1. Possible Graduate Accounting Theory Course Learning Objectives/Outcomes.

- Develop and demonstrate knowledge and understanding of financial accounting frameworks for business entities based on established theories, concepts, and standards
- Develop critical-thinking/analysis, research, and problem-solving skills and techniques to address complex accounting issues/transactions using generally accepted accounting principles (GAAP), FASB Conceptual Framework documents, and the International Federation of Accountants (IFAC) pronouncements
- Develop sound research and documentation skills focused on using FASB Conceptual Framework documents, FASB standards' codifications, and IFAC pronouncements
- Develop student appreciation of significant, relevant academic research that influences development of accounting theory, concepts, and standards
- Enhance teamwork, oral, and written communications skills through team projects focused on analyzing complex accounting issues with the context of accounting theory and principles and practice presenting their findings in class
- (If applicable) Prepare students for the FAR section of the CPA examination

In Table 11.2, we offer a possible list of topics for inclusion in an accounting theory class syllabus. These are each faculty member's choice for emphasis, but the order and context are important as the class moves from the theory/concepts/principles to application. In Table 11.2, we identify some resources that can be used to support such a course and later in the chapter identify other significant research that could be incorporated into this component of the course. All of these resources are germane to evaluating the impact of accounting information along with important factors such as uncertainty, relevance, and reliability for capital markets. There are also emerging areas such as "Corporate Social Responsibility" (CSR), "Environmental, Sustainability, and Governance" (ESG), and "Diversity, Equity, and Inclusion" (DEI) disclosures which may or may not be included in the quantitative sections of financial statements, but are important, emerging areas of financial reporting.

SOME POSSIBLE RESEARCH PAPERS

For the research component of the course, the focus should be on important, relevant, historical, and recent seminal publications. We recognize faculty members may have different preferences to include in this part of the course; however, we offer a list of some research publications that we think can be used.

Though a number of academic articles contain substantial methodological and statistical complexity, students can be advised to focus on the results and practice implications of the articles. Again, the readings should include samplings from the earlier literature as well as more recent articles.

Examples of earlier articles to assign include Ball and Brown (1968), the seminal capital markets study that examined the effect of accounting earnings announcements on stock returns; Akerlof (1970), which introduced the concepts of information asymmetry and adverse selection to the financial economics literature; Jensen and Meckling (1976), the seminal paper that introduces agency theory and conflicting incentives between shareholders and managers; and Thomas

Table 11.2. Possible Topical Outline for a Graduate Accounting Theory Class.

- Review key underlying concepts critical to financial accounting frameworks and standards, that is, the entity concept, money measurement concept, periodicity concept, accrual concept, matching concept, going concern concept, cost concept, conservatism, consistency, and materiality
- Review official documents issued by the FASB and prior organizations on financial accounting concepts to include Storey and Storey (1998), FASB Concept Statements (as updated 2023), and FASB Standards. Exploring consistencies and differences in domestic and international reporting standards by reviewing IFAC pronouncements also provides a basis for solid discussion analysis and recognition of differences in the application of accounting standards in a multinational context
- Review the evolution of uses of accounting information from the focus on solvency in the 1920s to capital market impacts and shareholder value in the current context as well as usefulness from a predictability perspective. Individual and/or team projects doing a financial analysis of the actual financial statements of different firms from different industries enables students to appreciate the differences or lack of differences captured in financial statements (Ball & Brown, 1968)
- *Based on the above, the following offers relevant, specific topical areas where supporting materials can include standards, underlying theories and concepts, and academic research publications relevant to the topical area*
- Measurement, valuation and recognition techniques for assets, liabilities, revenues, and expenses including fair value requirements and impairment assessments
- Income and expense recognition
- Earnings management, financial reporting quality, and research on the impact and uses of accounting information. Some resources may include (Ball & Brown, 1968; Dugan & Taylor, 2016; Dugan & Zavgren, 1989)
- Accounting for complex transactions supported with cases and/or real-world examples via individual and/or team projects. A solid resource is the Deloitte Trueblood Cases (Deloitte. 2022)
- Corporate governance, ethical issues, and accounting-related corporate failures
- The role of accounting research in theory development
- Current and emerging issues including multinational firms, ESG, CSR, DEI, etc. (Larcker & Watts, 2020)
- (If applicable) CPA exam questions analysis and review

(1975), which discusses the problematic nature of accounting allocations such as depreciation because of their inability to be verified or refuted.

Examples of more current studies that would generate interesting class discussion include Larcker and Watts (2020), who find that investors do not pay a premium for securities issued to finance environmentally friendly capital projects, which could lead to a discussion of ESG issues and reporting; Kim and Valentine (2021), who find that additional patent disclosures reduce the firm's innovation and increase the innovation of other firms, which calls to question the full disclosure principle; and Myers et al. (2018), whose findings indicate that the incremental market response to the issuance of a going concern qualification is not statistically or economically significant, which could lead to a discussion about whether managers should be so averse to receiving a going concern qualification.

CONCLUSION

We strongly support including a required financial accounting theory class in accounting degree programs. Such a course provides a synthesis of prior financial accounting and related classes with an advanced exploration of complex accounting issues in the contexts of established accounting standards, theories/ concepts, and the application of these. Such an approach also can incorporate key aspects of the intersection of accounting with economics, finance, and other business disciplines. The alternative of using the "theory" class as a CPA review class falls short in our opinion in developing advanced understanding, analytical, and problem-solving skills for accounting graduates.

We also see future research opportunities to enhance the content and structure of the graduate theory course. One such example is the application of artificial intelligence technology to the course. Such technology should prove useful in preparing for teaching case analyses by helping to focus on relevant questions to generate class discussion or even by assisting in the development of discussion points.

REFERENCES

Akerlof, G. (1970). The market for lemons: Quality uncertainty and the market mechanism. *The Quarterly Journal of Economics, 84*(3), 488–500.

Ball, R., & Brown, P. (1968). An empirical evaluation of accounting income numbers. *Journal of Accounting Research, 6*(2), 158–178.

Deloitte. (2022). *The trueblood case studies*. http://www2.deloitte.com/us/en/pages/noindex/shruti-test/trueblood-cases-studies-deloitte-foundation-new-html

Dugan, M., & Taylor, G. (2016). Ethical issues related to earnings management: An instructional case. *Journal of the International Academy of Case Studies, 22*(3), 84–89.

Dugan, M., & Zavgren, C. (1989). Bankruptcy prediction research: A valuable instructional tool. *Issues in Accounting Education, 3*(1), 48–64.

Jensen, M., & Meckling, W. (1976). Theory of the firm: Managerial behavior, agency costs and ownership structure. *Journal of Financial Economics, 3*(4), 305–360.

Kim, J., & Valentine, K. (2021). The innovation consequences of mandatory patent disclosures. *Journal of Accounting and Economics, 71*(2–3), 101381.

Larcker, D., & Watts, E. (2020). Where's the Greenium. *Journal of Accounting and Economics, 69*(2–3), 101312.

Myers, L. A., Shipman, J. E., Swanquist, Q. T., & Whited R. L. (2018). Measuring the market response to going concern modifications: The importance of disclosure timing. *Review of Accounting Studies, 23*, 1512–1542.

Storey, R., & Storey, S. (1998). *The framework for financial accounting concepts and standards*. Financial Accounting Standards Board.

Thomas, A. (1975). The FASB and the allocation fallacy. *Journal of Accountancy, 140*(5), 65–70.

www.ingramcontent.com/pod-product-compliance
Lightning Source LLC
Jackson TN
JSHW011917131224
75386JS00004B/241